John
Stuart
Mill
in Love

ABOUT THE BOOK

John Stuart Mill was the most
eloquent spokesman on the
women's question. He pursued it
tirelessly throughout his long
career. No one before or since has
ever equalled the cogency or the
intensity of his arguments.

Philosopher and politician, he
first met Harriet Taylor in 1830
when he was 24. She became the
love of his life. They were unable to
marry until her husband died 19
years later, but their passionate
attachment lasted until Mill's
death in 1873.

Apart from a remarkable story,
their relationship was the crucible
of Mill's interest in women's
rights. Josephine Kamm traces
back to his childhood to examine
the formation of his opinions. Her
remarkable book casts Mill's career
and the history of the women's
movement in an entirely new light.

ABOUT THE AUTHOR

Josephine Kamm was born and
educated in London. She has served
on the Executive Committee of the
National Book League and the
Committee of Management of the
Fawcett Library. She has published
more than 20 books for young
people, one of which *Return To
Freedom*, won the Isaac Siegel
Memorial Juvenile Award. Her
adult books include *How Different
From Us* about two famous
nineteenth-century
headmistresses, *Hope Deferred*
and *Indicative Past* about girls'
education. *Rapiers and Battleaxes*
about the women's movement in
England and a biography of
Gertrude Bell *Daughter Of the
Desert*.

John
Stuart
Mill
in Love

JOSEPHINE KAMM

GORDON & CREMONESI

The portraits of J. S. Mill and of Harriet Taylor shown in the
frontispiece were supplied by the British Library of Political
and Economic Science to whom grateful acknowledgment is
given.

Designed by Heather Gordon
Set in 10 on 11 pt Garamond
by Preface Ltd., Salisbury,
and printed in Great Britain
by The Pitman Press, Bath, Avon

British Library/Library of Congress
Cataloguing in Publication Data

Kamm, Josephine
    John Stuart Mill in Love
    1. Mill, John Stuart   2. Philosophers, English-
    Biography
    I. Title
    192   B1606   77-30051

ISBN 0-86033-020-6

Gordon & Cremonesi Publishers
New River House
34 Seymour Road
London N8 OBE

For Maria

Author's Acknowledgements

Two women played a decisive part in John Stuart Mill's life and career. The first, and by far the most important, was Harriet Taylor who ultimately became his wife; the second was Harriet's daughter Helen Taylor who acted as his helper, adviser and the guardian of his conscience after her mother's death. Mill's overwhelming love and admiration for Harriet were to a considerable degree the outcome of his ambivalent feelings towards his family, his domineering father and his intellectually inferior mother and sisters; they were also reflected in his attitude towards other women. The idea for this book, the influence of women on Mill's life and work, was suggested by my publishers Gordon & Cremonesi, to whom I am most grateful.

I should like to thank the British Library of Political and Economic Science for permission to quote from the letters in the Mill-Taylor Collection; the Provost and Fellows of King's College, Cambridge, for permission to quote from the manuscripts in the Keynes Library; the Library of University College, London, for permission to quote from manuscript material; and the Trustees of the Fawcett Library for similar permission. My special thanks are due to the archivists and librarians of these institutions, and to those of the Reading Room of the British Library, Chelsea Public Library, the National Portrait Gallery and the National Westminster Bank. The illustrations are reproduced by courtesy of the National Portrait Gallery, the British Library of Political and Economic Science, and the National Westminster Bank.

The most comprehensive biography of Mill is Michael St John Packe's *The Life of John Stuart Mill*, published by Secker & Warburg (1954). For the purposes of this book I am indebted to the authors, editors and publishers for permission to quote from the following: the *Collected Works of John Stuart Mill*, vols. II-III, *Principles of Political Economy*, Introduction by V. W. Bladen, Textual Editor J. M. Robson (1965), vols XII-XIII, *The Earlier Letters of John Stuart Mill*, 1812-1848, edited by Francis E. Mineka (1963), vols XIV-XVII, *The Later Letters of John Stuart Mill*, 1849-1873, edited by Francis E. Mineka and Dwight N. Lindley (1972), all published by the

University of Toronto Press and Routledge & Kegan Paul; *John Stuart Mill and Harriet Taylor: Their Correspondence and Subsequent Marriage*, edited by F. A. Hayek, Routledge & Kegan Paul (1951); *The Early Draft of John Stuart Mill's Autobiography*, edited by Jack Stillinger, the University of Illinois Press (1961); and *The Amberley Papers*, edited by Bertrand and Patricia Russell, George Allen & Unwin (1965). I am also indebted to Colombia University Press for permission to quote from the *Autobiography of John Stuart Mill*, published for the first time without alterations or omissions from the original manuscript, with a preface by John Jacob Coss (1924), and regret that a new definitive edition published by the University of Toronto Press was not available to me when this book went to press.

In addition I should like to thank John Allen for information about his great-grandmother Fanny Stirling; Anna Cooper of John Johnson for much help and advice; Betty Ellman for providing details of the law suit in which Helen Taylor was involved; and Antony Kamm for research in the Keynes Library.

J.K.

Contents

CHAPTER 1

A Boy's Best Friend

In pre-Freudian days it was commonly said that a boy's best friend was his mother. If this adage was accepted as axiomatic in many nineteenth-century homes it did not apply in the home of John Stuart Mill, the great philosopher, author and champion of women's rights. Mill's mother, Harriet, was the daughter of Mrs Burrow, a handsome widow who hailed from Yorkshire and conducted with competence and financial acumen her late husband's "establishment for lunatics"[1] in Hoxton in the City of London. Harriet, her eldest daughter, was a girl of startling beauty, small and slim, with fine aquiline features and a healthy complexion. In 1804, at the age of twenty-one, she became engaged to thirty-one-year-old James Mill, the brilliant, irascible Scotsman who had settled in London two years earlier to become in the course of his life well known as a philosopher, journalist, head of the India House (the offices of the East India Company), and author of a *History of India*.

For a brief period James Mill was very much in love with his Harriet. In the single letter which she preserved from the months of their engagement "the depth and tenderness" of his feelings "could not well be exceeded".[2] He had, however, made the mistake of assuming that one so beautiful would prove, if not his equal intellectually, at least an intelligent companion. He could not have been more wrong. Harriet, though loving, kind and practical, was totally lacking in brains. The marriage, which took place in 1805, was doomed from the start, except, presumably, on the physical plane, for during the next twenty years Mrs Mill bore her husband nine children—four boys and five girls. To John Stuart, the eldest and best loved, born the year after her marriage, she bequeathed an emotional temperament and the fine features and ruddy complexion which moved Carlyle at their first meeting to describe him as a "beautiful young man".[3]

Mrs Mill kept her place in the bedroom, nursery and kitchen. In the early days of her married life James Mill was still a struggling journalist and money was scarce except when Mrs Burrow came forward with help; and even later, after he had become Chief Examiner at the India House, she continued to slave for her home and children and remained "thoroughly obedient to her lord".[4]

This was the impression she made on her husband's friends on the rare occasions when she met them. Harriet Grote, the outspoken and domineering wife of George Grote, who became famous as the historian of Greece, declared that James Mill had married "a stupid woman 'a housemaid of a woman' & left off caring for her & treated her as his squah but was always faithful to her".[5]

Mrs Grote's description sums up the relationship between husband and wife very well. James Mill did not attempt to conceal the contempt that he held for his wife and for all his children except John, who was too clever to be ignored. He was not actively unkind, but "his entering the room where the family was assembled was observed by strangers to operate as an immediate damper. This was not the worst. The one really disagreeable trait in Mill's character . . . was the way he allowed himself to speak and behave to his wife and children before visitors." In letters to his friends he sounded a good family man, "putting forward his wife and children into their due place; but he seemed unable to observe this part in daily intercourse".[6]

All too easily John Mill came to accept his father's estimate of his mother. She may well have objected to the extraordinary system of education to which he was subjected: if she did, her objections were ignored. She may well have doubted the wisdom or propriety of denying her child a religious training or of driving him at the age of three to embark on Greek; but James Mill, who directed and carried out John's education himself, was bent on moulding a genius, and in this he succeeded despite his tyrannical methods. Mrs Mill could not follow her son into the Greek and Latin classics, still less into the study of philosophy and logic, which he began at twelve. And yet, despite a prodigious amount of learning, John Mill maintained that his "was not an education of cram", for his father would never permit lessons to "degenerate into a mere exercise of memory" but deliberately withheld information until the boy had exhausted every effort "to find it out"[7] for himself.

At seven, when he started Latin, the boy had to teach his five-year-old sister Wilhelmina—or Willie, as she was called—as he went along. In his *Autobiography,* that perennially fascinating but infuriating book which conceals so many aspects of his life which he might have revealed, he claimed that "from this time, other sisters and brothers being successively added as pupils, a considerable part of my day's work consisted of this preparatory teaching".[8] But his third sister, Harriet Isabella, who was born in 1812, recalling childhood memories after his death in 1873, could not remember ever learning Latin with John. Latin, she said, was "the only thing my father professed to teach us". After James Mill entered the India House "*we* could only see him in an evening, when we were always in disgrace over the hated Latin. We were never shown how to learn but had difficult books given us which we were ordered to translate! My father could not teach us as he had done John by companionship." Harriet Isabella had her own ideas about the nature of John's education: "how many of us would have lived through the same cramming I can only guess".[9]

Whether or not he actually taught his brothers and sisters Latin, John Mill had to supervise their work. It was a task he disliked and resented, although he confessed that it helped him to remember a considerable amount of information he might otherwise have forgotten. Like his sisters but unlike his brothers, he never went to school, and for him there were no holidays. Once, when the Grotes invited the boy to go on a holiday tour with them, Mrs Mill replied—doubtless at her husband's dictation—that John "could not be spared from the work of teaching the younger children".[10] He had a certain amount of leisure time but was always too mature intellectually to consider using it except in walking or further study.

In the version of his *Autobiography* which he finally approved there is no mention at all of his mother. In an earlier version she is criticized for being over-protective. He had, he said, the "misfortune of having, in domestic matters" everything done for him, so that he grew up without any practical ability or manual dexterity. He assumed that his father saw no need for him to learn to fend for himself: "& it would never have occurred to my mother, who without misgivings of any sort worked from morning till night for her children".[11]

An "evil" which he shared with the sons of other dictatorial fathers was to become subservient to a will so powerful that he was left with little will of his own. He was so accustomed to being told what to do and rebuked for disobedience that he "acquired a habit of leaving my responsibility as a moral agent to rest on my father, my conscience never speaking to me except through his voice".[12] As an adult his conscience was to speak to him through the voices of two strong-minded women, his wife and her daughter by her first husband.

As a boy John Mill took a normal elder brother's interest in his sisters' doings. Nine-year-old Willie, seven-year-old Clara, and Harriet Isabella, who was only five, had just begun music, he informed his grandmother Burrow in the autumn of 1817. Willie and Clara were also writing with the news that they had started on the first lesson but that Harriet had not yet "finished the treble notes ... How much Willie and Clara have improved [in their writing] you will know by reading their letters ... I believe my Mother has written to you a very long letter: and I suppose she has told you all the little news that we have." They were all well except for the baby, Jane, who was not yet a year old and had a cough. "I had lately the tooth-ache very bad. I hope that you are also in very good health. . . ."[13]

This letter was written from Ford Abbey, near Chard in Somerset, the country home of James Mill's friend Jeremy Bentham, the radical reformer and exponent of the doctrine of utilitarianism—in essence, the greatest happiness of the greatest number. The philanthropic Bentham had helped to move the Mills from their overcrowded quarters in Newington Green to the more gracious surroundings of Queen Square, Westminster, where he himself lived, paying half the rent and giving the Mill children the run of his garden.

Lessons continued at Ford Abbey as in London. The effect of James Mill's stern regime on John and his sisters and three-year-old James Bentham, the brother next in age to John, was closely observed by Francis Place, self-educated tailor, pioneer working-class leader and social reformer, who was also staying with Bentham in the summer and early autumn of 1817. The children did not seem unhappy and gave no trouble, he told his wife; but they had "a hard time of it", with lessons beginning at 6 a.m. and continuing with one or two breaks for meals until late afternoon. The younger children sometimes cried "when scolded or cuffed over their lessons, but [crying] is all but unknown on other occasions". There was crying one day when Willie and Clara were accused of falling behind with their work. At three o'clock they were still "plodding over their books, their dinner, which they knew went up at one, brought down again". John, who dined with his sisters, was also hard at work, "for having permitted them to pass when they could not say, and no dinner will any of them get till six o'clock. . . . The fault today is a *mistake in one word*." Place, who would never have been so severe with his own children, admitted that "the learning and reasoning" already acquired by the little Mills was "not equalled by any children in the whole world".[14]

At the time there were no career opportunities for highly educated women and even if James Mill's daughters had shown the precocity of their brother John they would have had little or no chance of living up to their early expectations. Harriet Isabella was probably the most promising. As she explained to one of her brother James Bentham's college friends, John had told her that, had it been feasible, she could "have taken the Senior Wrangler's degree at Cambridge. I believe", she added, "that mathematical training has been very useful to me".[15] How she used that training except for household accounts we do not know.

Mrs Place was fond of Mrs Mill but pitied her, the more so, as Place told James Mill, because "she, poor woman, as well as my wife, has 'a grumpy husband who bites her nose off' ". Place found Mrs Mill patient and gentle but "by no means meanly submissive", surely a sign that she had the courage to stand up to her husband on occasion. She was also "both good-natured and good-tempered, two capital qualities in a woman". She was, however, "not a little vain of her person" and endeavoured to "be thought to be still a girl".[16] It is true that Mrs Mill, who was thirty-four, had written to Mrs Place that she had recovered her youth following the birth of little Jane. James Mill's biographer, the Scottish philosopher and psychologist Alexander Bain, attributed this natural vanity to the fact that, having once been admired for her beauty, she had been deeply upset to discover her lowly position in marriage. Mrs Mill had little enough reason for complacency: she had lost her husband's love and he made no secret of his contempt for her. John Mill was aware that his father was ashamed of showing any emotion and rigorously concealed any affection he may have felt for his elder children. He thought too that in the right atmosphere James Mill "would have been tender & affectionate; but his ill assorted marriage", coupled with his uncertain temper, stood in the way. For his mother, who once reproved him mildly for excessive conceit, John Mill "never had the slightest regard". He spoke of "that rarity in England, a really warm hearted mother", who might have made his father "a totally different being, & . . . made the children grow up loving & being loved". But Mrs Mill, "with the very best intentions, only knew how to pass her time drudging for them. Whatever she could do for them she did, & they liked her, because she was kind to them, but to make herself loved, looked up to, or even obeyed, required qualities which she unfortunately did not possess." Most bitterly he added: "I thus grew up in the absence of love & in the presence of fear".[17]

These cynical remarks were deleted from the *Autobiography* at the instigation of John Mill's wife, who, while she barely knew Mrs Mill and had no reason to love her, had the perspicacity to see what harm they might do. The remarks were not only unkind: they were untrue. Mrs Mill, who doted on John, was too much in awe of her husband to display very much of the love and emotion she felt. Her daughters understood her position well enough: they looked at it not, as John did, from their father's point of view but from their mother's. "My poor mother's married life must have been a frightfully hard one", said Harriet Isabella. "Here was an instance of two persons, a husband and wife, living as far apart under the same roof, as the north pole from the south; from no 'fault' of my poor mother certainly." How was it possible for a woman with a large and growing family and, initially at any rate, very little housekeeping money, to be much more than a domestic drudge? Worse than that: "How could she intellectually become a companion for such a mind as my father?"[18]

Mrs Mill's status was apparent not only to her husband's friends but also to friends of the children. John alone had no friends of his own age; he was so conditioned to study that even when, at fourteen, he spent a year in France with the family of Jeremy Bentham's brother he could not drop the habit of continuous work. Isolation had been part of James Mill's regime; but the other boys—James Bentham, Henry and George Grote—were not secluded, and made friends in the ordinary way. Henry Solly, who was at University College, London, with James Bentham and was an observant sixteen-year-old when he first met the family in 1830, was pained by James Mill's attitude towards his wife, especially when he compared it with his own father's courtesy towards his mother, "and that of other gentlemen . . . in similar relations". He found Mrs Mill "a tall, handsome lady, sweet-tempered, with pleasant manners, fond of her children: but I think not much interested in what the elder ones and their father talked about".[19]

Mrs Mill might have been interested in the conversation had she been able to understand it, but no allowances were made for ignorance. Henry Solly also noted that James Mill took little notice of the children except for John, for they did not come up to his expectations. In later life he mellowed sufficiently to win the affection of the younger children—Henry (or Derry, as he was called), George, and Mary; yet Alexander Bain claimed that their love for their father "was never wholly unmingled with fear".[20]

Solly saw a good deal of the Mills in the early 1830s, both in London and in the country. In 1831 James Mill, now comparatively affluent, moved his family from Queen Square to a large detached villa in Vicarage Place, Church Street, Kensington. At the same time he bought a cottage in the pretty, straggling village of Mickleham, near Dorking, facing the Surrey hills. According to Carlyle, the cottage was made up of some " 'old carpenters' shops" joined together to form "a pleasant summer mansion (connected by shed-roofed passages), the little drawing-room door of glass looking out into a rose lawn".[21]

Henry Solly, who visited the Mills at Mickleham more than once, did not believe that John Mill despised his mother. John, everybody's favourite, he said, "was evidently very fond of his mother and sisters". Whatever John himself might think about growing up in the absence of love and in the presence of fear, Solly recorded that he "frequently manifested a sunny brightness and gaiety of heart, which was singularly fascinating". In later life he liked to recall John Mill's "warm affections ... in those happy days at Mickleham"[22] for the sisters he was later to treat so harshly. Writing in old age, Solly might have been tempted to cast too rosy a light on the past; but he had written in precisely the same way in the *Workman's Magazine* twenty years earlier, in 1873. Other friends were of the same opinion. The Mill children, said Bain, "besides having a fond, indulgent mother ... were very much attached to one another";[23] while the Rev. J. Crompton, another of James Bentham's University College friends, recollected that in the Mickleham days "John was devotedly attached to his mother and exuberant in his playful tokens of affection". Towards his father, however, "he was deferential, never venturing to controvert him in argument nor taking a prominent part in the conversation in his presence". John Mill, Crompton averred, "from pride and assumption was freer than most, yet the deference paid him by his brothers and sisters was profound. When unable to determine any matter for themselves the suggestion came from one or other of them as a matter of course, 'Ask John: he knows.' And whilst his juniors were eagerly contesting some point of history or philosophy ... and John was apparently absorbed as usual with a book on his knee in the corner, they would be startled from time to time at a sarcasm or an objection shot out by the recluse from his place of retirement which put one or other of the disputants completely hors de combat."

John Mill's sarcasm was an echo of his father's; yet, as Crompton noted, in his last years James Mill "softened into a very different being from the pedagogue of the *Autobiography*.... Though intolerant of adult bores he was gentle and even affectionate with young people in whom like Bentham he took a warm interest. Nor did Mrs Mill's life appear by any means a hard one at this time. There was noticeable indeed a certain repressive harshness of manner in the behaviour of her husband though the reviewers [of the *Autobiography*] have unquestionably represented it with gross exaggeration. In truth however the whole family regarded the head with a good deal of reverential awe."[24]

Crompton believed correctly that Harriet Isabella's strictures referred to the earlier period of his life. This is true, but it was in that earlier period that the older children as well as their mother suffered. At that time John Mill's feelings towards his mother were ambivalent: he was fond of her and knew himself to be loved; but he also admired his father and adopted his critical attitude towards his mother and sisters. Yet, while he admired his father he resented his domination, though powerless to escape it.

CHAPTER 2

Substitute Mother

Since Mrs Mill had failed to provide the understanding and the stimulating intellectual atmosphere in which her eldest son thrived the boy soon found himself a mother-substitute of a very different calibre. She was Sarah Austin, a near neighbour of Jeremy Bentham and the Mills in Queen Square.

Born in 1793, Sarah, whose maiden name was Taylor, belonged to an East Anglian family of Unitarians, relations of the well-known Martineau clan. She was the youngest of seven daughters, an intelligent, vivacious, attractive girl, and much admired. At nineteen, to the surprise of her family and friends, she became engaged to John Austin. He had been briefly a soldier, then a lawyer, but in 1825, at the age of twenty-five, was forced to retire from the Bar owing to ill health. Austin, a grave and solemn young man, diffident and self-critical, celebrated the betrothal with a pious letter, praying that the Lord might give them strength "to bear up under those privations and disappointments" against which they would all too likely be "destined to contend".[1]

In 1826 he was appointed Professor of Jurisprudence in the recently founded University of London and brought his wife from Norwich to Queen Square. He was plagued with illness, which hampered his career, but Sarah, who had been well educated by her mother, was an excellent linguist. She helped to balance the family budget and provide an outlet for her own gifts by working as a translator and, later, as a writer on Germany and on the education of girls. She also used her charm and good sense to gather about her a circle of writers, lawyers and wits, Carlyle, James Mill and Bentham among them. This comely, popular young woman very soon became one of the toasts of London society. She was "my best and brightest" to a future Lord Advocate, Francis Jeffrey of the *Edinburgh Post;* Sydney Smith called her "dear, fair and wise", Carlyle, "sunlight through waste weltering chaos".[2]

The marriage was a happy one, but Sarah, a romantic, carried on a passionate love affair, conducted entirely by correspondence, with the profligate Prince Puckler Muskau, whose book *Tour of a German Prince* she translated. She found the handsome, precocious John Mill immensely appealing. He was thirteen years her junior and she was soon calling him her "dearest child and friend".

Lucie (Lady Duff Gordon), the Austins' only child, was born in Queen Square when John Mill was fifteen. He had no friends of his own age but became very fond of the little girl. John "really doats on Lucie", declared the proud mother, who watched them play together in Jeremy Bentham's garden, "and can do anything with her."[3]

During the year John Mill spent in France Mrs Austin had obligingly taken over his role as his sisters' teacher. He wrote to thank her in French, presumably to show off his fluency: "Je ne sais si elles sentent toute l'entendu de cette bonté, mais je vous assure que je la sens, et que je ne manquerai pas de vous en remercier, à mon retour, de vive voix...."[4]

In John's absence James Mill had been urged by his friends to send him to Cambridge to read Law: he had refused, convinced that the boy already knew more than he could learn at university. Instead, he consented to allow John to study Roman law with John Austin, an acknowledged expert, and to go to Sarah Austin for lessons in German. In the long letter he had written her from France John had addressed her formally as "Madame"; but very soon he was writing in German to his "liebe, Mütterlein", signing his letters "Ihre Söhnchen". Sarah, who now wrote to him as her "dearest John", signed her letters "Your Mütterlein".

This idyllic friendship flourished for ten years or more. John was in and out of the Austins' house, talking to Sarah as he could never have talked to his own mother; and, when they were apart, they corresponded and made numerous plans to meet. In 1832, when she was in Cornwall with her husband after one of his illnesses, she wrote to her dearest John saying how dearly she would like to see him but realized that he was too busy to make the journey. "How could you so far misunderstand me as to suppose that it could be a question with me whether I would sacrifice two days to you?" he replied. "I thought that it would be sacrificing two days *of* you."[5] Some time later, after another illness, the Austins were staying nearer home, in Richmond, Surrey, and both were eager for a visit from their entertaining young friend. "And now, dear John," wrote Sarah, "I am going to make an earnest appeal to your friendship. It is nothing less than a little of your company & conversation *for him*....You are & continue the one & only person whose society he really craves for...."[6]

It may well have been Sarah Austin who first discussed with John Mill the idea of a system of universal education with equal opportunities for boys and girls. She felt so strongly about it that, when she translated a report on the educational system in Prussia, she argued the case in a preface of her own. In later life, when she was no longer his Mütterlein, she modified her views. In her *Letters on Girls' Schools and on the Training of Working Women*, published in 1857, she praised the old-fashioned method of teaching working-class girls little but industry, obedience, and reverence towards their betters. She had been, however, noted for her advanced views on women's rights and most probably fostered John Mill's latent interest, an interest born of an adolescent urge to rebel against his father. As a boy he must have heard James

Mill arguing against the enfranchisement of women with Jeremy Bentham, who took the opposite view.

The problem of enfranchisement in its wider setting—equal rights—had been debated for years. As early as 1739 a pamphlet had appeared under the high-sounding title, *Woman not Inferior to Man: or, short and modest Vindication of the natural Right of the Fair Sex to a perfect Equality of Power, Dignity & Esteem, with the Men*. The author, "Sophia, a Person of Quality", may have been the blue stocking Lady Mary Wortley Montagu. Sophia's pamphlet preceded by fifty years Mary Wollstonecraft's *A Vindication of the Rights of Woman*, that passionate, moving plea for a genuine partnership between men and women to replace a partnership resting on their sexual relations. During the intervening years other pamphlets had been published in England urging equal rights and opportunities, but very few people had taken them seriously. James Mill was prominent among the sceptics. In 1824 he wrote an article on government for the *Encyclopaedia Britannica* in the course of which he poured scorn on the arguments in favour of women's suffrage. In order to protect the rightful liberties of the people, he wrote, certain safeguards to the elective franchise were essential. All "those individuals whose interests are included in those of other individuals may be struck off [the electoral roll]. In this light women may be regarded, the interest of almost all of whom is involved in that of their fathers or husbands."

The article was read with furious indignation by one of Bentham's disciples, the Irish philosopher William Thompson. He wrote at once to James Mill, pointing out that he had been unjust and also inconsistent. Almost all women, he said, did not mean all women: Mill had therefore tacitly admitted that some women at least should be enfranchised. James Mill took not the slightest notice, whereupon Thompson consulted his inamorata, an unhappily married woman named Wheeler, who, incidentally, became the great-grandmother of one of the bravest of the militant suffragettes, Lady Constance Lytton. Together they produced a wordy but stinging reposte: *The Appeal of One Half of the Human Race, Women, against the Pretensions of the other half, Men, to retain them in political, and thence in civil and domestic slavery: in reply to a paragraph of Mr Mill's celebrated "Article on Government"*.

Mary Wollstonecraft had blazed the trail, declared Thompson; now the hand of another woman—Mrs Wheeler—"should have the honour of raising from the dust that neglected banner which a woman's hand nearly thirty years ago unfolded boldly, in face of the prejudices of thousands of years". For far too long

> has remained uncontradicted the anathema of a school of modern philosophy against the claim to the equal use and enjoyment of their faculties of half the human race. In the ponderous though enlightened volumes of the Supplement of the Encyclopaedia Britannica this

dastardly anathema might have remained concealed from all eyes but those of the philosophers themselves, had not some patriotic men, overlooking perhaps the interests of women in their zeal for those of men, or not weighing the tendency of the paragraph, extracted the "Article on Government" ... from the volume where its malignity towards half the human race slumbered, and re-printed it for gratituitous circulation [so that] the least amiable features

of James Mill's philosophy could now be read and gloated over by his admirers.

Thompson's *Appeal of Women* is interesting not only in itself but because in it are embedded the arguments which John Stuart Mill and Harriet Taylor were to put forward in more temperate language. The central theme is the unjust and unjustifiable enslavement of women by men. Thompson inveighs against the marriage tie which turned women into household slaves and, whether they liked it or not, into breeding machines. As for their political enfranchisement, in James Mill's article

six lines, out of 32 pages on the principles of government, are devoted to the pretensions of women and children, or rather of children and women—for children take the precedence in this new and enlightened nomenclature—of which two lines include the pretended principle of exclusion; two the application to children; and two more, last of all, the application to the hopelessly weak and helpless appendage to the race of man, women. And yet, such are to be the judges in the last resort of the political rights of women; *men!* inclined by their very nature, as the Article maintains, to the boundless misuse of uncontrolled power till its victims are reduced at least to the condition of negroes in the West Indies.

It might have been assumed, continued Thompson, that Mill, who advocated "the primary political rights of man", intended to include women "as forming part of the human race". But no! "On so presumptious a hope, the *veto* is placed."

Since they could expect no help from their lords and masters, the women themselves must protest, demand that "the same enlarged education, which ought to be afforded to all men", should also be applied to them; that they should have the same rights and privileges before the law and "the same political and civil rights that men enjoy". Women, now forced "to eat the tear-steeped bread of dependence as wives, sisters, hired mistresses or unpitied prostitutes", must escape from "the relentless yoke" which man's laws had prepared for them. "As your bondage has chained down man to the ignorance and vices of despotism, so will your liberation reward him with knowledge, with freedom and with happiness."[7]

John Mill came to know Thompson well and to respect him. As for his father's article, it was given a thorough airing in the debating society he had formed and, while·John and his "chosen associates" approved it as a whole as an example of political wisdom, their "adhesion by no means extended to the paragraph of it, in which he maintains that women may consistently with good government, be excluded from the suffrage, because their interest is the same with that of men". From such a doctrine John Mill and his chosen associates "most positively dissented".[8]

At nineteen, John was still too much under his father's thumb to do more than register dissent against the offending passage; but there is no doubt that, between them, Thompson and Mrs Wheeler had converted him to the cause of women's rights. He never forgot the debt he owed to them, to Mary Wollstonecraft and the other pioneers, refusing to permit people to speak of him—as they were often to do in the future—as the first advocate of women's suffrage. "Several of the most eminent philosophers and many of the noblest women for ages have done this",[9] he emphasized at a suffrage meeting in 1870. To him, naturally, the noblest woman of them all had been Harriet Taylor, his wife.

By the time Thompson's book was published, John Mill, who had been working at the India House for two years, had so far emancipated himself as to make a few friends; yet, in the office as at home, he remained very much under James Mill's critical eye.

At the start of a career which was to take him to his father's old post, he showed a flash of independence which not only shook the comparative calm of the Mill household but nearly put paid to his future as a civil servant. He was in the habit of walking to the City every morning from Kensington through the London parks, and more than once was horrified when he stumbled over the body of a dead baby, murdered or abandoned by its mother. His father's reforming friend Francis Place accepted the doctrine of Malthus that the population could be kept in check by moral restraint and late marriage; but he had recently come to the conclusion that these methods alone would not suffice. He had heard that in France, where women had smaller families, they practised a primitive form of birth control—the use of the sponge. He therefore took himself off to Paris, made various enquiries, and returned to write a pamphlet on the subject addressed to the married people of England, arranging for it to be circulated as widely as possible. When he learned from John Mill of the pathetic little corpses he had seen in the parks, Place immediately enlisted his help. So John Mill, with one of his "chosen associates", undertook to distribute copies. For years the story of their escapade was carefully hushed up on account of the taboo on the subject of birth control. Even by 1900 Leslie Stephen, the former editor of the *Dictionary of National Biography,* was prepared to mention it only obliquely. Place's pamphlet, he wrote, "called 'What is love?' [advocated] what are now called Neo Malthusian principles. The police interfered and some scandal was caused."[10] In other words, the two youngsters were apparently caught by the police throwing copies of the pamphlet down the area steps of houses in which unmarried maidservants were employed. They were brought before a magistrate and referred to the Lord Mayor, who sentenced them to fourteen days' imprisonment for distributing obscene literature. They were released within two or three days, probably because the Lord Mayor realized that their object was not to deprave or corrupt, only to do something to prevent the crime of infanticide, to which certain classes of unmarried women were all too prone.

Some years later the former Lord Mayor met John Mill, by then well known, at a dinner, "& some pleasantries passed between them in reference to their previous acquaintance. 'I have had the pleasure of sitting opposite to you before, Mr Mill' said the former Lord Mayor; 'you have' said Mill '& I wd have had a pleasanter recollection of the meeting if you had been quicker in perceiving opposites'."[11]

Although the scandal was passed over almost in silence, it was pointedly remarked on by the poet Thomas Moore in a jingle which after Mill's death also appeared in his obituary in *The Times:*

> There are two Mr M . . ls, too, whom those who like reading
> What's vastly unreadable, call very clever;
> And whereas M . . l senior makes war on *good* breeding
> M . . l junior makes war on all *breeding* whatever.

What James Mill said to his son in private we shall never know; nor do we know the name of the friend with whom he was caught. By this time he was beginning, with the utmost caution, to respond to the friendly advances of other young men; but he was too reserved by nature, too inhibited by his upbringing, to look on them as more than close associates. Of women, beyond his mother and sisters, he knew nothing at all.

One of these new associates was John Arthur Roebuck, the future politician, who had just arrived in England from Canada to read for the Bar and was introduced to John Mill at the India House. Another was George John Graham, a future Registrar General of Births and Deaths. James Mill, who never doubted his divine right to choose John's associates for him, decided to break up his growing friendship with Roebuck and Graham. He attempted this in a roundabout way, by seeking to infect his wife and children with the ridiculous notion that if the friendship were allowed to continue they would lose their beloved John. Once or twice John had taken the young men to spend Sunday at Mickleham, where they were undoubtedly pressed into joining the all-day walks which James Mill and his eldest son enjoyed. On the last occasion James Mill was sullen and impolite. The young men returned to London on the Sunday evening, leaving John to spend the night. He came back to London on the Monday morning and when next he saw his friends explained that he had had an argument with his father and had told him exactly what he thought and where he stood. And so he had; but the upshot was that, while the friendship remained intact, neither Roebuck nor Graham was ever invited to Mickleham again. Moreover, the younger Mills never forgot how their mother, weeping, had cried out that "John was going to leave the house, all on account of Graham and Roebuck".[12]

CHAPTER 3

John Mill, Eliza Flower and the Harriets

When he was twenty John Mill passed through an experience which, apart from its other consequences, retarded any interest he might have felt in the opposite sex. He had already begun to make a name for himself as a writer in the influential reviews of the day and as a skilful and brilliant debater. He had launched a literary magazine and founded the debating society already mentioned of young thinkers and writers who reinterpreted Bentham's doctrine of utilitarianism. All seemed set fair until in 1826, he suffered a curious form of nervous breakdown.

Alexander Bain, who came to know him very well, attributed the breakdown to overwork. "There was one thing that [Mill] would never allow, which was that work could be pushed to the point of being injurious to either body or mind. That the dejection . . . was due to physical causes, and that the chief of these causes was over-working the brain may I think be certified beyond all reasonable doubt."[1]

Leslie Stephen came nearer to the truth when he claimed that a young man who, like John Mill, "had been kept in a state of severe intellectual tension from his earliest infancy"[2] would be more prone to a nervous breakdown than one who was merely suffering from overwork. It is incontrovertible that sooner or later the conflicting pressures of his boyhood would take their toll; that his ambivalent feelings towards his father and mother, half smothered in work as they were, would lead to some crisis. For a time he lost all relish for life and, as he himself put it, he lapsed into "a dull state of nerves", was covered by a cloud which refused to pass away. He spoke of this to no one: to confide in his father was impossible; his mother would not have understood; he was not really intimate with his sisters, and the brother nearest him in age, James Bentham, was only twelve. He had friends, but none close enough to risk a confidence which might have proved embarrassing. "If I had loved any one sufficiently to make confiding my griefs a necessity, I should not have been in the condition I was. I felt, too, that mine was not an interesting, or in any way respectable distress. There was nothing in it to attract sympathy. Advice, if I had known where to seek it, would have been most precious."[3]

Even at its thickest the cloud of misery and depression did not, it appears, obscure his work or interfere with his normal life. Very slowly it began to lift. The process was hastened by the realization that his father's eighteenth-century philosophy and cool rational outlook were not enough for him: he must seek to enter a world in which feelings and emotions as well as arguments mattered. He was too naive and immature to understand that what he needed was a sympathetic young woman. What he found, or thought he found, was the ideal friend, a sincere, charming and most lovable young man. He was John Sterling, writer, poet and, briefly, a clergyman, the son of Edward Sterling of *The Times*, known as "The Thunderer".

There was nothing homosexual about the friendship: on Mill's side it was the delight of being able to speak and write frankly to another human being which counted. His sympathies with society, so he told Sterling three years after the onset of his breakdown, had always been weak but were growing slightly stronger; yet he still felt solitary and lonely. "By loneliness I mean the absence of that feeling... which one fellow traveller, or one fellow soldier has towards another—the feeling of being engaged in the pursuit of a common object, and of mutually cheering one another on, and helping one another in an arduous undertaking."[4] So self-searching was he—though entirely on the wrong track—that he was convinced that no human being existed with whom he could feel on terms of absolute equality, with whom he could work towards some common goal without the uneasy feeling that he was simply using him to further his own purpose.

Sterling, then, was not to become the perfect friend; neither was Carlyle, another likely candidate. When Mill did find the perfect friend, in a young woman, he deliberately placed himself not on terms of absolute equality with, but below, her.

Poetry, which his ideal friend loved dearly, proved another source of consolation. He found Byron's state of mind too like his own, but the poems of Wordsworth "seemed to be the very culture of the feelings, which I was in quest of. In them I seemed to draw from a source of inward joy, of sympathetic and imaginative pleasure, which could be shared in by all human beings." The first real "ray of light" to lighten John Mill's gloom was, however, the accidental discovery of *Mémoires d'un père* by the French novelist and dramatist François Marmontel. To Mill, the most pregnant passage was one "which relates his father's death, the distressed position of the family, and the sudden inspiration by which he, then a mere boy, felt and made them feel that he would be everything to them—would supply the place of all that they had lost. A vivid conception of the scene and its feelings came over me, and I was moved to tears."[5]

It has been suggested that the root cause of John Mill's breakdown was a suppressed death-wish towards the father who dominated and moulded him, that "by an act of empathy [he] identified himself with the bereaved Marmontel.... In experiencing his father's death and the freedom which this would mean to his own ego, but under the literary and imaginative circumstances which would absolve him of the guilty wishes themselves, Mill brought to the surface what had hitherto been laboriously repressed, and by this cathartic act spontaneously found the real solution for his mental crises."[6]

This is most certainly a satisfactory explanation, but it is one which Mill was naturally at pains to conceal. In the official version of his *Autobiography* he insisted that he was always loyally devoted to his father; but there is a passage in the early version of it (published in 1961 as *The Early Draft of John Stuart Mill's Autobiography*, ed. J. Stillinger) which reveals his true feelings: "In respect of what I am here concerned with, the moral agencies which acted on myself, it must be mentioned as a most baneful one, that my father's [elder] children neither loved him, nor, with any warmth of affection any one else."[7]

In fact, John Mill blamed both his parents: his father for the absence of genuine paternal love, which stultified his capacity for forming normal personal relationships; his mother for being intellectually limited, unimaginative, and obsessed with domesticity. He emerged from the shadow of his breakdown a diffident, inhibited, suspicious man. The diffidence and the inhibitions were gradually lightened, but the suspicion, which persisted at intervals throughout his life, caused him to behave on occasion with unreasoning cruelty, especially towards his mother and sisters and some of the women supporters of the suffrage movement.

His depression was finally relieved by his meeting in 1830 with the young woman who was to change the whole course of his life and work. It is true that even after this cataclysmic meeting Mill remained prone to attacks of melancholia, but these were in part the result of his unconventional relationship with another man's wife. "I will not if I can help it give way to gloom and morbid despondency", he wrote to Carlyle in 1833, at the onset of one of these attacks, which coincided with a period of crisis with his beloved. He felt, however, that a tendency to depression and self-examination was responsible "for all the most valuable of such insight as I have into the most important matters". The tendency also constituted a menace of which he was well aware: "I will and must . . . master it, or it will surely master me."[8]

John Mill owed his introduction to Harriet Taylor, the ideal friend, to a fellow writer, William Johnson Fox, who was at the time Unitarian preacher at the South Place Chapel in Finsbury, London. The two men most probably met as fellow contributors to the radical *Westminster Review,* which had been founded in 1824 by James Mill and financed by the wealthy, philanthropic Jeremy Bentham. (James Mill considered that his position at the India House precluded him from openly assuming the editorship, but his was always the deciding voice. In 1836 the *Westminster Review,* which had already been sold once, was bought by Sir William Molesworth, who amalgamated it with the recently founded *London Review.* The new *London and Westminster Review* was run at a loss until Molesworth disposed of it to John Stuart Mill the following year. Mill raised it to a high level of excellence and persuaded the most distinguished writers of the day to contribute. Like his father, he was responsible for policy and he also appointed an editor, John Robertson, to work under his direction. In 1840 Mill disposed of the review to a former shoe manufacturer, John Hickson, who was unable to sustain its former high standard. Hickson sold it in 1851 for £350 to John Chapman, who ran it, once more as the *Westminster Review*, with the assistance of Marian Evans—i.e. George Eliot.)

Fox was twenty years older than Mill; but the friendship prospered despite the difference of age and the more cogent fact that Mill had been brought up without any religious beliefs. No attempt was made by Fox to convert his young friend to his own beliefs. His religion, Mill explained, was "of the most unobtrusive kind, [it] is what the religion of all denominations would be, if we were in a healthy state—a religion of *spirit*, not of *dogma* and catholic in the best sense".[9] Fox edited the Unitarian magazine the *Monthly Repository*, which he bought in 1831, and was a magnetic preacher. Carlyle conceded his eloquence, even though he was suspicious of the Unitarian circle and noted in the preacher an unfortunate "tendency to pot-belly and snuffiness".[10]

One of the women in Fox's congregation to fall under the spell of his eloquence was Eliza Flower, to whom he introduced John Mill. Eliza and her younger sister Sarah were the lovely, gifted daughters of that champion of Dissenters, Benjamin Flower, editor of the *Cambridge Intelligencer*. Flower was sent to prison for the alleged libel of a bishop of the Church of England, and there he was visited by an independent-minded young woman who became his wife. Mrs Flower died when Eliza was seven, Sarah only five, and the little girls were educated by their father.

The Flowers and the Foxes were close friends, but, while Benjamin Flower had been happily married, Fox found his own wife incompatible and unsympathetic. The Flower girls were welcome visitors in the Fox household, and the preacher became "their friend and religious teacher [and] also their mentor in literary and cultural matters".[11] To Eliza he became something very much more.

Sarah Flower, who wrote poetry, is remembered today chiefly for the words of the hymn "Nearer my God to Thee". The enchanting Eliza, known to her friends as "Ariel", loved poetry and composed music even as a child. "She worshipped Mozart, Shakespeare, Milton, Burns, Byron, but if these had never existed she would still have been Eliza Flower", wrote Fox's biographer.[12] Both sisters contributed to Fox's *Monthly Repository*. Eliza won the adoring friendship of an incipient genius, Robert Browning, nine years her junior; but, although she appreciated poetry, music was her first love. As a natural, untrained musician she was considered one of the finest women composers of her day. He first published work was the *Fourteen Musical Illustrations of Waverley Novels;* and this was followed by a wealth of compositions, religious and secular, culminating in a musical service for the South Place Chapel. In addition she helped Fox in his editorial and journalistic work, copying articles and speeches and doing the necessary research. It is scarcely surprising that "the community of literary and cultural interests between them ripened by degrees into a romantic friendship". Lacking the companionship of an affectionate wife, he "seems to have turned more and more to the talented girl seventeen years his junior".[13]

Benjamin Flower died in 1829, leaving Fox as executor and trustee for his daughters. In the circumstances this was extremely rash, for, while Sarah married and moved out of the preacher's orbit, Eliza remained helplessly enmeshed.

It was at about this time, when Eliza Flower was twenty-six and John Mill twenty-three, that they first met. Fox's most distinguished successor at South Place, the American, Moncure Daniel Conway, biographer of Thomas Paine, believed that Mill was "an aspirant for her hand". He also believed that Eliza refused him on the improbable grounds that "she was the spouse of her art, consecrated to its ideal".[14]

If the two had been genuinely attracted there is no reason why they should not have married. Eliza Flower could have become Mrs John Stuart Mill and continued her career as a composer, for Mill, who was himself musical, greatly admired her work. Of one of her compositions, *Songs of the Months*, he wrote, "The March and August are the best, I think, in a high sense of the word. 'July', 'October' & 'November' are simpler & extremely beautiful. 'February' I admire exceedingly, & most of the others seem to me very good, each in its way."[15] He wrote a review of Eliza's *Songs* for the *Examiner* of 4 January 1835, remarking, a little belatedly in the circumstances, that they would be "a welcome Christmas present to any lover of music".

Mill was also something of a musician. According to his stepson, Algernon Taylor, who lived with his mother and Mill after their marriage in 1851, he used sometimes to play the piano in the evenings when especially asked to do so by his wife. He would then "play music entirely of his own composition, on the spur of the moment: music of a singular character, wanting, possibly, in the finish which more practice would have imparted, but rich in feeling, vigour and suggestiveness".[16]

It was of Eliza Flower that Mill was thinking when he wrote a certain passage in the early draft of his *Autobiography*. In a reference to his wife's circle of friends when he first knew her, he declared that "one only (a woman) was a person of genius, or of capacities of feeling or intellect kindred with her own".[17] That the woman in question was Eliza Flower was confirmed by Mrs Mill's daughter, Helen Taylor; but, at Mrs Mill's request, the word "woman" was replaced by "person" in the final version of the *Autobiography*.

If John Mill proposed marriage to Eliza Flower, which seems highly unlikely, she refused him not on account of her music but because of her devotion to William Johnson Fox. Fox was in love with Eliza and she with him. He may well have feared, however, that the disadvantage of being a married man, to say nothing of his age, pot-belly and snuffiness, would lead her to prefer the brilliant, highly eligible John Mill. If this were so, then the meeting he proceeded to engineer between Mill and a member of his congregation, Harriet Taylor, was deliberately planned in order to provide Mill with a counter-attraction.

Another woman with whom Mill was reputed by the diarist Charles Greville to be in love was Carlyle's adored Lady Harriet Baring (Lady Ashburton). Mill and Harriet Baring met shortly after his first encounter with Harriet Taylor, but before he had begun to experience the full impact of her personality. According to Greville, Mill was devotedly attached to Lady Harriet and, in return, she admired but did not love him.

In any event, here was only the vaguest hint of a romance, despite an ingenious theory which has recently been put forward by Professor Bruce Mazlish: that the prevalence of Harriets in Mill's life was not accidental but was the outcome of a submerged love of his mother—also a Harriet. This theory, though highly intriguing, fails on a number of counts. It is, of course, true that the love of Mill's life was named Harriet, but so were countless other women of his time. One was his grandmother, Mrs Harriet Burrow, after whom his mother was named. He was as fond of her as most small boys are of their grandmothers, but it is hard to equate her with Harriet Baring. Another Harriet was his sister Harriet Isabella, to whom, as to his mother and others among his sisters, he behaved most callously. There were at least two more Harriets in his life: one was Harriet Grote, with whom he quarrelled on Harriet Taylor's behalf; the other was the deaf, opinionated Harriet Martineau, whom he thoroughly disliked. These women all happened to be called Harriet. Then, too, it is difficult to think, as Professor Mazlish avers, that there is any connection between the age of John Mill's mother, who was twenty-three when she married his father, and Harriet Taylor, who was twenty-three when he met her.[18]

The much disliked Harriet Martineau was present at the fateful meeting between John Mill and his Egeria. Her career as a pioneer woman journalist had, in fact, been given a tremendous impetus by William Johnson Fox. She had published a few articles when her attention was drawn to an advertisement soliciting contributions for the *Monthly Repository*. She answered it and was flattered to discover that her name was already known to the editor, who promptly invited her to write regularly for him. For a woman to write under her own name was most unusual at the time; and it was from the Fox family pew in the South Place Chapel that Harriet Martineau first heard it spoken aloud in public. The British and Foreign Unitarian Association had offered three prizes for three separate essays on the means of diffusing their faith among Jews, Moslems and Catholics. It was announced that all three prizes had been awarded to Harriet Martineau.

Harriet Martineau was twenty-eight in the late summer or early autumn of 1830, when W. J. Fox escorted her to dinner at the house of a leading member of his flock, John Taylor: the other guests were John Mill, who had not yet met the Taylors, and his friends Roebuck and Graham. John Taylor was a prosperous drysalter, or wholesale druggist. He was a kindly, honourable man: according to Carlyle, who met him a year or so later, "an innocent, dull good man".[19] He possessed a cheerful disposition and was an admirable host, if rather too fond of the pleasures of the table; and, though far from uncultured, he was not an intellectual and lacked imagination and insight. His looks were indeterminate and in this, as in other respects, he was the complete antithesis of the dearly loved wife whom he had married in 1826, when he was twenty-nine and she only eighteen.

Harriet Taylor, born Harriet Hardy, was one of the seven children—five sons and two daughters—of a doctor, a member of the Royal College of Surgeons. The atmosphere in the Hardy household was neither peaceful nor pleasant. According to Harriet, her father was harsh and excessively mean. Between herself, her irritable, exacting mother, and her volatile younger sister Caroline, who married a licentious lawyer, Arthur Ley, there existed a tangled "emotional triangle which on occasion drove Harriet to the edge of exasperation".[20] It was to result in frequent quarrels, with Mrs Hardy and the Leys on one side, Harriet on the other. The only member of the family to hold a permanent place in Harriet's affections, as she in his, was her youngest brother, Arthur, who settled in Australia.

The marriage with John Taylor may well have been arranged by Dr Hardy, himself a Unitarian, but there can be no doubt that Harriet was thankful to escape from the tension and frictions of the Hardy household to a home of her own and a husband who worshipped her. She had grown into a beauty. With her huge, intelligent dark eyes, her finely-cut features, ringletted dark brown hair, and the long, pearly-skinned throat and sloping shoulders so fashionable in her day, she resembled a Jane Austin heroine. She was undoubtedly in love with her husband, at least for the first year or so of their marriage: she could not otherwise have written to him in 1828, a year after the birth of her elder son Herbert—or Herby as he was called—in the terms she used. She and the baby were in the Isle of Wight, her husband in London.

My dearest John,
　　Though I knew that I must not send you another letter for some days, as I only wrote yesterday, yet I cannot bear to defer the pleasure of writing, even tho' you should not see it at present. I received your letter my dearest ... last night—every letter you send me the mere sight of your writing, gives me great pleasure but the happiness the delight I have received from this can scarcely be imagined—every question I asked you, all that I have said is answered in the very words I would have chosen. . . . I put it under my pillow that I might read it to our dear little one as soon as he awoke this morning. . . . Oh my dear John, each hour that passes brings us nearer the day when we shall meet and I think from my present feelings that I shall never again consent to our parting. . . . I need not repeat the joy I shall feel when I perceive you on the boat for I know you will feel the same. Our little one is rather poorly again, but looks well and

will soon be so as his tiresome tooth does appear to be coming through at last. Adieu dearest till the happy moment comes—Adieu.[21]

What little Herby thought of his father's letters history does not relate, but John Taylor clearly was charmed by Harriet's.

The susceptible William Johnson Fox admired the lovely Mrs Taylor from a distance, not simply for her looks but also for her intellect. The year after her marraige he was absent for some time from London, owing to illness, and, when he wrote to John Taylor on congregational matters, he added a ponderously gallant message for Harriet. When "improving health & pleasurable sensation give me sufficient impulse for the production of a spontaneous letter Mrs Taylor shall profit—or suffer—by the occasion. Will she draw a practical inference from the position that reading is better for an Invalid than writing".[22]

A second son, Algernon—known as Haji or Hadji—was born at the beginning of 1830. By that time, however, Harriet had become disenchanted with her dearest John: in fact she was thoroughly bored with him. Largely self-educated, she had an earnest, inquiring mind, sensitive artistic and aesthetic tastes to which he could not respond. With the exception of the Flower sisters, Eliza and Sarah, who were her friends, she found the company of her Unitarian acquaintances narrow and limited and longed to spread her wings. It appears that she turned for advice on intellectual questions to Fox and, according to Carlyle, "he told her that John Mill was the man among the human race to relieve in a competent manner her dubieties and difficulties".[23]

And so, whatever his motives, Fox brought Mill to dine with the Taylors. It was as rash an act as Benjamin Flower's decision to confide his daughters to Fox's care: its consequences were as incandescent but, for posterity, far more significant.

The friendship between John Mill and his hostess developed more rapidly than he was prepared to admit, and even on that first evening there must have been an awareness of sympathy between them. John Roebuck could not afterwards recollect "what passed . . . , but it turned out that Mrs Taylor was much taken with Mill". Roebuck, who understood Mill as well as any man, soon had reason for concern. Mill, he affirmed, was "utterly ignorant of what is called society . . . ; of the world, as it worked around him, he knew nothing; and . . . , of *woman* he was a child".[24] Carlyle put the case more crudely. As he told the American man of letters and art historian Charles Eliot Norton, a good friend of writers and artists, Mill, "who up to that time, had never so much as looked at a female creature, not even a cow, in the face, found himself opposite those great dark eyes, that were flashing unutterable things while he was discoursin' the utterable concernin' all sorts o' high topics".[25] Carlyle, who had not been present at the dinner party, was, of course, fond of embellishing his stories. To another friend, Sir Charles Gavan Duffy, the Irish patriot, he described Harriet Taylor as "a shrewd woman, with a taste for coquetry, [who] took possession of Mill and wrapped him up like a cocoon".[26]

Harriet was shrewd but she was certainly not a coquette. If she wrapped Mill up in a cocoon it was because it was in a cocoon of her spinning that he most wished to lodge.

CHAPTER 4

Harriet Taylor and John Stuart Mill

Thousands of words have been written about the relationship of John Stuart Mill with Harriet Taylor, but it was not until the publication of their letters in 1951 (in F.A. Hayek's *John Stuart Mill and Harriet Taylor*) that the extent of her influence over him could be gauged. With very few exceptions Mill's contemporaries and early biographers, while admitting that to some extent she helped him in his work, saw her only as a designing woman of quick intelligence who exploited his infatuation and courted attention. Harriet Martineau, for example, waspishly dismissed her as one of "the mere pedants [who] were qualified for something better...and...ought to have been superior to the nonsense and vanity in which they participated".[1] W. J. Fox and the Flower sisters, on the other hand, saw her as Mill initially found her. Up to the time of their first meeting, Mill wrote, "her rich and powerful nature had chiefly unfolded itself according to the received type of feminine genius. To her outer circle she was a beauty and a wit, with an air of natural distinction, felt by all who approached her: to the inner, a woman of deep and strong feeling, of penetrating and intuitive intelligence, and of an eminently meditative and poetic nature." Although he claimed—wrongly it appears—that it was years before the friendship became really close, he "soon perceived that she possessed in combination, the qualities which in all other persons whom I had known I had been only too happy to find singly". Her intellect, her sensibility and imagination would "have fitted her to be a consummate artist, as her fiery and tender soul and her vigorous eloquence would certainly have made her a great orator, and her profound knowledge of human nature and discernment and sagacity in practical life, would, in the times when such a *carrière* was open to women, have made her eminent among the rulers of mankind. Her intellectual gifts did but minister to a moral character at once the noblest and the best balanced which I have ever met with in life."

Not content to extol her intellectual excellence alone, he wrote of her character in the same terms:

> Her unselfishness was...that...of a heart which thoroughly identified itself with the feelings of others, and often went to excess in

34

consideration for them by imaginatively investing their feelings with the intensity of its own. The passion of justice might have been thought to be her strongest feeling, but for her boundless generosity, and a lovingness ever ready to pour itself forth upon any or all human beings who were capable of giving the smallest feeling in return.

She also possessed, among other superlative qualities,

the most genuine modesty combined with the loftiest pride; a simplicity and sincerity which were absolute, towards all who were fit to receive them; the utmost scorn of whatever was mean and cowardly, and a burning indignation at everything brutal or tyrannical, faithless or dishonourable in conduct and character. . . .

To be admitted into any degree of mental intercourse with a being of these qualities, could not but have a most beneficial influence on my development. . . . The benefit I received was far greater than any which I could hope to give; though to her, who had at first reached her opinions by the moral intuition of a character of strong feeling, there was doubtless help as well as encouragement to be derived from one who had arrived at many of the same results by study and reasoning; and in the rapidity of her intellectual growth, her mental activity, which converted everything into knowledge, doubtless drew from me, as it it did from other sources, many of its materials . . . .[2]

For many years it was thought that the *Autobiography* (see below, chapter 23), which was not published until 1873, a few months after Mill's death, was one of his final works. In fact, since the publication in 1961 of the early draft, it has been clear that the bulk of it was written during 1853-4, so that Harriet Taylor, by that time Mrs John Stuart Mill, both saw and approved much of the praise which her doting husband chose to bestow on her. It is only natural that she should have been anxious to vindicate herself in the eyes of the world which had disapproved of their unconventional relationship; but a proper sense of proportion would have convinced her that she was doing herself no good. Mill wrote of her as he found her and as they both hoped posterity would see her. In so doing, he obscured instead of illuminating the crucial importance of her contribution to his work. Since no one could credit the existence of so celestial a being, no one could believe how greatly her radical views, so much more advanced than his own, had influenced his writing.

One of the first—if not *the* first—subject which drew them together was their common interest in women's rights. People might suppose, wrote Mill, "that my strong convictions on the complete equality in all legal, political, social and domestic relations, which ought to exist between men and women, may have been adopted or learnt from her. This was so far from being the fact, that those convictions were among the earliest results of the application of my mind to political subjects, and the strength with which I held them was, as I believe, more than anything else, the originating cause of the interest she felt in me."[3] Lest it be thought that in this field he led and Harriet followed, he hastened to add that she gave substance to what until then had been no more to him than an intellectual abstraction. Humble in all ways, he endowed her with a degree of perception which he did not consider he possessed himself. He said, for example, that he had found his friend Carlyle difficult to understand: "I never presumed to judge him with any definiteness, until he was interpreted to me by one greatly the superior of us both—who was more a poet than he, and more a thinker than I—whose own mind and nature included his, and infinitely more"[4] (see also chapter 8 below).

We do not know how long it was before the tyrannical James Mill realized that his eldest son had escaped from his domination and yielded to a personality as powerful but infinitely more compelling than his own. When he learned of the friendship he told John roundly that he should not "'be in love with another man's wife', to which John answered with strange simplicity, 'I have no other feeling for her than I would have for an equally able man.' "[5] John Mill was, indeed, strangely simple in some respects. It is not difficult to believe that he genuinely thought that it was Harriet's character and intellect, not her beauty, feminine allure and desire for admiration, which drew him to her. James Mill remained sceptical, as well he might. "John is still in a rather pining way", he wrote to his son James Bentham, who left England in about 1836 to join the Indian Civil Service; "tho as he does not choose to tell the cause of his pining, he leaves other people to their conjectures."[6] Mrs Mill and her elder daughters must have discussed John's pining, but what they said, or thought, is also pure conjecture.

There would, of course, have been nothing against the friendship had John Taylor been included, but he was not. As the person most intimately concerned, he suffered intensely. When John Mill first met Harriet, she and John Taylor were still physically man and wife, for their daughter Helen—or Lily as she was called—was not born until the summer of 1831. Helen was undoubtedly John Taylor's child although throughout the remainder of his life he was to see little of her and she for her part did not feel deprived. Meanwhile, when Harriet's relationship with Mill developed into something more than mere friendship, she refused to be anything but a wife in name to her husband.

About a year after Helen's birth, Harriet, distraught and torn by conflicting emotions, her love for John Mill and his growing dependence on her on the one side, her duty towards her husband and children on the other, made a futile attempt to break with Mill. On returning to London, laden with wild flowers for her, from a walking tour in the south of England, he found awaiting him a note of renunciation. It elicited from him an agonized cry of protest: "Benie soi la main qui a tracé ces caractères! Elle m'a écrit—il suffit; bien que je ne me dissimule pas que c'est pour me dire un éternel adieu. .... Elle sera obéie: mes lettres n'iront plus troubler sa tranquillité, ou verser une goutte de plus dans la coupe de ses chagrins ...."[7]

Harriet had said they must part. Mill utterly refused to accept the separation as final: at some time in the future they would surely meet again. And so they did, not in the distant but in the immediate future.

In this delicate situation Mill could rely on W. J. Fox to act as go-between, for he and Harriet were both contributors to Fox's *Monthly Repository* and Fox was a welcome guest in John Taylor's house. The preacher, who transformed the *Repository* from an essentially religious to a largely secular magazine, published anonymously some of Harriet's poems, sketches and reviews. He did not, however, view her literary efforts in the same exalted light as John Mill, who declared, "I have often compared her, as she was at this time, to Shelley; but in thought and intellect, Shelley, so far as his powers were developed in his short life, was but a child compared with what she ultimately became."[8] Harriet's poem "To the Summer Wind" which appeared in the *Repository,* and is reprinted, along with two other of her poems, in Hayek's *John Stuart Mill and Harriet Taylor* (pp. 271-5) might fairly be labelled "after" Shelley; but by no stretch of the imagination can it be called great poetry:

> Whence comest thou, sweet wind?
> Didst take thy phantom form
> 'Mid the depth of the forest trees?
> Of springs, new born,
> Of the fragrant morn,
> 'Mong the far-off Indian seas? ...

All the same, if Harriet was no great poet, she stimulated and developed Mill's appreciation of poetry, which had been brought to life by Wordsworth during his mental crisis. In 1833 he wrote a two-part essay "What is Poetry?" and also reviewed the poems of Robert Browning (Browning's first published poem, "Pauline", is said to have been inspired by Eliza Flower) and those of another rising star, Alfred Tennyson. The article and the reviews were written under Harriet's direction. Mill's essay on Tennyson, wrote Fox's biographer, "with its appreciation of other poets and discussions of the principles of poetry in general, would have been impossible ... when, not many years before, he had just sufficiently awakened to the mission of poetry to call in Wordsworth as a spiritual physician. The development can only be ascribed to the influence of Mrs Taylor".[9] Mill had told Fox that, subject to Harriet's agreement, he might publish the essay as well as the reviews. "You know it is hers—if she approves, it shall be yours." At the same time he confided in the older man, whose personal predicament resembled his own, something of the anguish he was enduring. When Harriet was depressed, as she often was, "it is always something amiss in *me* that is the cause ... it is because she sees that what ought to be so much easier to me than to her, is in reality more difficult—costs a harder struggle—to part company with the opinion of the world, and with my former modes of doing good in it; however, thank heaven, she does not doubt that I can do it . . . ."[10]

He hoped, he added, that he and Fox would meet frequently while Harriet was away. This was a reference to the fact that, after interminable discussions, John Taylor had yielded to his wife's persuasions and agreed to a six months' separation. Harriet duly departed for Paris: within a month she had been joined by Mill, who could not stay away. As he wrote ecstatically to Fox, a few days with Harriet had "brought years of experience to us—good and happy experience most of it. We never could have been so near, so perfectly intimate, in any former circumstances. . . . Not a day has passed without removing some real & serious obstacle to happiness. I never thought so humbly of myself compared with her, never thought or felt myself so little worthy of her, never more keenly regretted that I am not, in some things, very different for her sake."

He had promised to abide by any decision she might make, even if it meant his returning to London alone. Fox, who not unnaturally had surmised that the separation would be permanent and that Mill and Harriet would live openly together, had completely misjudged them, Mill now insisted. Harriet was convinced that if she chose separation she would ruin her husband's life. Instead, her affection for him had been strengthened by fresh proofs of his steady devotion, "& by the unexpected & (his nature considered) really admirable generosity and nobleness which he has shown under so severe a trial".[11]

Enclosed in this letter was a note from Harriet to Fox and Eliza, also upbraiding them: "It is sad to be misunderstood by you . . . my own dear friends . . . but it will not be always so. . . . He tells you quite truly our state. . . . To be with him wholly is my ideal of the noblest fate for all states of mind and feeling which are lofty & large & fine, he is the companion spirit and heart desire—we are not alike in trifles only because I have so much more frivolity than he . . . ."[12] What bliss it would be, she concluded, if the four of them could be together in Paris.

But Harriet had already made up her mind. At her command John Mill returned home, but she herself was back in England long before the stipulated six months had come to an end. John Taylor had been coerced into giving his consent to a continuance of the friendship on condition that the outward semblance of his married life was maintained. Making use of the valid excuse that his wife was delicate, he bought her a country house at Keston Heath, near Bromley in Kent. Harriet, with her little daughter Helen, spent more and more of her time at Keston. She returned to her husband's London home—17 Kent Terrace, a tall house with imposing Ionic columns, near Hanover Gate, Regent's Park—only during her sons' school holidays. When Harriet was in London her husband obligingly vacated the house when Mill was expected to call, leaving her to the chaperonage of her children and servants. Despite his loneliness and her preoccupation with

Mill, husband and wife contrived to remain on good terms. She wrote to him now as her "dear John"; he addressed her as his "dear Harry". "Your letter gave me the greatest pleasure, many thanks, dear John, for all the kind things you say in it", she wrote to her long-suffering husband in 1839. "Give my best love to the dear boys & tell them I am always thinking of them . . . ."[13]

Whether or not she was thinking of the dear boys, who were old enough to suffer from the arrangement, Harriet was thinking far more about herself and John Mill. His love and admiration were boundless. There are passages when the eulogies in his *Autobiography* and elsewhere are too far-fetched to be credible; others, such as the following passage, when he did her no more than justice: "Alike in the highest regions of speculation and in the smaller practical concerns of daily life, her mind was the same perfect instrument, piercing to the very heart and marrow of the matter; always seizing the essential idea or principle."[14] Harriet could, indeed, cut with ease to the root of the problem and, as will be seen, produce a solution which might surprise or alarm, but ultimately convince him. She was not, however, good at clothing her ideas in words, which make her letters confusing to read; nor was her intellect superior to Mill's whatever he might say to the contrary. What was remarkable was that this largely self-educated woman could, and did, speak and correspond with him on equal terms and, when she felt strongly enough, force him to accept her ideas. When they worked together on the *Autobiography* his intention to vindicate and glorify the woman who was now his wife was admirable. He would have been horrified to think that, instead, he had done her a good deal of harm.

A generation earlier, with equally good intentions, William Godwin had harmed the posthumous reputation of his wife, Mary Wollstonecraft, not by putting her on a pedestal but by his frank disclosure of her love affairs, her pregnancies and suicide attempts. Indeed, as her recent biographer suggests, this account of "her sexual transgressions" not only damaged her reputation but also caused the next generation of Dissenting women to guard their morals with peculiar care. Harriet Taylor, for one, she says, "certainly felt obliged to put an extraordinary restraint upon her own sexual behaviour".[15]

But did she? The question of whether Harriet and John Mill were lovers in the full sense of the word has been argued at length, and the accepted conclusion is that they were not. Nevertheless, they were wildly indiscreet. Mill was a constant weekend visitor at Harriet's country house; they travelled together in England and on the Continent, often with one or more of Harriet's children; they were seen everywhere together. And yet, to use Harriet's expression, they remained *Seelenfreunden*. Had they become lovers and behaved more discreetly, their relationship would have been less strained and tense and John Taylor might have been less hurt. Did they remain soul-mates because they were too idealistic to become lovers, because Mill was impotent, or because Harriet found the physical act distasteful?

Naturally they were at pains to prove that their restraint was mutual and based on the highest of motives. In 1854, while Harriet was abroad for her health and Mill, in England, was at work on the *Autobiography,* he consulted her, as he had done for the past year, on the wording of the draft. It contained "a full writing out as far as anything can write out, what you are, as far as I am competent to describe you, & what I owe to you—but, besides that until revised by you it is little better than unwritten, it contains nothing about our private circumstances, further than shewing that there was intimate friendship for many years, & you only can decide what more it is necessary or desirable to say in order to stop the mouths of enemies hereafter". If the book were not to be published for another century he would say, "tell all, simply and without reserve". In the meantime, "will you not my own love in one of your sweetest letters give me your general notion of what we should say or imply respecting our private concerns. As it is, it shews confidential friendship & strong attachment ending in marriage when you were free & ignores there having ever been any scandalous suspicions about us . . . ."[16]

Harriet considered the problem and came to the conclusion that all that was required was about a dozen lines telling the story of their lives from 1830 onwards in all "its genuine truth and simplicity"; close affection and friendship but "no impropriety". This would paint "an edifying picture for those poor wretches who cannot conceive friendship but in sex—nor believe that expediency and the consideration for feelings of others can conquer sensuality".[17]

Mill declared himself unequal to the task. "Could you not my own love write it out your darling self & send it in one of your precious letters . . . ."[18]

The passage, as it eventually appeared in the *Autobiography,* explained that Mill had visited Harriet in the country, where she lived with her daughter, and also, very rarely, in London.

> I . . . was greatly indebted to the strength of character which enabled her to disregard the false interpretations liable to be put on the frequency of my visits to her while living generally apart from Mr Taylor, and on our occasionally travelling together, though in all other respects our conduct during those years gave not the slightest ground for any other supposition than the true one, that our relation to each other at that time was one of strong affection and confidential intimacy only. For though we did not consider the ordinances of society binding on a subject so entirely personal, we did feel bound that our conduct should be such as in no degree to bring discredit on her husband, nor therefore on herself.

Of their marriage he had this, among his tributes to Harriet, to say: "Ardently as I should have aspired to this complete union of our lives at any time in the course of my existence at which it had been practicable, I, as much as my wife, would far rather have foregone that privilege for ever, than have owed it to the premature death of one for whom I had the sincerest respect, and she the strongest affection . . . ."[19]

The remark that the relationship was one of affection *at that time* could be interpreted as an indication that the marriage was indeed a *complete union*, as Mill states. If we knew whether their interpretation of their earlier relationship was the correct one, we should be better informed. Mill was forty-five when they married, Harriet forty-four, although he made out that she was a year younger. Both had been in poor health for years, Harriet especially so, which makes consummation after so long a delay improbable, child-bearing out of the question.

As to the supposition that Mill was impotent, the nervous complaints which afflicted him makes this sound more than possible, but there is no direct evidence either way. A letter to Harriet written in 1857, the year before she died, provides an indirect clue. He had dreamed the previous night, he said, that he had been sitting at table opposite a young man and with a woman seated on his left. In conversation the man quoted a saying, " 'there are two excellent & rare things to find in a woman, a sincere friend & a sincere Magdalen.' I answered 'the best would be to find both in one'—on which the woman said 'no, that would be *too* vain'—whereupon I broke out 'do you suppose when one speaks of what is good in itself, one must be thinking of one's own paltry self interest? no, I spoke of what is abstractedly good & admirable . . . .' "[20] In another letter he told her of a terrifying dream. He had been separated from her, as he was at the time, on a six months' journey for his own health; he had returned "& she was sweet & loving like herself at first, but presently she took a complete dislike to me saying that I was changed much for the worse—I am terribly afraid sometimes lest she should think so".[21] Harriet, then, was unattainable, though whether as a consequence of Mill's incompetence or because he imposed an iron discipline on his natural urges we do not know.

Whatever the nature of their physical relations, Mill's complete dependence on Harriet shows him as emotionally immature. He enjoyed being dominated by her, as other men before and after him have enjoyed being dominated by strong-minded women. There is a parallel here to be drawn between John Stuart Mill and the late Duke of Windsor, who enjoyed being dominated by the Duchess. Harriet bewitched Mill as Mrs Simpson bewitched the King: the influence of these two highly intelligent women was overwhelming.

The suggestion has been made that Harriet, not Mill, was responsible for the restraint in their physical relations, that she was obsessed with "cases of wife-beating, of cruelty towards women, at home and in factories, of sexual assaults, and of corporal punishment", to an extent which pointed to a "deep-seated masochism unfitting her for normal physical love".[22] It is perfectly true that in the record which Mill kept of his published articles and letters to newspapers there were a number of references to crimes of this kind and that against these entries he noted down such comments as "a joint production with my wife", or "very little of this was mine"; but these entries are relatively very few, many of the rest being concerned with India, a subject in which Mill was, of course, the expert and on which joint production with

Harriet could not be expected. Then, too, Harriet was deeply concerned with all questions of injustice, not only towards defenceless women but towards the underprivileged classes as a whole, in an age when they suffered much injustice. There seems no valid reason, therefore, why she should not have suggested and helped in the composition of an unsigned article—"very little of which was mine"—arguing that "the administration of corporal punishment by representatives of the law should be made illegal".[23] Nor does there seem any reason why she should not have proposed and provided substance for a letter commending Queen Victoria for her refusal to sanction flogging for a young man who had fired at her with an unloaded pistol. Mill found her suggestions both valuable and important. In an undated letter which probably refers to an assault committed in 1850 he thanked his "dearest dearest angel" for her comments on a draft he had submitted to her. Her note contained "a really important addition . . . & I have put it in nearly in your words, which as your impromptu words almost always are, were a hundred times better than any I could find by study. What a perfect orator you would make—& what changes might be made in the world by such a one, with such opportunities as thousands of male dunces have . . . ."[24]

Harriet, then, may have been moved only by humanitarian concerns. On the other hand, it is possible to read in her contributions the deep-seated masochism which unfitted her for normal physical love or, indeed, a degree of mental masochism which forced her to refuse what she most desired. It seems likely, however, that, as she appeared blissfully happy with John Taylor for the first two years of their married life, she began to dread the physical act with him after the conception of her second son, or, later still, when some months after her meeting with John Mill she discovered that she was pregnant for the third time.

John and Harriet Taylor had been, albeit briefly, man and wife in the full sense of the term. Whether John and Harriet Mill were ever man and wife in that sense remains open to doubt, but it seems almost certain that they were not. What is indubitable is that during the long years of friendship their relationship was often strained or clouded by guilt. When Harriet decided that she dared not live openly with Mill but must at all costs retain the shreds of her marriage, she wrote to him, "I do not hesitate about the certainty of happiness, but I do hesitate about the rightfulness of, for my own pleasure, giving up *my* only earthly opportunity of 'usefulness'. *You* hesitate about your usefulness & that however greater in amount it may be, is certainly not like mine *marked out* as a duty. I should spoil four lives & injure others. . . ." She was aware that the inevitable scandal aroused by their behaviour, whether technically innocent or not, might well compromise not only his social life but also his career as a civil servant. He must have expressed anxiety on this score, for she turned on him savagely:

Nothing I believe could make me love you less but certainly I should not admire one who could feel in this way except from mood. Good heaven have you at last arrived at fearing to be "obscure & insignificant"! What *can* I say to that but "by all means pursue your brilliant and important career". Am *I* one to choose to be the cause that the person I love feels himself reduced to "obscure & insignificant"!...you will never be that—& still more surely *I* am not a person who...could give you cause to feel that *I* had made you so...."[25]

Harriet, when she chose, could wound him in his most vulnerable spot or raise him to the heights of ecstasy. Some of her letters, judged by today's standards, would prove beyond a doubt that they had been lovers, but, judged by the language and sentiments of the time, it would be wrong to assume anything of the sort. "... for me", she cried, "I *am* loved as I desire to be, heart and soul take their rest in the peace of ample satisfaction." If there were to be no more happiness ahead she had already received enough to last a lifetime. "O my own love...you need never regret for a moment what has already brought such an increase of happiness and can in no possible way increase evil.... Far from being unhappy or even low this morning, I feel as tho' you had never loved me half so well as last night...." The days between one meeting and the next are endless. "Adieu my only & most precious", she wrote, "till Saturday—Dear Saturday." And again: "When I think that I shall not hold your hand till Tuesday, the time is so long & my hand so useless. Adieu my delight, je baise tes jolies pattes *cher cher cher*."[26]

In the early stages of their friendship Harriet had sensed a certain verbal restraint in Mill, a tendency of which he was well aware, to weigh every word for fear of being misunderstood; and yet, with so many partings, misunderstanding was inevitable. As Mill wrote despairingly, "I have been made most uncomfortable all day by your dear letter sweet & loving as it was dearest one...because of my having given you pain...You cannot imagine dearest how very much it grieves me now when even a small thing goes wrong now that think heaven it does not often happen so, & therefore always happens unexpectedly...." It was always Mill who abased himself, never Harriet; but to this letter she added in her own writing, "my *own* adored one!"[27] In her reply she said, "I don't know why I was so low when you went this morning. I was so LOW I could not bear your going my darling one: yet I should be well enough accustomed to it by now. O you dear one! dear one!"[28]

And so the long years of happiness and turmoil rolled by.

CHAPTER 5

A Quadrilateral

At the beginning of their long years of friendship, Harriet Taylor and John Mill drew very close to Eliza Flower and W. J. Fox, who, for their part, found strength in the companionship of the other "guilty" couple. "I hope we shall meet oftener—we four or rather five, as we did on Tuesday", wrote Mill to Fox when Harriet had returned from Paris. The fifth member of the party must have been Eliza's sister Sarah. In 1834 she married the railway engineer William Bridges Adams, a staunch feminist and, under the pen name of "Junius Redivivus", the author of *The Producing Man's Companion*. "I do not see half enough of you", Mill continued, "and I do not, half enough, see *anybody* along with her [Harriet]—*that* I think is chiefly what is wanting now—that, and other things like it." "Health and peace and blessing and love to both", he wrote after he had reviewed Eliza's *Songs of the Months*, "and continue to give some love to me as I do to you." In more than one of his letters to Fox he mentioned the nervous strain imposed by the nature of his relationship with Harriet; "a time perhaps is coming when I shall need your kindness more than ever", he wrote in the summer of 1834, "—if so, I know I shall always have it."[1] That time never came, for Mill and Harriet established their *modus vivendi*. Instead, Fox and his Eliza made demands on the kindness of the other pair and of the compliant John Taylor.

Eliza, if she had ever for a moment thought seriously of Mill, lavished an extravagant amount of affection on Harriet. Though the elder by some four years, she regarded Harriet more as a goddess than as a friend. "If you will really like to see me—think how stupid I was—but I will try & be better next time—I will come", she cried in one of a series of highly emotional and often incoherent letters which she sent Harriet in the early 1830s. "It was so gracious of you to write—& so kindly too!"[2] She could scarcely endure it when some temporary indisposition kept her from Harriet's side at a moment when Harriet herself was unwell. She was, she protested, almost unbearably moved by "the mere thought of your bewitching beauty. . . . Why were you ill—the old longing of nursing you quite came back when you said you had been ill . . . ."[3]

Harriet, susceptible to adoration, was fond of Eliza but found such slavish devotion somewhat cloying. In view of her own equivocal position, she was also nervous of being seen too often with a young woman whose unconventional behaviour was already giving rise to scandal. She made tentative efforts to withdraw, but the wounded Eliza was not easily detached and dashed off a reproachful letter:

> As to my being so "well off" as not to want you, as never to have wanted you (for so your words translate) . . . you know how it was with me when I found you, and how your smile fell like a ray over a troubled sky. . . . You know how I cling to you, how the world was enriched by you. You know too how often you have kept me from fainting by the rugged roadside. . . . You know me & what I live for . . . & the effort I have made to be contented & to seem happy, & how grateful I am when love comes to me . . . but that you should talk of my throwing away affection—your affection. . . . How could you write so. And I take "no interest" in you — have no "care" about you or yours. You believe . . . me to be so selfish—so capricious . . . ."[4]

Harriet, who had clearly been clumsy, relented, for soon Eliza was writing that "I feel I shall be quite well when I get to that sweetest presence again. Your note was as welcome as it was needed."[5] As few of her letters were dated or signed it is difficult to know when each was written. On another occasion she wrote, in words which Mill might have used "I *do long* to see *you*—I must have all the rest or rather unrest till I do—if possible this evening".[6] After one of their meetings, when Harriet had been more than usually responsive, Eliza was moved to write "If it were not for fear of accidents & making Mr Taylor jealous, I could say how 'I would I were a man' to have laid my heart at your feet while you were talking yesterday—but no more at present, from your true & affectionate E. F."[7] It was not at all uncommon for women to address one another in these extravagant terms: they indicated a strong emotional attachment but not, in the majority of cases, a physical one. In this instance it was not Mr Taylor who was jealous of Eliza but Mrs Fox. In 1832 matters in the Fox household had come to a head. Mrs Fox wrote her husband a formal letter of complaint and, as a result, although they continued for a while to inhabit the same house, to all intents and purposes they lived apart.

For Mrs Fox, as for Harriet Taylor, divorce was out of the question even had they desired it. The official dissolution of a marriage, a divorce *a vinculo matrimonii*—from the bond of matrimony—could be obtained only by Act of Parliament on the plea of an injured husband: the ecclesiastical courts were merely empowered to grant a decree of judicial separation, *a mensa et thoro*—from board and bed.

Eliza Flower, who lacked Harriet's resolution, was beside herself with anguish: "O you—no not even you can imagine what the wretchedness of this state is—I mean when one *must* bear & so quietly too! & one's whole existence is condensed into the mere effort of enduring. You say you wouldn't stand it—sometimes I believe twill sink me dead . . . sweet friend I am so sick at heart."[8]

Some time during 1834 Mrs Fox told her side of the story to several members of the South Place congregation, after which she left her husband for good, accepting from him suitable financial provision. The affair was now an open scandal and Fox was called on to justify his conduct.

In this dilemma he turned for advice to the Taylors and John Mill, who, despite their own dilemma, united to support him. They were firmly convinced, so Mill told Fox, that the attitude of a proportion of the congregation was caused by an erroneous belief that he and Eliza were lovers. Fox himself was partly responsible for the belief, for in the columns of the *Monthly Repository* he had openly advocated freedom for unhappily married couples to divorce, a subject he would have done well to avoid in the circumstances. Mill, on behalf of himself and the Taylors, now urged him to make it plain that, in his case, there was no question of adultery. Even if he had to resign, "the effect on your future prospects will entirely depend upon that fact being denied or not—& whether you feel it consistent, or not, with your personal dignity to deny it, we are quite convinced that we, and all your friends, ought". To refuse, as Fox had suggested, to deny the charge, on the grounds that his personal conduct was his own affair and no one else's, would be fatal to his cause. "We all think it of great importance that every public mention of the charge should be accompanied by mention of your denying it . . . ."[9]

While Mill composed this letter Harriet went to see her father, a member of South Place, in order to enlist his help. It is possible that Dr Hardy intervened, impossible to doubt that John Taylor's influence weighed heavily with the congregation. Fox proffered his resignation. It was refused, and the crisis was resolved by the secession of the dissident minority. Fox continued to preach in the chapel, but his links with the Unitarian Association—forerunner of the Ethical Movement—had been loosened and he spent an increasing amount of time in journalistic, editorial and political activities.

Meanwhile, in January 1835, Mill, the Taylors and those other friends who had stood by him, learned with consternation that he had taken a step which, to quote his biographer, "though innocent in intention, fatally compromised him in the opinion of many good men". In other words, with two of his three children he moved from Finsbury to Bayswater, then a country village. When the move was accomplished Eliza Flower appeared "at the head" of the household. The step "involved no blemish of personal purity". Eliza, who had inherited the sturdy independence of her father, would never "have submitted to an ambiguous relation. She would have assumed his name, and declared herself his wife in the sight of Heaven. Her omission to do so ought to have convinced all who knew her of the true state of the case. . . ."[10]

There is no absolute proof; but some of Eliza's friends, even though they believed her innocent, could not resist the strict conventions of the day and ostracized her. One of these, not surprisingly, was Harriet Martineau, who owed so much to Fox. Among Unitarian friends to defy convention was Peter Alfred Taylor (no relation to John Taylor), an upholder of every movement for the promotion of freedom, later a colleague of John Stuart Mill in the House of Commons. Another was Clementia Doughty, a future leader of the women's suffrage movement, who married Peter Taylor in 1842.

Relations between Fox and Eliza, Mill and Harriet now became tense and awkward. There was no open breach between them, but Harriet, conscious of her own ambiguous standing in society, saw to it that they met only rarely. By 1839 Eliza was ill with tuberculosis, the scourge which had already killed James Mill, was to kill two of his sons and Harriet herself. Eliza, thankful for small mercies, was pathetically grateful when Harriet called on her. "Mrs John Taylor has been and gone", she wrote to her sister Sarah. "She was very sweet and tender, and looked at me with eyes full of real love."[11]

Eliza remained with Fox, caring for his children, running his home, composing a musical service for the chapel. She endeared herself to the ladies of South Place, who refused to think ill of her and in 1843 "expressed their affection and gratitude . . . by presenting her with an alabaster vase". Three years later she was dead. Those present in the chapel heard Fox, who was conducting her memorial service, utter the single word "God", then pause, "as if in an agony of struggle". He controlled himself, and continued more calmly, "God! with Whom are the issues of life and death. . . . Not our will, but Thine be done."[12]

If, for the sake of argument, John Mill had married Eliza Flower, the course of his life would have been entirely different. Eliza's would have been a gentler influence than Harriet's but for that very reason largely ineffectual. Where Harriet was intellectual, determined and, on occasion, ruthless, Eliza was too excitable and erratic to give Mill what he so patently needed, the masterful guidance and sense of direction once supplied by his dictatorial father. If Harriet, rightly or wrongly, has been accused of physical masochism, there seems no doubt at all that Mill was a mental masochist. Harriet was in every sense his master: to her, as time went on, he was to submit his life, his thoughts, even his conscience.

CHAPTER 6

Broken Friendships

Secure in the knowledge of their sexual innocence, John Mill and Harriet Taylor had seen no reason why they should conceal their friendship from the outside world, although it was some time before they appeared together in public. Among the first of his friends to whom Mill introduced Harriet were Thomas and Jane Welsh Carlyle.

Mill and Carlyle had first met in the autumn of 1831, when Carlyle, eleven years Mill's senior, came to London from Craigenputtock, Dumfriesshire, to try to arrange for the publication of his *Sartor Resartus*. He had read with approval some of the young man's articles and was anxious to meet him, so one of his friends suggested that he should ask Sarah Austin for an introduction. The friend was Charles Buller, a member of parliament who had once been a private pupil of Carlyle's. Buller, like Mill, was said by Charles Greville to be in love with Carlyle's Lady Harriet Baring (Lady Ashburton). "To Lady Ashburton, John Mill was 'sentimentally attached'", declared Greville on very doubtful evidence, "though 'she did not in the slightest degree return his passion. Her other lover was Charles Buller with whom she was extremely intimate but without ever reciprocating his love.'"[1]

Mill and Buller were already friends and Carlyle acted on Buller's suggestion. He admired Sarah Austin's knowledge of the German mystics and, when she invited him to tea to meet John Mill, he accepted with alacrity. "The Frau Austin herself was as loving as ever—a true Germanical spiritual Screamikin", he wrote to his wife after the meeting. John Austin, though worthy, he considered rather limited; but John Mill "I fancy and hope is 'a baying you can love'. A slender, rather tall and elegant youth, with small clear Roman-nosed face, two small earnestly-smiling eyes; modest, remarkably gifted with precision of utterance, enthusiastic, yet lucid, calm; but not a great, yet distinctly a gifted and amiable youth." He also noted, after the first of many evenings spent in talking and walking the streets of London, that Mill's "fancy is not rich; furthermore he cannot *laugh* with any compass".[2]

Mill, an excellent conversationalist, was also an admirable listener, something which naturally appealed to the older man. But, if Carlyle did not foresee a great future for this gifted and amiable youth, in other respects his assessment was fair enough. Lack of imagination was to lead Mill into the most appalling blunders in his dealings with his mother, his sisters and his friends. He could be playful but he lacked Carlyle's robust sense of humour, just as Harriet lacked Jane Carlyle's wit. His initial estimate of Carlyle was as wide of the mark as most of his character assessments. Carlyle, he told John Sterling of that masterful, cantankerous genius, "has by far the largest & widest liberality & tolerance . . . that I have met with in any one".[3] Charles Buller, who was more perceptive, pointed out that they differed "as widely as the poles" but thought that they might "well meet in that point where all clear spirits find each other, the love of truth".[4]

When the Carlyles settled in Chelsea in 1834 Mill was a frequent visitor at their house in Cheyne Row, as welcome to Jane as he was to Thomas. Yet the close friendship which burgeoned between the two men was based on a false premise: they were, as Buller had noted, poles apart. Jane, normally so shrewd and observant, shared her husband's misconception that Mill was at heart a mystic. "Among all the literary people who come among us", she told her cousin Helen Welsh, "the one I like best is Mr Mill (son of Mill the Utilitarian) but *he* is no Utilitarian—he belongs rather to the class to which my Husband belongs and which for want of a fitter name has been called 'the Mystic School'."[5]

The Carlyles had not yet been introduced to Harriet, nor had Mill as much as mentioned her name, when Carlyle, calling on the Austins, was welcomed by Sarah "with a kiss and a 'Niagara of gossip'. The most important item was that a young Mrs Taylor, though encumbered with husband and children, had ogled John Mill successfully, so that he was 'desperately in love'." A day or so later Charles Buller, questioned on the subject, "corroborated hilariously, the news was true".[6]

Thomas Carlyle, vastly amused, reported the news to his brother John. Under Mr Taylor's very eyes, he wrote, Mill was violently, though platonically, in love with his wife. Although Mill's friends disapproved of the relationship they none of them seemed to imagine that it was anything but platonic. As Sarah Austin assured Carlyle, John Mill and his "young philosophic beauty" were in love "with the innocence of two sucking doves".[7]

Only his lack of imagination can explain Mill's failure to suspect from the outset that his friends would gossip or that, when they met his Egeria, they would not necessarily share his estimate of her. The Carlyles, agog to meet this paragon, were introduced to Harriet in the summer of 1834 and responded with qualified admiration. She was, the susceptible Jane informed her brother-in-law John, a woman " I could really love; if it were safe and she were willing—but she is a dangerous looking woman and engrossed with a dangerous passion and no useful relation can spring up between us". If Jane was moved by Harriet's solemn beauty, she was equally, if not more, moved by the appeal of that other clever woman, Sarah Austin. "If I 'swear everlasting friendship' with any woman here", she said, "it will be with her." Carlyle, highly intrigued with their new acquaintance, told his brother that she was "a living romance heroine, of the clearest insight, of the royalist volition".[9] In a letter to his mother, however, he was more cautious. For the present Mrs Taylor seemed " 'all that is noble' and what not. We shall see how that wears."[10]

In August the Carlyles dined with the Taylors at Kent Terrace, together with John Mill and W. J. Fox. Carlyle thought Taylor a genial host but found fault with Harriet. She did not, so he told his brother John, "yield unmixed satisfaction, I think, or receive it. She affects with a kind of sultana noble-mindedness, a certain girlish petulance, and felt that it did not wholly prosper. We walked home, however, even Jane did, all the way from Regent's Park, and felt that we had done a duty." It was certainly a long walk for Jane; and when, a week or so later, Carlyle walked from Chelsea to call on the Taylors he himself felt tired enough to sit down and rest on a seat in Regent's Park. Presently he saw them walking past, too lost in their personal crisis to notice him: "pale she, and passionate and sad-looking; really felt a kind of interest in her".[11]

Harriet remained a fascinating enigma, but her attitude towards John Mill and his to her were entirely foreign to the Carlyles. In company Jane subdued her own undoubted qualities to her husband's, quietly directing the conversation to the point at which he could deliver one of his famous monologues. Mill, in his humility, only wanted Harriet to shine, to prove to his friends what he himself believed, that she was his superior in every way. It was not long before Harriet compromised herself in Carlyle's eyes. Either from nervousness, from which she did not as a rule suffer, or from a sense of superiority, she was almost as patronizing towards Jane as she was to Eliza Flower. Fortunately this did not last. Carlyle, calling her "a very will-o'-wispish 'irridescence' of a character" who "at first considered my Jane to be a rustic spirit fit for rather tutoring and twirling about when the humour took her", was relieved to find that she "got taught better . . . before long".[12]

The Carlyles were not, of course, the only friends to meet Harriet in Mill's company. The others, too, were intrigued, but, either through her fault or Mill's, or because they considered the friendship dangerous, they looked on Harriet as more an encumbrance than an addition. And naturally they continued to talk among themselves of Mill's overwhelming interest in another man's wife.

To Mill, the first indication of this gossip was given him at an evening party held by Mrs Buller, Charles's mother. John Roebuck anxiously watched his friend enter the drawing-room, Harriet Taylor's arm in his. "The manner of the lady, the evident devotion of the gentleman, soon attracted universal attention, and a suppressed titter went round the room."[13] Mrs Buller herself may well have joined in the general amusement, for she was prone to uncontrollable fits of giggling. As Harriet Grote noted of another party, given by the Austins, Mrs Buller, for some reason or other, was seated " 'sniggering' on the sofa".[14]

The laughter was quickly subdued but not until the damage had been done. Mill was furious; John Roebuck determined, whatever the cost, to warn him that his infatuation could do him nothing but harm. He therefore called at the India House and told Mill frankly what he thought. Mill received his warning with indifference, and Roebuck, not realizing how deeply he had offended, called again the following day. "The moment I entered the room I saw that, as far as he was concerned, our friendship was at an end. His manner was not merely cold, but repulsive; and I, seeing how matters were, left him. His part of our friendship was rooted out, nay destroyed, but mine was left untouched." It was only natural for Roebuck to ascribe the rupture of their friendship to his intervention; but Mill, incredibly, put it down to a dispute over the rival merits of Byron and Wordsworth. Hot in his championship of Harriet's good name, he refused all Roebuck's overtures of friendship. Many years later—in 1865—when Mill entered Parliament and Harriet had long been dead, Roebuck, a seasoned politician who had played an active part in Mill's election campaign, approached him in the House of Commons with an offer of help to the novice. Mill received him as a stranger and, on the specious grounds "that he was so much engaged that he had no time,"[15] curtly refused an invitation to dine with their old friend Graham. During the last year of his life, however, Mill made a sincere if belated gesture of goodwill. He sent Roebuck a book which had once been his, an old school Virgil which he had found among his belongings, with a letter referring nostalgically to the long-distant past. Although they never met again, Roebuck was deeply moved when, after Mill's death, his stepdaughter and companion, Helen Taylor, assured him that she had never heard Mill mention him "but with esteem and affection".[15]

The rupture with Roebuck, whatever Mill may have said to the contrary, was directly attributable to his friendship with Harriet. It is possible that George Grote or, more probably, his wife, who had an almost parental affection for John Mill, also intervened. Alexander Bain, who did not meet Mill until 1842, noticed at once that he was "completely alienated from Mrs Grote", though not from "the historian", as Harriet Grote always called her husband. Since she was not, as Bain rightly declared, "the person to have an opinion without freely expressing it", he "inferred that the estrangement had some reference to Mrs Taylor".[17]

Harriet Grote, who was noted for her interference in other people's affairs, may well have thought it her duty to try to separate John Mill from Harriet Taylor. Whether she did or not, she was placed under a ban of excommunication. "As for Mrs Grote," Mill wrote scathingly to Sarah Austin, with whom he had not as yet quarrelled, "you know her, & would not expect either good feeling or good taste from her...."[18] In 1854, when Harriet Taylor had been Harriet Mill for three years, Mrs Grote, longing to be friends once more, wrote to thank Mill for a favourable article he had contributed to the *Edinburgh Review* on Grote's *History of Greece*. Mill forwarded the letter to Harriet, who was convalescing in the south of France. It was, he said, "little worthy" of the honour of her perusal. "The impudence of writing to me at all & of writing in such a manner is only matched by the excessive conceit of the letter."[19] He supposed he must answer it, but how? Harriet gave him the benefit of her advice, but this letter, like so many others, was destroyed by Mill at her urgent request. She must have told him to be pacific if not cordial, for he answered, "my darling is I dare say right. It did not escape me that there was an amende, & I should have felt much more indignant if there had not." But he still considered it impudent "that after the things she has said & done respecting us, she should imagine that a tardy sort of recognition of you, & flattery to me, would serve to establish some sort of relation between us & her".[20]

The breach with Harriet Grote was to be repaired in time at Helen Taylor's instigation. The break with Harriet Martineau, on the other hand, was final; but it cannot be attributed directly to Harriet Taylor. Mill had never cared for Miss Martineau; quite the reverse. As early as 1833 he had complained to Carlyle that she was "*narrow,* and *matter-of-fact* I should say, in the bad sense". Her only redeeming qualities were her industry and tireless quest for knowledge. "She has . . . the faculty of making herself personally disliked, by means it would seem of inattention to Christ's precept 'judge not, that ye be not judged' . . . ."[21]

Harriet Martineau, who had witnessed the first meeting between Mill and the Taylors, was an incurable gossip, but what she said we do not know. The tittle-tattle, which had died down over the years, was revived when Mill and Harriet married, and Miss Martineau provided John Chapman, by that time editor of the *Westminster Review,* with "the history of J. S. Mill's relation with Mrs Taylor, now his wife".[22] Alexander Bain, who knew far more than he was prepared to reveal, remarked with his usual caution that she had had "special opportunities of knowing the history of the connection".[23]

Although Mill refused to see again or to correspond further with Harriet Martineau, the breach owed as much to his contempt for her work as to his defence of Harriet Taylor's good name. He and Carlyle agreed that she lacked the mental equipment for some of her self-imposed tasks. Writing to Carlyle of her nine-volume *Illustrations of Political Economy,* which appeared between 1832 and 1834, Mill complained that she had contrived to reduce "the *laissez faire* system to absurdity as far as the *principle* goes, by merely carrying it out to all its consequences".[24]

It is most unlikely that Harriet Taylor suggested this criticism; it is far more probable that she inspired Mill's violent reaction against an effusive, chatty article which Miss Martineau submitted to the *London and Westminster Review* in 1837 on the occasion of Queen Victoria's accession. Mill told John Robertson, who was editing the review under his direction, that he had read and reread the article with the firmest intention of doing it justice, but could find nothing to say in its favour. In her account of the girlhood of the Queen and her future prospects, he declared, the author insisted on treating her as an artless young woman. "Now the Queen cannot be young, except in ignorance of the world, and kings and queens are that even at sixty. . . . She cannot be artless, as a person full of anxieties . . . doing her duty to her subjects." He found the whole tone of the article childish in the extreme, without "an opinion or observation that you may not drive a coach and six through".[25] The article would do the review more harm than good and, if published at all, which he did not recommend, must appear with a strong note of editorial dissent. Robertson bowed to the inevitable and rejected the article; but Mill remained annoyed with him for approving the idea in the first place and corresponding with the author without his permission. "She and I are not upon terms, and I know her too well to make it likely that we ever shall be." Nor did he wish her to be "identified with the Review more than its interest requires."[26] He was wise enough—perhaps on Harriet's advice—not to place an outright ban on future contributions from such a well known and popular author—giving his approval, for example, if in tepid terms, to an innocuous review of the works of the American novelist Catherine Maria Sedgwick. This he found "quite unobjectionable, though there is less in it that I expected, & the extracts given do not inspire me with any admiration for the books praised".[27]

Although Harriet Taylor was not openly connected with the *London and Westminster* there seems little doubt that Mill was in the habit of consulting her and of submitting contributions for her comment and criticism. She also acted as an intermediary between Mill and her husband. In September 1837 she asked Mill, at John Taylor's request, to solicit contributions from the Italian refugee Mazzini and his friend Angelo Usiglio. Mill did as he was asked. "I find that Usilio's [sic] article is to be in the next number", Harriet wrote to her husband. Mill had called on the publishers and found both men discussing their ideas with the editor. As a result, Robertson "has undertaken to do all the revising that is necessary to Usiglio's article & has engaged him to write another on new Italian books & Mazzini to write one on Italian politics since 1830".[28]

Jane Welsh Carlyle says that a French refugee who was living in London at the time, may also have contributed to the review and certainly suspected Harriet's influence on its policy, nicknamed her "the Armida of the 'London and Westminster' ".[29] He was the Carlyles' friend Godefroi Cavaignac, brother of General Cavaignac the future French head of state. He must also have been thinking of Harriet's personal influence on Mill, for Armida is the enchantress heroine of Tasso's *Gerusalemme Liberata*.

It is probably true that, had she been given any choice in the matter, the strait-laced Harriet Martineau would have closed her doors to Harriet Taylor as she had to Eliza Flower. It is almost impossible to imagine that Sarah Austin would have refused to receive her dearest John and his Harriet, however much she might deplore the relationship. She was, and remained, devoted to Mill; and, apart from anything else, she was well aware that she herself would be open to censure if ever the knowledge of her epistolary love affair with Prince Puckler Muskau became public property. Sarah did not meet the prince until she was in her fifties: by that time their passionate correspondence had petered out and, with it, her futile love for a dissolute man.

When, in due course, John Mill quarrelled with Sarah Austin, it was not only, as will be seen, because he realized that she had been a "Niagara of gossip". It may well be that Harriet, whose social life was inevitably restricted when she separated from her husband, was jealous of Sarah Austin's continuing success as a hostess and writer and would have been glad to hear Francis Jeffrey's irreverent description of her in later life as "the bearded beauty".[30] She may also have resented the longstanding affection between "mother" and "son". At any rate, she disliked Mrs Austin personally and, as always, where she led John Mill followed.

For some years, however, Mill and Mrs Austin remained on the best of terms. In 1836, for example, he fell ill with what Bain described "as an obstinate derangement of the brain": in other words, a nervous breakdown brought on by over work and the strains of love. This illness, which, so he told Sarah Austin, had started with a slight stomach disorder, left him with a distressing facial twitch from which he was to suffer for the rest of his life. He was treated by a Dr King, who subsequently married Mill's sister, Willie, but died very young, leaving her with one daughter.

Dr King recommended a period of convalescence in Brighton, from which John Mill returned prematurely, owing to his father's illness. James Mill died a lingering death from tuberculosis in June 1836. His son was still very ill, as Carlyle noted when he visited the stunned, bereaved family at Mickleham. He was struck by the lack of communication between them. "There was little sorrow visible in their house, or rather none, nor any human feeling at all; but the strangest unheimlich kind of composure and acquiescence, as if all human spontaneity had taken refuge in invisible corners", he wrote to Jane. John Mill, though only thirty, seemed to have withered in body and mind. "His eyes go twinkling and jerking with wild lights and twitches; his head is bald, his face brown and dry."[32]

At Dr King's request the India Office granted Mill three months' leave of absence. He spent it travelling on the Continent with Harriet, accompanied part of the time by his young brothers Henry and George and their friend Herbert, Harriet's son.

On his return Mill wrote to his "dear Mütterlein", "You may wonder that I have been so long in writing to you—though after all, I write first: but you would not wonder if you knew the endless drudgery I have had upon my hands, with arrears of India house business, & private affairs, without counting review matters or any other writing...."[33] He asked her for a contribution to the review, and she replied with characteristic affection and generosity:

My dearest John,
    Of course I shall do all I can.... You did right to apply to me, I should

have been jealous if you had not and miserable if you had sacrificed your rest when I could help you—I shall put aside all for this and with pleasure. It is a small earnest dearest John of what I should be glad to do for you if I could—and if you get any satisfaction from that I am more than rewarded. . . .

Your Mütterlein.[34]

During the following spring Mill wrote to ask her if her husband would be interested in the post of Professor of Moral Philosophy at Glasgow University: if so, there should be no difficulty in obtaining it for him. For the last time his letter was signed "Your Söhnchen"; thereafter he signed himself "truly" or, more rarely, "affectionately" "JSM", and addressed her as "Dear Mrs Austin". Perhaps, at thirty, he judged it proper to emancipate himself from the old mother-and-son relationship; perhaps Harriet had ridiculed it as childish. It is also possible that at long last he was beginning to suspect that Sarah was an incurable gossip.

The correspondence continued for several years, albeit on a far less intimate note. In October 1841, for example, when Mrs Austin was in Germany, Mill consulted her about German doctors and the possibility of treatment for Harriet: "Mrs Taylor bids me tell you how one fine day . . . she suddenly & with hardly any warning lost the use of her legs almost entirely—this was in June, & since, the little power of moving them that was left has become still less, in spite of all manner of remedies".[35]

On the basis of an entry in the diary which Helen Taylor kept from 1842 onwards it has always been thought that the paralysis was the result of a carriage accident, in May of that year, in which Harriet and her husband were involved. By citing Mill's letter to Mrs Austin, however, Professor Mazlish has made it clear that the paralysis preceded the accident.[36] It was therefore hysterical in origin, caused by the exigencies of her life, most probably one of the numerous disputes with her mother and Mrs Hardy's allies, Caroline and her objectionable husband Arthur Ley. Although she appears to have had no love for her mother, Harriet was undoubtedly jealous of the strong emotional tie between Mrs Hardy and her younger daughter. The paralysis itself disappeared in due course, but Harriet's health continued to decline.

Three years later, still in touch with the Austins, Mill gave them an introduction to the founder of Positivism, the French philosopher Auguste Comte. Mrs Austin, he wrote, "est non seulement très aimable mais vraiment supérieure, quoique je connaisse des femmes qui la dépassent infiniment. C'est par le bon sens des idées et par la clarté et l'élégance de l'expression qu'elle excelle le plus, soi dans la conversation, soi dans le peu qu'elle a écrit . . ."[37] Comte thanked Mill "for procuring me such a pleasant acquaintance", and wrote fulsomely to Sarah, praising her as the only woman he knew "in whom moral delicacy and mental elevation are so happily united".[39]

"Comte's taking to you is what I should have expected",[39] Mill wrote to

Sarah in what was to prove his final expression of goodwill towards her. By now their political views had begun to diverge and the gulf widened with the French uprising of 1848. The Austins, who were in Paris at the time, were appalled by what they considered a disaster; to Mill, and still more to Harriet, it was an inspiring bid for liberty. In September, when Harriet was house-hunting in Surrey, she learned that the Austins were looking for a country cottage in Weybridge and immediately removed herself from the district. As the years passed, political dissension grew more and more pronounced. Harriet's dislike and possible jealousy of Sarah was a contributory factor in the death of a warm, rewarding friendship: it was not decisive.

John Austin died in 1859, one year after Harriet. Mill, who possessed a strong streak of vindictiveness, could not bring himself to write Sarah even a conventional letter of sympathy. He wrote instead to her granddaughter Janet, the seventeen-year-old child of his old friend Lucie. Janet was naturally upset; her grandmother was hurt beyond measure. John Mill, Janet recalled in later life, who had read Roman law with Professor Austin and studied German with his wife, "of whom he was very fond and always wrote to as *Liebes Mutterlein*, never even mentions her. I saw that the evidently intentional slight cut her to the heart."[40]

Mill was obliged to write to Mrs Austin once more. She was proposing to edit her husband's unpublished lectures, some of which he had attended, and wrote to ask his advice. Mill submitted the letter and a draft reply to his stepdaughter Helen, who had slipped into her mother's place as mentor. The request, he said, "seems to involve the unpleasant necessity of writing to her. My principal anxiety is to do as exactly as I am able what would have been done if I had still my darling to guide me. . . . I enclose for your remarks & suggestions what I think of saying . . . ."[41]

Mill's letter, though helpful, was formal in the extreme. "I am very glad you thought I hit the right mark in my answer", he told Helen, who had made some pungent remarks on Mrs Austin herself. "You have very truly characterized her letter." It was, he added caustically, much the same as the others and, if Helen had seen the letters of Sarah's daughter Lucie, "you would say she was an apt pupil. Only the daughter has the grace to mention *my* loss though in a very inadequate manner."[42] So much for Lucie, who had called him Brother John when they played together in Jeremy Bentham's garden! Although additional information about the lectures was required, Mill chose to send it, not to Sarah Austin, but to the nephew who was assisting her.

In the early draft of his *Autobiography* he gave vent to his spleen, stigmatizing Sarah as a social climber and a pseudo-intellectual, scorning their old relationship: "Having known me from a boy, she made great profession of a kind of maternal interest in me. But I never for an instant supposed that she cared for me; nor perhaps for anybody beyond the surface; I mean as to real feeling, not that she was not quite ready to be friendly or serviceable . . . ." And then, recalling with unquenchable bitterness her tendency to gossip, he accused her of possessing "a very mischievous tongue, which sowed *médisance* far & wide by expressions so guarded as almost to elude responsibility for any distinct statement".[43]

Fortunately for Sarah's reputation, Mill had second thoughts and deleted the entire passage from his final draft. In the published version of his *Autobiography,* Sarah Austin, like his own mother, is passed by without a single mention.

CHAPTER 7

Who was the Guilty Party?

Ever since his boyhood visit to France, Mill had been fascinated by the history of the French Revolution. He corresponded with French historians, built up a comprehensive library of books, and in 1828 wrote a defence of the early revolutionaries for the *Westminster Review*. He began seriously to consider writing a history, but realized that Carlyle, to whom the revolution represented an instance of divine government, a terrifying example of God's vengance on the rich for oppressing the poor, was thinking along the same lines. Carlyle knew, however, that Mill, who had lent him his books, was already an expert and first in the field; he could do no less than advise his young friend to tackle the "grand *work* of our era",[1] a subject still so imperfectly understood in their own country.

The two men tossed the idea backwards and forwards between them, each courteously egging the other on, suggesting new ideas and varying characterizations. In one of many letters Mill unwittingly revealed both the source of his adoration of Harriet and the undeniable feminine aspect of his own nature. Carlyle had suggested that Madame Roland, perhaps the finest personality of the Revolution, was more like a man than a woman; but, Mill asked, "*is* there really any distinction between the highest masculine & the highest feminine character?" By this he did not mean the purely "mechanical *acquirements*," which frequently differed between the sexes. "But the women, of all I have known, who possessed the highest measure of what are considered feminine qualities, have combined with them more of the highest *masculine* qualities" than he had met with in all "but one or two men, & those . . . were also in many respects almost women".[2]

In the course of the correspondence Mill admitted that he had serious reservations. It was not only the complexity of the subject which worried him, but the fact that the religious susceptibilities of the vast majority of his countrymen would make it impossible to describe Christianity, as it could be described in France, "as by far the greatest and best thing which has existed on this globe, but which is gone never to return", even though its finest aspects might reappear one day in a higher guise. If he could not reveal his own feelings on this point, he could not "tell the *whole* truth". He had not, howver, entirely relinquished the project, for "it is highly probable I shall do it sometime if you do not".[3]

Carlyle took this as permission to go ahead. He was already working on his sketch of "The Diamond Necklace", about the scandal of Marie Antoinette's famous necklace, and when he had difficulty in finding a publisher Mill offered to print it at his own expense, "that he might have the pleasure of reviewing it!"[4] (Carlyle refused and "The Diamond Necklace" was published in *Fraser's Magazine* in 1837.) The great Sage of Chelsea was in literary and financial troubles at the time. He would have liked to spend some weeks in Paris but could not afford it; instead Mill, who had gone there to join Harriet, hunted down obscure books for him and supplied him with useful comments on contemporary French life and thought.

And so, with the help of Mill's library and with many groans and verbal creakings, Carlyle embarked on the history which was to make his name. "The French business grows darker and darker upon me: dark as Chaos. *Ach Gott!*"[5] he wrote to Mill.

Despite his misgivings Carlyle had completed the first volume of his *History* within five months and had started on "The Feast of Pikes", the first book of volume II. The whole world knows the sequel. As the work proceeded, said Carlyle, Mill "began to think there never had been such a book written in the world ... a verra foolish piece o' friendliness,—and ... nothing would serve him but that he should have it."[6] Mill read the manuscript with intense excitement and enthusiasm: here, he was convinced, was a work of genius in the making.

Then, on that fatal evening in early March 1835, Carlyle, who had been working all day on "The Feast of Pikes", was sitting quietly with his wife in the first-floor drawing-room which Jane had constructed by knocking two small rooms into one. They heard a rap on the front door, a step on the stairs, and Mill came in, pale as Hector's ghost, as Carlyle put it, or, in another version of the story, as the ghost of Hamlet's father. "Why, Mill," he cried, "what ails ye, man? What is it?"[7] He forced the quaking, staggering man into a chair. In one version Mill was speechless, could no nothing but clutch at a fragment of paper which he held in his hand; in another, he implored Jane "to go and speak to a lady sitting in a carriage at the door. 'Something dreadful has happened, she'll tell you what.' "[8]

Husband and wife naturally assumed that "a thing which they had long feared must have actually happened and that Mill had come to announce it and take leave of them".[9] In other words, as Jane said to herself as she hurried downstairs, "Gracious Providence, he has gone off with Mrs Taylor."[10]

As she expected, Harriet was the occupant of the carriage. She was as incoherent as Mill: all that Jane could deduce was that this was no elopement.

"Oh! you'll never speak to him again!" whimpered Harriet. Jane, utterly mystified, "sped back to the gentlemen, and saw Carlyle emblematically rolling a paper match. 'Tell me what has happened!' 'What? [cried Mill] hasn't she told you? Your husband's manuscript is entirely destroyed!' "[11]

And so it was, save for one or two useless fragments.

The Carlyles insisted that their immediate reaction was one of relief that Mill and Harriet were not eloping. Yet, from their own point of view, the truth was disastrous. Carlyle's method was to read until his mind was saturated with his subject, to write at white heat, and then to throw away his notes. Of the completed volume he could now remember nothing.

Harriet had not followed Jane upstairs, and presently the carriage was heard clip-clopping away. In the drawing-room Mill, "the very picture of desperation", was explaining in broken sentences that the precious manuscript, "left out in too careless a manner after it had been read", had been, except for the fragments, "irrevocably annihilated". He might have had the sense to see that all Carlyle and his Goody wanted was to be left alone to face this tragedy together: instead, he stayed on interminably, talking endlessly of "indifferent things". When at length he had taken his departure Carlyle turned to Jane. "Well, Mill, poor fellow, is terribly cut up; we must endeavour to hide from him how very serious this business is for us."[12] Jane flung her arms impulsively round her husband's neck, "openly lamenting, condoling, and encouraging like a nobler second self".[13]

Mill, penitent and abashed, wrote next day that there was nothing he would not do to rectify his tragic blunder, if only this were possible. All he could do was to offer his friend financial compensation, which, in the circumstances, he knew would be useful. "I beg of you with an earnestness with which perhaps I may never again have need to ask anything as long as we live", he wrote, "that you will permit me to do this little as it is, towards remedying the consequences of my fault & lightening my self-reproach. . . ."[14]

Even before he heard from Mill, Carlyle had written to console him. "You left me last night with a look which I shall not soon forget." The volume had perished; its contents could not be recalled; but that "I *can* write a Book on the French Revolution is (God be thanked for it) as clear to me as ever; also that if life be given me so long, I will".[15]

Pressed by Mill, Carlyle accepted £100 and a copy of the *Biographie Universelles*. As proof of his confidence, he now offered to lend Mill the manuscript of "The Feast of Pikes", "provided you durst take it: with me it were no daring: for I think of all men living you are henceforth the least likely to commit such an oversight again".[16]

Mill demurred. He did not believe for a moment that a similar disaster could occur "but for the sake of retributive justice I would wear the badge of my untrustworthiness". If, however, Carlyle wished to give him the great pleasure of reading the manuscript he should lend it to Mrs Taylor: "in her custody no harm could come to it—and I can read it aloud to her as I did much of the other—for it had not only the *one* reader you mentioned but a second as good".[17]

The manuscript was not lent to Harriet, which seems to suggest, although Carlyle gave no indication of it at the time, that he thought she might have had something to do with the disappearance of volume I.

The questions of exactly how the manuscript came to be destroyed and in whose keeping it was at the time have never been decisively answered. Mill's reaction was clear: he was deeply penitent and the fault and the responsibility were entirely his. The story most generally accepted was that he left the papers lying in an untidy heap one evening in the library and then went up to bed. Next morning, when the maid came in, she mistook the manuscript for waste paper and used it to light the fire. This is the story Mill told the Carlyles and his own family, although he did not mention the incident in his *Autobiography,* and Carlyle did not mention it in his *Reminiscences.* Another story, which gained credence as time went on, was that Mill had lent the manuscript to Harriet and that it was in her house that it was destroyed. After his death this story was revived in an obituary article in the *Daily Telegraph* and repeated in a memorial tribute, Harriet being named as "the heroine of one of the most extraordinary incidents in the unrecorded 'Curiosities of Literature' ".[18] When Mill's sister Harriet Isabella read the obituary she wrote at once to Carlyle, "As far as my recollection goes, the misfortune arose from my brother's own inadvertence, in having given your papers amongst waste paper for kitchen use. I can, perfectly well, remember our search, and my dear brother's extreme distress, and I fancy, although of this I do not feel so sure, that some pages were found." To this Carlyle replied that his impression was "that Mrs Taylor's house and some trifling neglect there, had been the cause of the catastrophe".[19]

It seems incredible that Mill, who was accustomed to handling official documents and was himself a writer, would have treated another man's work in so cavalier a fashion. It is conceivable that, overcome with regret that he had failed to seize the chance of writing the book himself, his action had been deliberate. Yet this, too, is unbelievable, entirely out of character. He was invariably generous in his praise of works of genuine merit and to destroy one would have been sacrilege. But the manuscript had been lent to him and he was solely responsible for its safe-keeping. He had no right to lend it to Harriet, if this is what he did; and, if so, the letter to Carlyle asking him to let her see "The Feast of Pikes" must be read not as an affirmation of her innocence, but as a piece of bluff intended to conceal the truth.

Carlyle was the first to hint that the manuscript had not been in Mill's hands when it was destroyed. He told the story in a variety of ways—one of the most explicit, but also the most confusing, of them being the version he gave to a friend of his,

A friend desired that he might have the reading of it; and it was committed to his care. He professed himself greatly delighted with the perusal, and confided it to a friend, who had some curiosity to see it as well. This person sat up, as he said, perusing it far into the wee hours of the morning; and at length recollecting himself, surprised at the flight of time, laid the manuscript carelessly upon the library table, and hied to bed. There it lay, a loose heap of rubbish ... So Betty, the housemaid, thought when she came to light the library fire in the morning. Looking round for something suitable for her purpose, and finding nothing better than it, she thrust it into the grate, and applying the match, up the chimney, with a sparkle and roar, went "The French Revolution".[20]

There are several inconsistencies in this story. Carlyle, with unwonted tact, concealed the sex of the friend; he invented the name of the housemaid (unless, indeed, Harriet had a housemaid named Betty); and he denied that he was immediately apprised of the tragedy. In another version he made no attempt to conceal the identity of the friend, remarking sourly that Mill "needs must take [the manuscript] to that woman, Mrs Taylor, in whom he had discovered so much that no one else could."[21]

In his letter to Harriet Isabella Mill, Carlyle assured her that her brother's conduct "to me in this matter, as indeed in all others, then and afterwards, was conspicuously nobel, generous and friend-like".[22] Harriet Isabella then began to have second thoughts. She had not witnessed the destruction of the papers and could no longer believe that they had been burned in her own home. In 1881, after Carlyle's death and when John Mill had been dead for eight years, the canard was revived. In a letter signed "F. W. R." (F. W. Reynolds) and published in *The Times* on 12 February, the incident was recalled as told by "Mrs Carlyle to a friend of mine". Mill, said Reynolds, called on Carlyle,

and stated that he had heard he was engaged in writing the history . . . , adding that he had himself intended to write on that subject, and that he would be glad to see what was already done in order that he might judge of the advisability of commencing the work or not. Mr Carlyle readily lent his manuscript. But it happened shortly afterwards that Mr Mill's cook had occasion to bake some cakes, and finding the precious manuscript lying about, she concluded that she might turn it to good account, and accordingly as fuel and partly as lining for the cake tins, she used up the whole of the manuscript. Horrified at the accident, Mr Mill and Mrs Taylor called on the great historian . . . Carlyle . . . soon afterwards began again at the beginning, scarcely saying a word about his misfortune at the time, but afterwards grumbling about it often.

Incensed by the tone of this letter, Harriet Isabella Mill rushed indignantly into print on 17 February:

Any one with the slightest knowledge of either Mr Mill or Mr Carlyle must see at once that the narrative of your correspondent . . . could not be correct; it is indeed a misstatement throughout. Valuable papers were not left lying about in Mr Mill's house, nor was the disaster owing to him, beyond the fact that he had lent the manuscript to the person at whose house it was destroyed. Having heard Mr Carlyle's own account of all that passed between him and Mr Mill, when the latter carried him the fatal news, and also of the alarm felt by himself and Mrs Carlyle at the state of Mr Mill's distress, I can safely say that none of the statements made in the letter ... agree with the facts

The incident was also resuscitated in ambiguous forms in the *Daily News* and the *Westminster Review*.

In 1837, when *The French Revolution* appeared, Mill praised it unstintingly. And Harriet Taylor? On the day after the tragedy Carlyle had written to Mill, "Thanks to Mrs Taylor for her kind sympathies. May God guide and bless you both."[23] Yet, grumbling as was his wont as the years went by, he complained, "I never heard that it very much diminished her content in life."[24] One or two recent writers, John Stewart Collis among them, have suggested that the destruction of the manuscript was not accidental: "There were 170 pages of closely written foolscap—for [Carlyle] wrote 600 words to a page. It would be difficult to mess up a manuscript of that kind so as to make it look like waste paper; but Mrs Taylor achieved this, for next morning a servant lit the fire with it."[25]

There is no use trying to evade the fact that Harriet had a motive. Mill was still only a man of promise and she was ambitious for him, thinking, perhaps, that, since the original idea had been his, he should be allowed to produce the masterpiece. Yet, despite her faults, among them the ability to hoodwink herself into believing that the way of life she had chosen was the best for all concerned, such an act of deliberate malice is foreign to her character. Instead, it is possible to visualize her reading, with reluctant admiration, far into the night, then rising wearily and half asleep, giving the papers as she passed a gentle push which sent them fluttering to the floor. The subconscious wish to destroy them may have been there, and that in itself would have been enough to cause the accident.

New queries continue to arise. Another recent writer, Ian Campbell, thinks that it would have been easy enough "to mess up" Carlyle's manuscripts: "He altered [them] to the extent that some printers refused to set them in type. . . . The piles of loose paper, written and re-written, altered times without number and with frequent pasted-on additions looked for all the world like scrap paper, and it is not surprising that the maid should have torn them up and used them to light the fire . . . ."[26]

Obviously, both writers have seen some of Carlyle's original manuscripts, which makes it clear that they were not uniform. A fragment of *The French Revolution,* one of the charred pieces rescued from the holocaust, is to be seen in Carlyle's Chelsea home, as are a few pages from his *Frederick the Great.* Judging only from these, it is true that his handwriting is difficult to decipher and that he made frequent use of deletions and insertions. And yet it is impossible to believe that, unless they were on the floor or in the wastepaper basket, anybody could have taken them for rubbish. The puzzle therefore remains unsolved.

CHAPTER 8

Poles Apart

Friendship with the Carlyles, which might well have been brought to a violent end by the incident of *The French Revolution,* continued, apparently as warmly as before. Carlyle was intrigued by Harriet, but she and Jane, so different in personality and outlook, remained wary of one another. When John Carlyle was in London in 1836 the brothers "called one day at Kent Terrace; but the Lady was not there", so Carlyle told Mill, who had probably been with Harriet at the time. Yet, however friendly he might appear, Carlyle could never resist his tendency to gossip. "Is it not strange," he wrote to John Sterling, "this pining away into desiccation and nonentity, of our poor Mill, if it be so, as his friends all say, that this charmer is the cause of it?" He underlined with malicious glee the current rumours. "They are innocent, says Charity; they are guilty, says Scandal: then why in the name of wonder are they dying broken hearted?" He himself protested that he believed them "innocent . . . as sucking doves, and yet suffering the clack of tongues, worst penalty of guilt".[1]

It may have been at this time that Carlyle began to concoct the stories with which he regaled his friends in later life. The much-abused John Taylor, so he told his Irish friend Charles Gavan Duffy, had remonstrated with his wife about the affair. To this she had proudly replied (although Carlyle cannot possibly have known whether she had or not) that he "might blow up the house if it seemed good to him",[2] but in no circumstances would she relinquish her friendship with Mill.

Jane Carlyle, as fascinated as her husband with this strange romance, informed her "ever dear" John Sterling early in 1837 that "John Mill and Mrs Taylor get on as charmingly as ever. I saw them together very lately looking more ecstatically 'moony' at one another and sublimely superior to the rest of the world".[3]

It was this air of superiority, conscious or unconscious, which annoyed Jane and induced her with more than a dash of spleen to tell Duffy that Harriet "was not the pink of womanhood, but a peculiarly affected and empty body".[4]

This estimate has echoed down the years. As recently as 1952, on the evidence of her published letters and papers, she was called "one of the meanest and dullest ladies in literary history, a monument of nasty self-regard, as lacking in charm as in grandeur".[5] She was not the paragon Mill thought her, but, had she been so dull and charmless, he would surely, besotted as he was, have tired of her long before the end.

Mill's comparative ignorance of the ways of the world had blinded him to the obvious fact that Carlyle was gossiping. In 1839 John Sterling received a letter from Carlyle which tacitly accused Mill and Harriet of carrying on a liaison. Mill had informed him that Mrs Taylor "is not living at the old abode in Regent's Park, but in Wilton Place, a street where as I conjecture there are mainly wont to be *Lodgings*. Can it be possible? Or if so, what does it betoken?"[6] Sterling, a loyal friend, answered that he had heard from Mill by the same post and had received no hint of anything untoward. The truth of the matter was that Harriet had come to London to see her sons and was staying in rooms while repairs and redecorations were being carried on at the house in Kent Terrace.

Harriet was also ignorant of the gossip, for three years later, in June 1842, she wrote to ask Carlyle "a great favour". At the time she was having a peculiarly violent altercation with her family about her brother-in-law Arthur Ley's trusteeship of her marriage settlement. Ley was untrustworthy but refused to resign; a second trustee, John Taylor's brother-in-law, was going to live abroad and could no longer act, and Harriet was anxious that the vacancy should be filled, "so that I shall leave this portion of my young ones interests in the surest hands". She assured Carlyle that, if he consented to accept the position, there would be very little work involved, otherwise she would not have felt entitled to ask him. "May I hope that you will not disappoint me in this?" She sent her kind regards to Mrs Carlyle and added a message from her husband: "Mr Taylor joins in this request & proposes to take an early opportunity of calling at Chelsea to make it in person."[7]

Carlyle accepted—then, on second thoughts, declined:

What you ask me is very flattering; and seemed so small a matter, in regard to "trouble" or the like, that I could not but at once accede to your request when Mr Taylor came, that same evening, to enforce it and receive my answer.

During these two days, however, there have various doubts arisen. . . . The fact is, you have not among all your friends any person, possessed of common sense and arrived at the years of discretion, who is so totally unacquainted with every form of what is called Business; nor, I think unlikelier now ever to become acquainted with it. . . .

Of my trustworthiness to do what I undertake, and of my true readiness to serve you in a much larger matter, I will not raise any doubt . . . .[8]

Nevertheless he begged his "dear Friend" to look elsewhere for a trustee.

Such a protestation of friendship sounded genuine enough. It was not until 1846 that Mill grasped the extent of Carlyle's duplicity, although Carlyle himself put the rupture at a later date. In 1846 the American critic and essayist Margaret Fuller, author of *Woman in the Nineteenth Century,* came to London with an introduction to Carlyle from Emerson. In conversation with his American friend Charles Eliot Norton after Mill's death, Carlyle recalled that he decided to invite some congenial friends to meet her at dinner, Mill among them. "And I went one day to the India House to invite him, and before I got there I met him coming along the street, and he received me like the very incarnation o' the East Wind, and refused my invitation peremptorily. And from that day to this I've never set eyes upon him, and no word has passed between us . . . ."[9]

Carlyle had not only got his date but also one of his facts wrong. In 1851 Duffy came to London and asked him for an introduction to Mill. Carlyle complied, but warned Duffy that "I must understand that Mill and he had ceased to see much of each other in later times, as in fact they had nothing in common."[10]

By 1851 Margaret Fuller was dead. She had been drowned the previous year, together with her Italian husband and their infant son, on the return voyage from Europe to America. If Carlyle and Mill were still meeting even occasionally in 1851, the "incarnation o' the East Wind" meeting could not have taken place in 1846.

To Norton, Carlyle, the old hypocrite, complained that he could really never account for Mill's frosty behaviour:

And many a night have I laid awake thinkin' what it might be that had come between us, and never could I think o' the least thing, for I'd never said a word nor harboured a thought about that man, but of affection and kindliness. . . . Never could I think 'o the least thing, unless maybe it was this. One year . . . . Godefroi Cavaignac . . . was over here from Paris, an' he told me o' meeting Mill and Mrs Taylor somewhere in France not long before, eatin' grapes together off one bunch, like two love-birds. And his description amused me, and I repeated it, without thinkin' any harm, to a man who made trouble with his tongue [Charles Buller (see Hayek, *J. S. Mill and Harriet Taylor,* pp. 89 and 293)], and I've thought that he might perhaps have told it to Mill, and that Mill might have fancied that I was making a jest o' what was most sacred to him; but I don't know if that was it' but it was the only thing I could ever think of that could ha' hurt him.[11]

Godefroi Cavaignac must have seen Mill and Harriet together during the Taylors' trial separation in 1833. He came to London two years later and made friends with the Carlyles. It is hard to believe that this particular piece of gossip, extremely stale by 1850 or thereabouts, was the real cause of Mill's coldness or that Carlyle himself imagined that it was.

Norton made no comment on Carlyle's specious excuse, but Duffy, when told something of the same kind, was more perspicacious. Carlyle had told Norton that he "never could find out what more than ordinary there was in the woman he cared for so much".[12] Duffy, when told by Carlyle that he could not account for the abrupt ending of their friendship, since neither he nor Mill "had altered in fundamentals, nor were they further from agreeing than they had always been", replied dryly "that if Mill had heard his estimate of Mrs Taylor, there need be no difficulty in accounting for the change".[13]

Duffy had also, of course, heard Jane Carlyle call Harriet "a peculiarly affected and empty body". To illustrate her mannerisms she had added that Harriet "was not easy unless she startled you with unexpected sayings. If she was going to utter something kind and affectionate, she spoke in a hard, stern voice. If she wanted to be alarming or uncivil, she employed the most honeyed and affectionate tones." From something else Jane said at the time it seems probable that the Carlyles were still on visiting terms with Mill and Harriet after their marriage in 1851: " 'Come down and see us,' she said one day (mimicking her tone), 'you will be charmed with our house, it is so full of rats.' 'Rats!' cried Carlyle. 'Do you regard *them* as an attraction?' 'Yes' (piano), 'they are such dear, innocent creatures.' "[14]

The mention of rats indicates a meeting as late as 1854. The house in Blackheath Park, Kent, to which the Mills retreated after their marriage was infested with them. Towards the end of the previous year Harriet had gone to the south of France on one of her periodic trips abroad in search of health. Whatever the nature of her previous illnesses, she was by now in an advanced stage of tuberculosis, the disease transmitted by James Mill to John and his two youngest sons and, in all probability, from John Mill to Harriet. Mill had accompanied his wife as far as Nice, where, but for the care of an English resident doctor, Cecil Gurney, she would probably have died from a severe haemorrhage of the lungs. When she recovered, Mill returned to England and his work at the India House, leaving Harriet with her daughter Helen. Bereft of his competent wife and her daughter, with only the maid, Kate, and the doubtful assistance of his listless, delicate stepson Haji, he allowed the housekeeping affairs to get into an inextricable muddle. Too much money was being spent on meat, coal and potatoes; he misunderstood Harriet's careful instructions about the payment of bills and taxes, for he was quite helpless without her, a fact which he attributed to the lack of practical training in his youth; and—to return to the Carlyles—he was involved in an inconclusive struggle with his next-door neighbour, a Mr Powell, about the infiltration of rats from Powell's house to his. Having first described his physical symptoms to Harriet, on this occasion a cough and a "mucous secretion", which had not as yet been correctly ascribed to tuberculosis, he went on to tell her that he had been assured by Kate that not a single rat had been seen on the premises until after the local ratcatcher had visited the next-door house, since when a "populous colony" had infested both properties. "You will tell me what is to be done", he cried, as always. In the meantime he had sent Haji with a note to Powell, "in these words: 'Mr J. S. Mill is obliged to Mr Powell for his information & will have his side of the garden wall examined': that seemed safe & *un*committing . . . ."[15]

It was not, of course, for, as Harriet was quick to note, her husband had tacitly admitted that the infestation might have started in his house. She did not agree either that, since Mill had lost the key of the outhouse in which the rats were now making "a great uproar", he should sit back and "leave things as they are till we meet". "I am so sorry the few words I wrote to Powell vexed her", he wrote humbly, resorting to the whimsical use of the third person as he so often did in his leters to Harriet. "I was much annoyed at having to write or do anything . . . without having time to consult her for I know I always miss the proper thing & above all the proper tone. I shall now do at once what my dearest one recommends."[16]

Harriet's instructions, which he hastened to obey, were to get hold of a locksmith to break open the outhouse door, obtain the ratcatcher's address from his neighbour, and make it quite plain to Powell that the infestation had started on his premises and that he alone was responsible for its spread.

It seems most likely, therefore, that some time after her return to Blackheath in the spring of 1854, with the rats still in partial possession of the house, she had paid a visit to Cheyne Row and quaintly described the vermin as "dear, innocent creatures".

There is certainly no truth in Carlyle's assertion to his friend Norton that, after the abortive invitation to meet Margaret Fuller, "no word has passed between us"; for the two men continued to correspond fitfully even if they did not meet. After his marriage and the revival of the old gossip, Mill had made it abundantly clear to almost all of his one-time friends that he and Harriet wished for no visitors to disturb their wedded bliss. "I respect your solitude", wrote Carlyle, "and indeed find it necessary myself to cultivate the same, as years grow upon me. No truer wish for the happiness of you both dwells anywhere than here,—which is of some use to myself if none to any other body."[17] Yet only a few months earlier he had written maliciously to Lady Ashburton that "John Mill . . . is wedded to his widow Taylor; a fact in biography: poor good Mill".[18] The news had sent the courteous Lord Ashburton to ask Mill if he might call on his wife: the offer was refused.

Carlyle and Mill sent messages of goodwill to their respective wives whenever one or the other of them had occasion to write. In the summer of 1858 Mill went as far as to make a half-hearted attempt at a rapprochement. Carlyle had taken refuge from the heat in Annan, and, so Mill wrote, "You are well out of dusty London at this dusty season, though we by no means find it necessary to go so far as Annan for the calm and silence you speak of. We have a quiet corner down here, where we shall be at any time happy to see you."[19] It seems unlikely that Carlyle took the invitation seriously. In any event the visit never took place, for within four months Harriet Mill was dead.

Not very long before his own death Mill received a friendly gesture from Carlyle, now himself a widower. The older man had found two volumes of Evelyn's *Diary*, which he fancied had once belonged to James Mill, and sent them to John by way of Mrs Grote, who had been readmitted to favour. John Mill replied that, while he had forgotten about the books, the note which accompanied them "would have revived, if they had ever been dormant, many old memories and feelings". He was shortly going abroad with his stepdaughter but would be back in England before long, "and any communication from you—not to mention your bodily presence—would be always most welcome to yours truly, J. S. Mill."[20]

Carlyle's bodily presence could have acted only as an irritant. The rift between the two men had been caused only in part by Carlyle's malicious gossip. If Harriet Taylor had never existed they would inevitably have reached breaking point sooner or later. The first serious clash had occurred in 1849, sparked off by Carlyle's extremist views on the black population of the West Indies. In December of that year he published an article in *Fraser's Magazine*, "Occasional Discourse on the Nigger Question", in which he argued that the use of black labour on the sugar plantations was necessary for the benefit of the world. He was not in favour of slavery but thought that emancipation had been a mistake. The people should be treated like the English serfs of old, and throughout their lives should, together with their families, be guarded against cruelty and oppression and protected from want, provided that they worked as directed.

The very title was enough to raise Mill's hackles. In the next issue of *Fraser's,* Mill, the apostle of freedom, attacked Carlyle's thesis and upheld the great ideal of human progress—the long struggle of humanity against the iniquitous power of the law of might.

The dispute rumbled on until the final clash in 1865, when Governor E. J. Eyre suppressed the Jamaica riots with ruthless force. A report criticizing his conduct was published in the spring of 1866 and he was recalled to England. Two opposing factions then emerged: one, with Carlyle among its most vociferous adherents, maintained that Eyre's conduct was justified by the need to preserve law and order and the colony's economy; the other, led by John Stuart Mill, MP, unsuccessfully campaigned to bring the Governor to trial. As before, Carlyle and Mill attacked one another bitterly in print, and it is hard to imagine that any real semblance of friendship could have survived the dispute.

When he learned of Mill's death, however, the old man became positively maudlin. "I never knew a finer, tenderer, more sensitive or modest soul among the sons of man",[21] he assured Norton. But when he read Mill's *Autobiography* he reacted with understandable fury. Mill had referred to their differences, the fact that he was not, as Carlyle had hoped, "another mystic", and that, as the years passed, their views continued to diverge. Carlyle was a poet and a man of intuition, which Mill confessed he was not: "I knew that I could not see round him, and could never be certain that I saw over him; and I never presumed to judge him with any definiteness, until he was interpreted to me by one greatly the superior of us both—who was more a poet than he, and more a thinker than I—whose own mind and nature included his, and infinitely more."[22]

The comparison already mentioned between Harriet and himself was too staggering to pass. As he wrote to his brother John, he had never read "a more uninteresting book, nor I should say a sillier, by a man of sense, integrity, and seriousness of mind. . . . As a mournful psychical curiosity, but in no other point of view, can it interest anybody . . . ." He was still more incensed to read two newspaper eulogies of the man who had once been his friend. "Two more blustrous bags of empty wind I have seldom read. 'Immortal Fame!' 'First Spirit of his Age!' 'Thinker of thinkers!' What a piece of work is man with a penny-a-liner in his hand."[23]

There is only one conclusion to be drawn from such a letter: the old man was jealous, fearful that when his own time came he would not be rated so highly as Mill.

CHAPTER 9

A Working Partnership

Like many lesser women Harriet Taylor displayed the most disagreeable aspects of her nature to those who failed to credit her with unusual gifts. It is reasonable to suppose that, had the Carlyles respected her intellect, they would have found her less patronizing, affected and vain. Also, in common with other women, she expanded in the sunshine of uncritical admiration, responding graciously to the pompous overtures of W. J. Fox; Eliza Flower's schoolgirl adoration of her; and, above all, John Stuart Mill's worship of her. His adoration and deference, the submission which his friends and critics found so nauseatingly exaggerated, elicited from her the ideas, thoughts and analyses which had such a decisive effect on his later work.

Most of his early critics followed John Roebuck's estimate of Harriet, given despite the fact that he scarcely knew her, that Mill "believed her an inspired philosopher in petticoats; and as she had the art of returning his own thoughts to himself, clothed in her own words, he thought them hers, and wondered at her powers of mind, and the accuracy of her conclusions".[1] Alexander Bain, however, came nearer the truth when he said that what Mill most enjoyed "was to have his own faculties set in motion, so as to evolve new thoughts and new aspects of old thoughts. This might be done better by intelligently controverting his views than by merely reproducing them in different language."[2] Bain had no doubt that Harriet responded in this way. He was in a better position than Roebuck to assess her effect. He remained on friendly terms with Mill (since he aspired to be his biographer this was essential even if he had been less attached to him than he was), although, after Mill's marriage, he saw him only when he called at the India House. Mill's other friends and members of his family were forbidden to mention Harriet's name in his presence, but, according to his own account, Bain broached the forbidden subject twice, once before and once after the marriage, without causing any offence. With his customary infuriating caution he makes no mention of what was said on either occasion. But he underestimated Harriet when he claimed that she was Mill's "intellectual companion, only in a very small portion of his range of studies".[3] The range may have been comparatively small, but Harriet, not Mill, was the master.

71

Once she got her teeth into an idea she never let go: she argued, cajoled, persuaded, and, when he demurred, forced him to think again.

As the relationship grew in intimacy, so Mill came to rely more and more on Harriet for direction. It is true that, beyond a few stylistic suggestions, she made no contribution towards his widely acclaimed *System of Logic,* published in 1843; but she played a decisive part in his later works, notably the *Principles of Political Economy* and the books for which he is best remembered today, *On Liberty* and *The Subjection of Women.*

The *Political Economy* was called by Mill a joint production. It arose from five *Essays upon Some unsettled Questions of Political Economy,* published in 1844, and has its value for students today even if it was not, as one authority has put it, "conspicuously original".[4] It owed something to earlier political economists, to James Mill's friend David Ricardo, for example, the first economist to give clear expression to the quantity theory of money; to Adam Smith's *Wealth of Nations,* the basis of all works on political economy; and to the doctrines of Malthus, which, of course, Mill had studied at an early age. Mill favoured the private ownership of property, though not necessarily the right of inheritance; he considered competition essential to economic health and was opposed to State intervention in the economy, except where it was absolutely necessary. He believed that income tax should be imposed, above a minimum exemption level, in such a way as to exact an equal sacrifice from everyone. Above all, he was severely critical of socialism and communism, on the grounds that people would not trouble to work if they knew for certain that whatever happened their own livelihood was secure.

Despite his concentration on the rest of his work, the first draft of the *Political Economy* was finished by the early spring of 1847. It lacked the chapter which, Mill said, "had a greater influence on opinion than all the rest, that on 'the Probable Future of the Labouring Classes' ", a chapter which was "entirely due" to Harriet's prompting. "She pointed out the need for such a chapter, and the extreme imperfection of the book without it: she was the cause of my writing it; and the more general part of the chapter, the statement and discussion of the two opposite theories respecting the proper condition of the labouring classes, was wholly an exposition of her thoughts, often in words taken from her own lips."[5]

As a recent authority has described it, "The warm-hearted Mrs Taylor did not permit him to leave the toiling masses without an especially addressed word of encouragement as to their share"[6] in a brighter future. At her suggestion he wrote, "The poor have come out of leading-strings, and cannot any longer be governed or treated like children. To their own qualities must now be commended the care of their destiny.... Whatever advice, exhortation or guidance is held out to the labouring classes, must henceforth be tendered to them as equals, and accepted by them with their eyes open. The prospect of the future depends on the degree in which they can be made rational beings."[7] The "toiling masses" must be shown how they could contribute towards the progress of humanity by forming themselves into co-operative societies; by reading the newspapers and attending lectures and discussion groups; by joining trade unions, though these had not yet secured adequate legal recognition; by limiting the size of their families, a form of restraint which would be rewarded by educational facilities for their children and the mothers' release from domestic servitude. In due course, therefore, there would no longer be an identifiable working class, since men and women of all classes would have learned to work together for the common good.

"The purely scientific part of the Political Economy I did not learn from her", Mill admitted. Indeed, she was not equipped to provide it. But "it was chiefly her influence that gave to the book that general tone by which it is distinguished from all previous expositions of Political Economy that had any pretension to being scientific, and which has made it so useful in conciliating minds which those previous expositions had repelled."[8]

As embellished by Harriet, the book was sent to John W. Parker, publisher, at the end of 1847. She had taken exception to the terms Mill had accepted for his *Logic,* and although these—based on half the net profits—were repeated, Parker's rights in the new book were to be limited to one edition. This was Harriet's idea, and Mill was delighted with her business acumen: "The bargain with Parker is a good one & that it is so is entirely your doing—all the difference between it & the last being wholly your work, as well as all the best of the book itself so that you have a redoubled title to your joint ownership of it . . . ."[9]

Harriet's preoccupation with the book is reflected in letters to her husband. "I do certainly look more like a ghost [than] a living person", she told John Taylor shortly before the book went to press. She had been on the point of going to Brighton, which always agreed with her, but "I think I shall not be able to go before the end of next week being just now much occupied with the book". She was still busy in February 1848, entirely "taken up with the Book, which is near the last & has constantly something to be seen to about binding &tc.". In March she was able to report that the *Political Economy,* "which has been the work of all this winter is now nearly ready and will be published in ten days."

Mill, eager to give adequate expression of his debt to his beloved, added a highly appreciative dedication: "To Mrs John Taylor as the most eminently qualified of all persons known to the author to originate or to appreciate speculations on social improvement, this attempt to explain and diffuse ideas many of which were first learned from herself, is with the highest respect and regard dedicated." Harriet, convinced that she had earned this praise, took the precaution of consulting her husband on the propriety of allowing it to appear in print. John Taylor, who already had troubles enough, registered strong disapproval. He was, he said, averse to dedications on principle, but this one evinced "a want of taste & tact which I could not have believed possible."

Having asked his advice, Harriet had to submit, at least as far as the general public was concerned; but the dedication appeared on slips of paper pasted into a few presentation copies. One of these she sent to W. J. Fox's daughter Eliza, because the girl sympathised in the cause to which she herself was devoted, "justice for women. The progress of the race *waits* for the emancipation of women", she wrote to Fox. (Eliza Bridell Fox, who married the landscape painter, Frederick Lee Bridell, was herself a portrait painter.) Artists alone were free to compete with men on equal terms; the vast majority of women were still condemned to the most menial and poorly paid occupations. "Political equality would alone place women on a level with . . . men".[10]

The first edition of the *Political Economy*— 1,000 copies—appeared in 1848 (It also appeared in America in 1848. Six editions, each with fresh revisions, were published during Mill's lifetime. Since then it has been reprinted many times, appearing in a number of languages. Details of the variations in the editions of the *Political Economy* appear in the introduction and comments by Sir W. J. Ashley (Longmans Green, 1909). The 1849 edition, collated with the first edition of 1848 and the manuscript, is published in the *Collected Works of John Stuart Mill,* vols. II and III (University of Toronto Press and Routledge and Kegan Paul, 1965), and was exhausted within a year). When a second edition was published the following year, a drastic revision had been made to a vitally important chapter, *Of Property,* the first chapter of Book II. 1848 was the year of revolutions and Harriet, as we saw, was captivated by the revolution in France. She had previously assented to Mill's assertion that under existing conditions socialism and communism were unrealistic and undesirable: they placed too much emphasis on the importance of security. Mill had written, "Those who have never known freedom from anxiety as to the means of subsistence, are apt to overrate what is gained for positive enjoyment by the mere absence of that uncertainty."[11] This argument no longer applied, she now said. Mill had a set of proofs of the first edition; he could make the necessary revisions and send them to the printer. He protested mildly that the paragraph (it appeared on pages 247-8 of the first edition) "which you object to so strongly & totally, is what has always seemed to me the strongest part of the argument . . . —& as omitting it after it has once been printed would imply a change of opinion, it is necessary to see whether the opinion has changed or not". Harriet's opinion had changed, at any rate in some respects, for she now "marked strong dissent"[12] from the passage which read,

> The necessaries of life, when they have always been secure for the whole of life, are scarcely more a subject of consciousness or a source of happiness than the elements. There is little attractive in a monotonous routine, without vicissitudes, but without excitement; a life spent in the enforced observance of an external rule, and performance of a prescribed task: in which labour would be devoid of its chief sweetener, the thought that every effort tells perceptibly on the labourer's own interests or those of some one with whom he identifies himself; in which no one could by

his own exertions improve his condition, or that of the objects of his private affections; in which no one's way of life, occupations, or movements, would depend on choice, but each would be the slave of all....[13]

This passage, to which she now objected so strongly and totally was, as Mill reminded her, "inserted on your proposition, & very nearly in your words". It had previously seemed to him so strong an argument against socialism and communism: now she was asking him to modify it. Whatever his own feelings in the matter, he could not bring himself to refuse. Her theory, he said, most likely reflected no more than "the progress we have been always making, & by thinking sufficiently I should probably come to think the same—as is almost always the case. I believe *always* when we think long enough".[14]

"Always" was the operative word. The passage which Harriet found so offensive was replaced by one which, by himself, he would probably never have proposed: "On the Communistic scheme, supposing it to be successful, there would be an end to all anxiety concerning the means of subsistence; and this would be much gained for human happiness. But it is perfectly possible to realize this same advantage in a society grounded on private property; and to this point the tendencies of political speculation are rapidly converging."[15]

This was not all. In the first edition, with Harriet's concurrence, Mill had argued that only those activities which could not "be done by individual agency" should be entrusted to collective action: "But the proper sphere for collective action lies in the things which cannot be done by individual agency, either because no one can have a sufficiently strong personal interest in accomplishing them or because they require an assemblage of means surpassing what can be commanded by one or a few individuals. In things to which individual agency is at all suitable, it is almost always the most suitable."[16]

As Harriet now objected to this passage he concluded that he had not made his meaning clear. What he had intended to say, he told her, "was that whether individual agency or Socialism would be best ultimately—(*both* being necessarily very imperfect now, & *both* susceptible of immense improvement) will depend on the comparative attractions they will hold out to human beings with all their capacities, both individual & social, infinitely more developed than at present.[17]

The offending passage was replaced by one which concluded, "We are as yet too ignorant either of what individual agency in its best form, or Socialism in its best form, can accomplish, to be qualified to decide which of the two will be the ultimate form of human society."[18]

Elsewhere Mill had likened a socialist state to a "well-regulated manufactory". He believed that "the majority would not exert themselves for anything beyond this, and that unless they did, nobody else would, and that on this basis human life would settle itself in one invariable round".[19] When

Harriet ordered him to change this sentence, he murmured that, if it was "not tenable, then all the two or three pages of argument which precede & of which this is but the summary, are false, & there is nothing to be said against communism at all—one would only have to turn round and advocate it". This, he suggested hopefully, would be done better as "a separate treatise"[20] to precede publication of the second edition of the *Political Economy*.

Nevertheless the sentence had to go. Mill sent "the dear one" a revised draft of all the passages to which she objected: "I saw on consideration that the objection to Communism on the ground of its making life a kind of dead level might admit of being weakened (though I think it never could be taken away) consistently with the principle of Communism, though the Communistic plans now before the public could not do it. The statement of objections was moreover too vague & general. I have made it more explicit as well as more moderate; *you* will judge whether it is now sufficiently one or the other." After a proviso concerning the "present applicability" of the socialist doctrines of Fourier, which, if she insisted, he would also delete, he added, "I feel that I never should long continue of an opinion different from yours on a subject which you have fully considered."[21]

Further concessions were demanded and obtained. "I have followed to the letter every recommendation", Mill assured Harriet in March 1849; and later in the month he accepted her rewording of passages on the need for population control as "so very good that . . . get them in I must & will".[22]

When the third edition appeared, in 1852, it was clear that Mill's recantation had been complete. If, he now declared in the chapter "Of Property",

> the choice were to be made between Communism with all its chances, and the present state of society with all its sufferings and injustices; if the institution of private property necessarily carried with it as a consequence, that the produce of labour should be apportioned as we now see it, almost in an inverse ratio to the labour—the largest portions to those who have never worked at all . . . , the remuneration dwindling as the work grows harder and more disagreeable, until the most fatiguing and exhausting bodily labour cannot count with certainty on being able to earn even the necessaries of life; if this or Communism were the alternative, all the difficulties, great or small, of Communism would be as dust in the balance. But to make the comparison applicable, we must compare Communism at its best, with the regime of individual property, not as it is, but as it might be made.[23]

Mill's claim that the chapter which Harriet had initiated, "On the Probable Future of the Labouring Classes", made more of an impact on public opinion than the rest of the book gained credence in 1854 when the Christian Socialist editor Frederick J. Furnival asked permission to reprint it. Mill had no objection; but "what does my angel think? I did not expect the Xtian

Socialists would wish to circulate the chapter as it is in the 3^d edit. since it stands up for Competition against their one-eyed attacks & denunciations of it...."[24]

His angel was willing, subject to certain modifications and additions which she now considered essential and the translation of a number of passages which had originally appeared in French. Once more Mill bent himself to the task. "I think I agree in all your remarks & have adopted them almost all...."[25]

Alexander Bain, writing within ten years of Mill's death, admitted that the *Political Economy* owed something to Mill's discussions with Harriet, but did not agree that the chapter on the working classes could not have developed from his own, independent thought and studies. If Professor Harold Laski had seen some of the letters now lodged in his own London School of Economics, he would surely have revised his estimate of Harriet. In 1923 he reread the *Political Economy* and wrote to a friend, "I thought its tone and temper simply admirable; and it goes with a broad swing that nothing else save Adam Smith possesses." Yet he seems to have had no inkling of the strength of the woman who had forced Mill to change it. Of Harriet he could only surmise, "I should guess that she was a comfortable and sympathetic person and that Mill... had never met a really soft cushion before. If she was what he thought, some one else at least should have given us an indication."[26]

Mill had put a false gloss on his beloved's character, on her potentials as poet and orator, but not on her intellectual dominance over him. In some portions of his *Autobiography* he allowed his adoration to lead him into expressions of undue enthusiasm and exaggeration, but not in the following:

> She was much more courageous and far-sighted than without her I should have been, in anticipation of an order of things to come, in which many of the limited generalizations now so often confounded with universal principles will cease to be applicable. Those parts of my writings, and especially the Political Economy, which contemplate possibilities in the future such as, when affirmed by Socialists, have in general been fiercely denied by political economists, would, but for her, either have been absent, or the suggestions would have been made much more timidly and in a more qualified form.[27]

CHAPTER 10

John Taylor versus John Mill

Following the publication of the *Principles of Political Economy* in 1848, John Mill, Harriet and John Taylor were all ill, with complaints of varying severity. Mill, on his usual morning walk from Kensington to the India House, stumbled and fell over a loose brick near a pump in the park and injured one hip. The injury was treated with belladonna plasters, which seem to have affected his eyesight, and for some weeks he was both lame and half blind. "I never say him in such a state of despair", wrote Alexander Bain. "Prostration of the nervous system may have aggravated his condition."[1] Harriet's ailments were numerous—among them, rheumatic pains in the head and legs, partial paralysis, and palpitations. John Taylor felt wretchedly ill with constant diarrhoea. His wife was sympathetic but bracing. "I am glad to hear that your Doctor has changed his medicines & I hope that combined with the more healthy weather they will soon make much change for the better", she wrote from Worthing on the south coast, where Mill was visiting her, in November. "That sort of ailment is so very tedious—it is always returning again after a few days interval of improvement."[2] She herself, she added, felt too feeble to venture out of the house as often as she wished.

John Taylor was more solicitous. "I regret very much to hear so sad an account of your health. I hoped that you would not have a return of stiffness in the leg—but I suppose that has been affected by the general state of health...."[3] Harriet, now contemplating a winter in the sunshine of the south of France, was impatient as well as sorry to learn that her husband was no better. "Surely you ought to take some tonic for the purpose of *confining* the bowels—all the Doctors say that you must pass through a period of confined bowels before they will act healthily after stomach derangement...."[4]

The derangement was obdurate, and John Taylor, importunate for once, was pathetically anxious for his wife to remain near at hand. Her father was seriously ill; her favourite brother, Arthur, in London from Australia, would have to travel north to visit him. Harriet wanted to see as much as possible of Arthur, but she had no wish to see the rest of her family. "The near relationship to persons of the most opposite principles to my own produces excessive embarrassments",[5] she told her husband in explanation of her refusal to change her plans. She was going abroad, she said, "not for any pleasure to myself but because I think it necessary".[6]

Husband and wife wrote frequently to one another but, towards the end of March 1849, when Harriet's health had improved, John Taylor confessed that he was not getting any better. She replied, "If I only consulted my own inclination I should come back to England immediately . . . in hopes of being able to be of use to you—the reason I cannot do this is that I have arranged with Mr Mill to meet me on the 20th of April when he is to have three weeks holiday on account of his health which has been the whole winter in a very precarious state . . . ." Mill's sight was still giving him so much trouble that he could neither read nor write with ease, and she considered it "a duty" to do everything she could to ensure his recovery. She promised to return to England as soon as she was free and, in the meantime, asked her husband not to reveal her whereabouts. Mr Mill, she said, "does not tell even his own family *where* he goes for his holiday as I do so hate all tittle-tattle".[7]

It is true that Harriet did not realize that John Taylor was gravely ill, but she had emphasized most cruelly that there was no comparison between his welfare and John Mill's. When she finally reached London in the middle of May she learned the truth: her husband was dying from cancer.

For the last two months of his life she nursed him obsessively, giving the unfortunate man all the comfort she could, herself enduring the pains of guilt and contrition. At first she refused to accept the doctors' verdict. Forced to admit at length that there was no hope, she wrote to John Mill of his courage and patience; he who "never hurt or harmed a creature on earth. . . I feel as if he beside you is the only life I value in this wretched world . . . ."[8]

In an effort to distract her, Mill misguidedly suggested that it might help if she refrained from writing exclusively about her husband's illness. "Good God," she stormed, "sh[d] you think it a relief to think of somebody else some acquaintance or what not while *I* was dying? If so . . . I feel it sacrilegious to enter into any account of what I feel & suffer . . . my heart is wrung with indignation and grief."[9] In her hysterical anguish she could not resist this display of power over over the man who loved her so deeply; and she tormented him further by insisting, against all the evidence, that cancer was contagious and that she might herself contract it. Between the storms she was as loving and affectionate as ever. She would not see him; but "I have so much to say to you that no one but you could understand. Tell me how you are. Take care of yourself for the world's sake."[10]

Deprived of her physical presence, Mill could not exist without the benefit of her advice, and so, partly to divert her, partly to help himself, he put one or two pressing problems to her as the weeks of John Taylor's dying dragged by. The first concerned George Jacob Holyoake, the free-thinking, left-wing editor, mainstay of the co-operative movement. Holyoake, well aware of Mill's sympathies, had asked for financial help towards his support while he worked for a university degree. Mill begged Harriet to tell him what he should say. She advised him to advance the money, together with a homily pointing out that the acquirement of a degree did not automatically entitle a man to call himself learned.

A second problem struck nearer home. John Sterling had died in 1844, to the grief of his many friends. Now Captain Sterling, his brother, had written to ask Mill if he might use some of his letters and some references to him in a volume of John Sterling's letters which he planned to publish. The mere possibility that Sterling's letters might give rise to the tittle-tattle she so detested terrified Harriet. Mill must not allow himself to be associated with the venture which she could not believe would be free of all mention of his long friendship with a married woman. Mill hesitated: John Sterling had been a loyal friend and he found an outright refusal difficult. Harriet then flew at him, accusing him of vanity and madness. "That you c^d be willing to have these things printed hurts me more deeply than anything else I think c^d do...."[11]

In the course of a lengthy tirade she had sought to denigrate John Sterling as foolish and weak enough to accept any adverse comments on her relationship with Mill which his other correspondents might have cared to make. In fact, this was not so, as his reply to Carlyle's malicious rumour proves. But she had made her point: Mill refused his consent and Captain Sterling had to abandon his project.

John Sterling was not the only one of Mill's friends to be denigrated in this moment of crisis. If she had ever feared the influence of women such as Sarah Austin, Harriet Grote or Harriet Martineau, she had no fear of it now; but in her hysteria she sought to lessen almost everyone for whom Mill had shown any liking or respect. Alexis de Tocqueville, she now declared, "is a notable specimen of the class which includes the Romillys [Sir John (later Baron) Romilly had been a friend of Mill's for many years] Carlyles Austins—the gentility class—weak in moral, narrow in intellect, timid, infinitely conceited and gossiping. There are very few men in this country who can seem other than more or less respectable puppets to us."[12]

Mill accepted all her strictures with the utmost meekness. Even if in his heart he did not believe that most men were puppets, Harriet was his beloved; she could say what she pleased. Guilt and weariness had made her more splenetic than usual, but her strictures had at least diverted her thoughts momentarily from her obsession with her dying husband. Mill was relieved, too, when she found time to expatiate on corporal punishment in connection with William Hamilton's mock attempt on the life of the Queen and to urge him to write an article on the subject.

By 16 July it was clear that John Taylor was sinking: two days later he died. "I find I am quite physically exhausted & faint after two nights & a day of most anxious and sad watching",[13] she wrote to Mill. But practical arrangements about the funeral had to be made and she also had to decide whether or not it would be prudent for Mill to be present. She consulted her elder son, Herbert, who was inclined to think that Mill should stay away; but

Herbert, like his father, she said, had "a sort of Ostrich instinct, like morally timid people, always *not to do*—while my instinct is always to *do*".[14] The latter part of this statement sums up Harriet very neatly. Whether or not John Mill attended his predecessor's funeral, however, we do not know.

Harriet received nothing but kindness from John Taylor's relations, who were grateful for her last-minute behaviour towards him. In no state to write letters beyond a few scribbled lines to Mill, she had instructed Herbert to inform her brother Arthur of her husband's death and to ask him to let the rest of the family know. Mrs Hardy, a tempestuous woman, took violent exception to this roundabout way of receiving the news and wrote an angry letter to her daughter. In her quarrels with her mother and sister John Mill naturally took Harriet's side; but on this occasion he was not available when she replied,

> I could not have thought it possible that you could have written so unkind & as I think it so unjust a letter. Your subject of offence with me if I understand it rightly is that I did not write to you immediately on my dear John's death. Whether this is sufficient ground of offence with one who has acted in this life to her mother as I have done to you I am willing to leave to the judgment of every person of taste or feeling. This offence you visit by a note in which sympathy or feeling for me is mentioned only incidentally . . . .[15]

Although Harriet's sister Caroline had earlier shown signs of wanting to heal the breach in the Hardy family, she had only succeeded in widening it, until eventually Harriet was not on speaking terms with either her sister or her mother.

John Taylor had been accused by his wife of ostrich-like behaviour; yet how otherwise could he have tolerated her conduct over a period of eighteen years? His tolerance and generosity extended beyond the grave. A few months before his death he had made a will leaving her a life interest in his entire estate. It can be truthfully said of him that, of the three people involved in the triangular relationship, only he emerged with unimpaired dignity.

Harriet could now feel not only that her feelings of guilt and remorse had been purged by her tireless attendance on her dying husband, but also that, in his own way, he had never ceased to love her.

The question in everybody's mind—the question which revived all the old gossip—was whether, now at last she was free, Harriet would marry John Mill. In fact, nearly two years elapsed before she decided that the period of conventional mourning had passed and they took the step which, so Mill was to write, added "to the partnership of thought, feeling, and writing which had long existed, a partnership of our entire existence".[16] It seems that only two letters from Mill to Harriet, and none from her to him, have survived from that period. Presumably they were often together; and "while you can love me as you so sweetly & so beautifully shewed in that hour yesterday", he wrote, "I have all I care for or desire for myself—& wish for nothing except not to disappoint you—& to be so happy as to be some good to you (who are all good to me) before I die...."[17]

CHAPTER 11

"The Enfranchisement of Women"

Once Harriet had established her ascendancy over Mill's mind, she remained the final judge and arbiter of his actions and his words.

In 1843, for example, he crossed swords, not for the first time, with Auguste Comte, on this occasion over the controversial question of feminism. Comte, a feminist in the past, had persuaded himself that women, as undeniably physically weaker than men, were also, on account of the supposed smaller size of their brains, mentally inferior. Mill, who was prepared to concede that their brians were smaller and that, with a few notable exceptions such as Queen Elizabeth I, they had not as yet proved themselves the equals of men, ascribed this inferiority entirely to circumstances. Woman's intellectual advancement was restricted, not by the size of her brain, but by the domestic servitude in which she was forced to live and by her lack of educational opportunities; her innate capacity to direct and control was blocked by official denial of her right to enter any of the professions; in the only spheres in which she could compete on equal terms with men—literature and art—her abilities had been demonstrated beyond all question. Mill's letters were courteous and deferential. Comte swept his arguments aside contemptuously. One day, he declared, Mill would discover, as he himself had done, that any attempt to champion women's rights was nothing more nor less than a waste of time.

The correspondence came to an end with an admission that the two philosophers must agree to differ. Mill had the letters bound in a volume, possibly for the edification of posterity (for it appears that he showed it to Alexander Bain), and certainly for Harriet. Her reaction was one of indignation against Comte and, to a lesser extent, against Mill, for being too conciliatory. Comte's fallacious arguments were only to be expected; but

> I am surprised in your letters to find your opinion undetermined where I had thought it made up—I am disappointed at a tone more than half-apologetic with which you state your opinions. & I am charmed with the exceeding nicety elegance & fineness of your last letter. Do not think that I wish you had said *more* on the subject, I only wish that what was said was in the tone of conviction, not of suggestion.

This dry sort of man is not a worthy coadjutor & scarcely a worthy opponent.... You are in advance of your age in culture of the intellectual faculties, you would be the most remarkable man of your age if you had no other claim to be so, than your perfect impartiality and your fixed love of justice.... [1]

The letter to which Harriet referred was most probably the one with which Mill ended the correspondence:

Puisque vous jugez que la discussion qui a tenu dernièrement une si grande place dans notre correspondence, est maintenant parvenue au point au delà duquel elle ne peut plus être portée avec avantage, je m'abstiendrai de la prolonger en y ajoutant des observations quelconques sur votre derniere lettre. Cette lettre n'a nullement ébranlé ma conviction, comme, en effet, elle n'y était pas destinée, mais seulement à mieux constater les points de divergence entre nos deux manières de penser.... [2]

According to Bain, Harriet's judgement rendered Mill so "dissatisfied with the concessions he had made to Comte" that he made up his mind that "he would never show [the correspondence] to any one again". [3] A few years later—in 1848—he told a friend who had written to him about Comte's *Discours sur l'Ensemble du Positivisme* that "in all his doctrines about women, I think and have always thought him in a radically wrong road and likely to go farther and farther wrong". [4]

Harriet had won a major triumph: she had persuaded Mill to consign the volume of correspondence to oblivion and, at the same time, ensured that his own thinking became more positive.

There were times when they argued, but on almost every occasion Harriet's was the deciding voice. Sometimes he accepted her actual wording, as when in 1854 he thanked her for "three beautiful sentences about 'disorder' "[5] which he promised to insert as they stood in his *Three Essays on Religion*. Sometimes he sought, and she gave, advice on public issues. In the same year he consulted her about a report which had been submitted to him by one of its authors, the politician Sir Charles Trevelyan. The report advocated stringent qualifying examinations for would-be recruits to the civil service; and, as Mill explained to Harriet, it was being opposed on the snobbish grounds "that it will bring low people into the offices! as, of course, gentlemen's sons cannot be expected to be as clever as low people". Harriet gave her opinion of the report in detail. "I need hardly say how heartily I feel all you say", he replied, "& the contempt I feel for the little feeling shewn for [the plan], not to speak of actual hostility...."[6] As a result he had promised Trevelyan his support and, when necessary, his considered comments, although he had to tell Harriet that at this stage all that Trevelyan needed was a general expression of approbation.

For some time now he had been trying to persuade Harriet to write something of her own, something which would show the world that she was worthy of his estimate of her. He was busy with the reversal she had demanded of his former strictures on socialism and communism in the *Political Economy* when he told her that he thought nothing could be written which "would do nearly so much good ... as the finishing your pamphlet—or little book rather, for it should be that".[7]

The germ of the piece sprang from the chapter in the *Political Economy* which Harriet had originated—"On the Probable Future of the Labouring Classes", with its emphasis on the need to liberate women from domestic slavery. The actual work was held up during John Taylor's last illness and the conventional period of mourning which followed his death.

In the second of Mill's two surviving letters to Harriet during 1850 he referred to two recent conferences on equal rights held in America—one in Ohio, the other in Massachusetts—with men and women speakers. The *New York Tribune* carried a report of the Massachusetts convention which in tone was "almost like ourselves speaking—outspoken like America, not frightened & servile like England—not the least iota of compromise—asserting the whole of the principle & claiming the whole of the consequences". Mill was hopeful that the campaign would gather momentum and that he and Harriet might live "to see something decisive really accomplished".[8] In the meantime, the unexpected success of the American conventions gave Harriet the necessary impetus to complete her "pamphlet" and also a topical peg on which to hang it.

"The Enfranchisement of Women", which appeared in the *Westminster Review* of July 1851, was a reasoned and powerful indictment of the inferior status accorded to women and a rational claim for equal rights in every sphere, in politics, property, education, work, and in the family. It is more radical in its approach than anything Mill had yet produced, which points to Harriet's overriding authority.

Opening with an account of the Massachusetts convention, the "Enfranchisement" claimed unequivocally that in the United States there were women "seemingly numerous, and ... organized for action on the public mind, who demand equality in the fullest acceptance of the word, and demand it by a straightforward appeal to men's sense of justice, not plead for it with a timid deprecation of their displeasure."

British radicals and chartists and European democrats were also claiming for women "what is called universal suffrage as an inherent right, unjustly and oppressively withheld from them. For with what truth or rationality could the suffrage be termed universal, while half the human species remain excluded from it? To declare that a voice in the government is the right of all, and demand it, only for a part ... is to renounce even the appearance of principle."

The theory that the vast majority of women wanted nothing more from life than to be wives and mothers was totally rejected. Many were housewives "only because there is no other career open to them ... To say that women must be excluded from active life because maternity disqualifies them from it, is in fact to say that every other career should be forbidden them, in order that maternity may be their only resource." Women were not only condemned to domestic slavery and denied their political rights; they were also excluded from many of the ordinary rights of citizenship. "It is an axiom of English freedom that taxation and representation should be co-extensive. Even under the laws which give the wife's property to her husband, there are many unmarried women who pay taxes." It was "one of the fundamental doctrines of the British constitution", the article continued, in what was indubitably Harriet's voice, "that all persons should be tried by their peers; yet women ... are tried by male judges and a male jury ... It is an acknowledged dictate of justice to make no degrading distinctions without necessity.... A reason must be given why anything should be permitted to one person and interdicted in another. But when that which is interdicted includes nearly everything which those to whom it is permitted most prize ...; when not only political liberty but personal freedom of action is the prerogative of a caste; when even the exercise of industry, almost all employments which task the higher faculties in an important field, which lead to distinction, riches, or even pecuniary independence" are denied to women, "the miserable expediences which are advanced as excuses for so grossly partial a dispensation, would not be sufficient, even if they were real, to render it other than a flagrant injustice ... We are firmly convinced that the division of mankind into two castes, one born to rule over the other, is ... an unqualified mischief." Throughout the ages great thinkers had claimed, though without any support from their rulers and governments, equality with men for women. In the present age, such thinkers "deny the right of any portion of the species to decide for another portion, or any individual, what is and what is not their 'proper sphere'. The proper sphere for all human beings is the largest and highest which they are able to attain to. What this is cannot be ascertained without complete liberty of choice.... Let every occupation be open to all, without favour or discouragement to any, and employments will fall into the hands of those men and women who are found by experience to be most capable of worthily exercising them." Men need have no fear of unfair competition: women would not compete for any occupations for which they were palpably unfitted. "By a curious anomaly" women, debarred from every form of public office, had shown "a decided vocation" as reigning monarchs. "Concerning the fitness, then of women for politics, there can be no question." The emancipation of women was in the interests of mankind as a whole and should not be delayed. It was often argued in England that women did not desire or seek "what is called their emancipation". This was true only of those women who had been conditioned to acquiesce in their conventional role as wives and mothers. It was true, however, that opposition was so strong that it required "unusual moral courage" for a woman to press for enfranchisement, at least until there was some likelihood of obtaining it.

It was equally true that, without proper educational facilities, they could never reach their full potential. "High mental powers ... will be but an exceptional accident, until every career is open to them and until they as well as men, are educated for themselves and for the world, not one sex for the other." Women did not want special treatment; they did not ask for "a position apart, a sort of sentimental priesthood. . . . The strength of [their] cause lies in the support of those who are influenced by reason and principle."

There were hopeful indications "that the example of America will be followed on this side of the Atlantic; and the first step has been taken ... in the North. On the 13th February, 1851, a petition of women, agreed to by a public meeting at Sheffield, and claiming the elective franchise, was presented to the House of Lords by the Earl of Carlisle."9 It is needless to add that this first petition, like so many of its kind, yielded no concrete results.

Fortunately for themselves, neither Harriet nor Mill had the remotest idea of the long haul which lay ahead, that the single issue of women's suffrage was only a dot on the far horizon. The article was the fruit of their combined thinking, dominated in essence by Harriet. At the time there was some doubt as to the actual authorship. In March 1850 William Hickson of the *Westminster Review* had asked Mill for an article on one aspect of women's disabilities. He would not care to undertake it, replied Mill, as if it were to be "limited to the question of divorce. I should treat that as only one point in a much more extensive subject—the entire position which present laws & customs have made for women." He was aware that his views were not generally acceptable, and so he asked Hickson for time to consider how much or how little it would be expedient to say. "When I have made up my mind I will write again . . . ." He let the matter rest for almost a year. In March 1851, however, he told Hickson that, if he would care for an article "on the Emancipation of Women, a propos of the Convention in Massachusetts which I mentioned to you ... I have one nearly ready". Hickson expressed interest, but Mill was still pondering over a suitable title when he wrote two months later, "The best I have thought of is 'Enfranchisement of Women.' The one you propose with the word 'sex' in it would never do. That word is enough to vulgarise a whole review. It is almost as bad as 'female'."

The article, under its title "The Enfranchisement of Women", was finished and delivered in June. When Mill saw the proofs he noted two unauthorized alterations in the text. He had, he informed Hickson with asperity, given him the article on the express understanding, "the only one on which I ever write, that no alterations should be made by any one but myself, & from this condition I cannot depart".10 He therefore recorrected the text before returning the revised proof to the printer.

These letters suggest that "The Enfranchisement" was actually written by Mill. He may well have thought that Hickson would be unwilling to publish unless this were so; but there seems no reason to doubt his later assertion that Harriet was both inspirer and author and that he was the editor. He gave substance to this theory in 1854, when John Chapman, by now in charge of the review, asked permission to reprint it. Mill told Harriet that he had sent Chapman "the letter you drafted, exactly as it was, only choosing the phrases I preferred where you gave me the choice of two". They had agreed to turn down the request, because "I should not like any more than you that the paper should be supposed to be the best we could do, or the real expression of our mind on the subject . . . I only wish the better thing we have promised to write [*The Subjection of Women*] were already written instead of being in prospect".[11] Had Harriet lived longer, he wrote in his introduction to the article in his *Dissertations and Discussions,* published the year after her death, he felt sure that she would have improved the article "immeasurably". She lived for seven years after it was first published in the *Westminster,* which, even with failing health, should have given her ample time for any improvements she cared to make. Mill's nervousness points inescapably to the fact that, while Harriet was an inspirer, she was not a natural writer and needed far more help from her editor than he was willing to admit. Mill, realizing that time was running out, was anxious for as much as possible of their work to appear in print while they still had life and strength. "About our plans, dearest", he wrote to her in the south of France where she was wintering in 1854, "they should all be made on the supposition of living. We should do what will be best on the supposition that we live . . . ."[12]

"The Enfranchisement of Women" appeared as Harriet's work in the *Dissertations and Discussions.* In his introduction Mill wrote,

> All the more recent of these papers were the joint productions of myself and of one whose loss, even in a merely intellectual point of view, can never be repaired or alleviated. But the following Essay is hers in a peculiar sense, my share in it being little more than that of an editor and amanuensis. Its authorship having been known at the time, and publicly attributed to her, it is proper to state, that she never regarded it as a complete discussion of the subject it treats of: and, highly as I estimate it, I would rather it remained unacknowledged than it should be read with the idea that even the faintest image can be found in it of a mind and heart which in their union of the rarest, and what are deemed the most conflicting excellencies, were unparalleled in any human being that I have known or read of . . . .[13]

Despite Mill's statement that the authorship was known at the time, the general impression seems to have been that the article was his. One highly intuitive reader, Charlotte Brontë, who read "The Enfranchisement" when it first appeared in the *Westminster,* fancied she detected the influence of another mind. As she wrote to her friend and future biographer, Elizabeth Gleghorn Gaskell, in September 1851, the article was "well-argued . . . , clear, logical, — but vast in the hiatus of omission; harsh the consequent jar on every finer chord of the soul . . When I first read the paper, I thought it was the work of a powerful-minded, clear-headed woman, who had a hard, jealous heart, muscles of iron and nerves of bend [strong ox] leather ... I believe J. S. Mill would make a hard dry, dismal world of it; and yet he speaks admirable sense through a great portion of his article ... In short, J. S. Mill's head is, I dare say, very good, but I feel disposed to scorn his heart."[14]

Mrs Gaskell received a number of complaints about her *Life of Charlotte Brontë*, chief among them the threat of a libel action on behalf of Branwell Bronte's inamorata, the former Mrs Robinson, which caused the withdrawal of the second edition prior to printing and of the few remaining copies of the first. Her publication of Charlott's strictures on "The Enfranchisement" apparently passed without comment until Mill read the book in 1859, two years after it first appeared. The publication had been tactless and Mill, incensed at the implied slur on Harriet's character, wrote a bitter letter of reproach to Mrs Gaskell.

"When you look at the signature of this letter", Mrs Gaskell replied, "you will probably be surprised at receiving it, as the only communication I ever received from you was couched in terms which I then thought impertinent, unjust and inexcusable." Since that time, however, she had read the more recently published *On Liberty*, a work conceived and modelled by Mill and Harriet jointly and completed by him after her death. In the light of her new found knowledge Mrs Gaskell considered Mill's tirade "simply unjust", and she was obviously moved by the dedication (see below pp. 110-11) the most touching of all Mill's tributes to his wife. She explained that she could appreciate "how any word expressing a meaning, only conjectured that was derogatory to your wife would wound you most deeply. And therefore I now write to express my deep regret that you received such pain through me". Neigher she nor Charlotte had known the true identity of the author of "The Enfranchisement"; her sole reason for publishing the unfortunate letter had been that it revealed Charlotte's quality of imagining a personality and that from this "a good deal might be learnt of Miss Brontë's state of mind and thought on such subjects". She would trouble him no further on so distressing a topic. "Only please do not go on thinking so badly of me."[15]

This perfectly genuine apology failed to satisfy the infuriated Mill. He replied uncompromisingly that Mrs Gaskell had "disregarded the obligation which custom founded on reason had imposed", of omitting material which might offend the susceptibilities and possibly injure "the moral reputation" of the individuals concerned. The idea that a biographer was free to publish anything "which could possibly throw light on the character of the sayer or writer ... is one which the world, and those who are higher and better than the world, would, I believe, perfectly unite in condemning".[16]

Mrs Gaskell naturally sought to defend herself. "You do me an injustice, I think, and I shall try once more to set myself partially right in your opinion, because I value it." She had explained herself badly if he still imagined that she had wilfully flouted convention; but no one else had made any complaint about the inclusion of any of Charlotte Brontë's letters; and "I do not feel that a just and reasonable person ought to have been offended by the publication of a mere conjecture as to possible character...."[17]

If Mrs Gaskell thought that this would be the end of the matter she was very much mistaken. Indignation upsetting his spelling, Mill answered on Harriet's behalf that it was "a sense of truth & Justice" which had made him so angry. "Even *now* I shd feel that I was acting contraryly [*sic*] to her wishes & character by any partiality or unreasonable sensitiveness, much more therefore at a time when I could afford to regard these things with indifference." He would not allow Mrs Gaskell to escape: she had abused her editorial responsibility by not "omiting [*sic*] all that might be offensive to the feelings of individuals". If the original letter had referred only to himself, its publication "would have been equally unjustifiable. Miss Brontë was entitled to express any foolish impression that might occur to her in a private letter—It is the Editor... who is alone to blame."[18]

Elizabeth Gaskell had been injudicious. She had struck Mill at his most vulnerable point, but, even so, there was surely no need for him to pursue her so relentlessly. He was equally intemperate with George Jacob Holyoake, who had the temerity to reprint "The Enfranchisement of Women" in pamphlet form in 1856 under the title *Are Women Fit for Politics?* Mill claimed that Holyoake had printed the pamphlet with its irritating title without Harriet's permission, although Holyoake denied that this was so; and, as printed, it contained a number of inexcusable errors. "One particularly offensive is the excessive vulgarity of substituting 'Woman' for 'Women'." One of the chief reasons which had prompted Harriet to write the article in the first place had been her desire to try to persuade American women to separate their claim for the suffrage "from the feeble sentimentality which exposes it to contempt & of which the stuff continually talked & written about 'woman' may be taken as a symbol & test".[19]

The attempt to impose the use of the American title "woman suffrage" on the women's suffrage movement in England was, it will be seen, to prove as much of a red rag to Helen Taylor as to her mother and stepfather.

Mill was paternally proud and delighted when anybody showed what he considered a proper appreciation of "The Enfranchisement". As he told an old friend, the social reformer Edwin Chadwick, who was supporting his candidature for Parliament in 1865, he would be glad to reprint any of his articles which the committee of electors thought suitable. He would be especially happy to reprint "The Enfranchisement", "but it must be as my wife's, not as mine".[20]

He was particularly proud to learn that the article, coupled with Harriet's name, was remembered in America, where the "woman suffrage" cause continued to make headway. "The author of... 'Enfranchisement of Women' would have been well rewarded by the progress that question is making, had she lived to see it",[21] he wrote to Moncure D. Conway in 1865. The article had been used as the basis of resolutions on women's rights very soon after its original publication, and it clearly exercised considerably more influence in the United States than it did in England when the suffrage movement came into being. In 1869, more than ten years after her death, Harriet's name, together with Mill's, was honoured at a suffrage convention in Newport, Rhode Island. Mill wrote to the woman's rights leader, Mrs Paulina Wright Davis, that, pleased as he was by the mention of his own name, he was still more pleased by the tribute to his wife. She had been devoted to the cause from girlhood upwards, had rendered it great service, "as the inspirer and instructor of others, even before writing the essay so deservedly eulogized in your resolution. To her I owe the far greater part of whatever I have been able to do for the cause", for though he, too, had been an advocate of women's suffrage from his youth, it was from his wife that he had learned so much about its wider implications—"the great moral and social interests"[22] enshrined in the claim for the equality of women.

The following year, writing to Mrs Davis of his pleasure that "The Enfranchisement" "has had so much effect, and is so justly appreciated in the United States", he added that, owing to paucity of details, it was unfortunately impossible to write Harriet's biography. This would have been "as valuable a benefit to mankind as was ever conferred by a biography.... What she was I have attempted, though most inadequately, to delineate in the remarks prefaced to her Essay, as reprinted with my 'Dissertations and Discussions'...."[23]

No biography could have been written without the title-tattle to which Harriet so strongly objected. Mill, of course, believed every word that he himself wrote about her; but, had he tried a little less hard to represent her to posterity as a combination of all the virtues, it would have been far easier to discount many unjust criticisms and to resurrect her as a flesh-and-blood woman, with undeniable failings but a most powerful intellect and drive.

CHAPTER 12

Family Strife

In the early spring of 1851 Alexander Bain, on a visit to France, called on John Mill's sister Jane, the wife of Marcus Paul Ferraboschi, an Italian banker and stockbroker resident in Paris. Staying with the Ferraboschis was John Mill's elder sister Clara, who gave him the long anticipated news "of the pending marriage of John to Mrs Taylor, which he had just communicated to his family".[1]

John Mill had never set up house for himself. He had remained at home with his mother and sisters, coming and going as he pleased, refusing to allow them to mention Harriet's name although they were well aware of the situation. The family home since James Mill's death in 1836 had been a tall eighteenth-century terrace house, 18 Kensington Square. Living there in 1851 were John, old Mrs Mill and her two unmarried daughters: Clara—later Mrs Digweed—and Harriet Isabella, who never married. John's eldest sister, Willie, who had married Dr King, was now a widow with a small daughter; Jane lived permanently in Paris; Mary, the youngest sister, sixteen years John's junior, was married to Charles Colman and lived in Clifton, Bristol.

From his boyhood upwards John had relied on his mother to supply him with all his creature comforts. He might criticize her for doing too much, for failing to foster his non-existent practical bent, but he could not manage without her. Before the move it was Mrs Mill who had seen to the sale of the old house in Vicarage Place. "I have no doubt you did the best you could", he wrote to her from Paris in November 1836. The house in Kensington Square might not prove to their liking; it was always possible they would find another they preferred. In the meantime, "I shall have the bookshelves put up. You may as well do it before I come unless you have any doubt how I should like it done . . . ."[2] Mrs Mill had not only to see to the bookshelves but also to make arrangements to accommodate the collection of plants and other botanical specimens which John had amassed in the course of botanizing (walking being his favourite spare-time pursuit). All this she did as a matter of course.

John Mill was happy enough to make his mother's home his base. He was still fond of his family, glad enough to dine and spend the evening with them when not otherwise engaged. Carlyle, as we saw, had noted an absence of communication between them when he visited the family at Mickleham immediately after James Mill's death, "as if all human spontaneity had taken refuge in invisible corners"; but this was the result more of shock than lack of sympathy. By 1840 there had certainly been a revival of family feeling, as a new young friend had noticed. She was the shrewd twenty-one-year-old diarist Caroline Fox, sister of Robert Barclay Fox, a prosperous, philanthropic Quaker from Falmouth, Cornwall.

Friendship between the Mill and the Fox families began that same year. Mrs Mill had decided to take her young son Henry, now critically ill with tuberculosis, to winter in Madeira, and Clara was to go with them. They reached Falmouth, where they were to embark, only to find that they had missed the boat. There they found John Sterling, himself a sick man who had also planned a visit to Madeira but was wintering in Falmouth instead. Sterling had already made friends with Fox, and was to make something more than friends with Caroline, who was very much in love with him; but Sterling was married and Caroline was virtuous and so the relationship remained severely cerebral.

Mrs Mill had gone to Sterling for advice in her predicament. Sterling approached Fox, and between them they settled the Mills in comfortable lodgings, with room for the rest of the family—John, Harriet Isabella and young George—who joined them.

Clara Mill and Caroline Fox were soon close friends and, when Clara introduced her brother John to Caroline, the girl was considerably impressed. She found him "a very uncommon-looking person—such acuteness and sensibility marked in his exquisitely chiselled countenance... His voice is refinement itself, and his mode of expressing himself tallies with voice and countenance." She greatly admired his looks, despite the loss of his hair, which, so he told her, had fallen out "when you were quite a little girl and I was two-and-twenty".[3]

Henry Mill, dearly loved by his whole family, died early in April. John Mill had to return to his work at the India House; the rest of the sorrowing family followed later.

Caroline Fox was in London with her sister during the summer. They went with Harriet Isabella Mill to one of Carlyle's famous lectures, then returned with her to Kensington Square, where they were "most lovingly received by all the family. John Mill was quite himself...." After dinner the girls were taken to see John's books and his herbarium. Mrs Mill, embarrassingly proud of her brilliant son, was "anxious to show everything, and her son so terribly afraid of boring us". Afterwards John read aloud a passage from Carlyle's *Sartor Resartus*; and the talk then turned to "the eccentricities of their friend Mrs Grote, whom Sydney Smith declares to be the origin of the word Grotesque". As Mrs Grote was out of favour with John Mill, he was obviously glad to make fun of her. On a second visit to London, Caroline Fox, dining again with the Mills, found John "in glorious spirits; too happy to enter much into deep things". The cause of Mill's elation was the completion of his *System of Logic,* with which he was justifiably pleased. "He is going to mark the best passages for me with notes of admiration", wrote Caroline. Playfully he told her "My family have no idea how great a man I am!" He promised to send the Fox sisters a copy of the *Logic* when it appeared, but warned them that they would understand very little of it. "He forbids my reading it, except some chapters which he will point out. 'It would be like my reading a book on mining because you live in Cornwall—it would be making Friendship a burden!' "[4]

The book duly arrived in Falmouth. Caroline, on her mettle, read the first part, then wrote enthusiastically to the author. Mill replied, "I do not know what to say to such a flaming panegyric as that bestowed on my unworthiness by a young lady who has done me the honour to learn fallacies under my tuition. In spite of so much encouragement I cannot in conscience take off my injunction against reading the remainder . . . (which however is, I assure you, quite as clever) so whoever does read any of it . . . does it at her own risk & responsibility."[5]

Caroline Fox, who remained close friends with Clara Mill, had observed John in a contented, harmonious setting, and there is no reason to suppose that she was mistaken. The harmony was shattered violently and for ever by the events of 1851. Looking back on her girlhood, Harriet Isabella Mill recalled that her eldest brother had given his sisters "all the few pleasures we ever had. Up to the time of his marriage he had been everything to us, and it was a frightful blow to lose him, without one word of explanation—only in evident anger."[6]

John had curtly informed his mother and sisters that he was to be married and then left them to their own devices. They had never yet met his enchantress, but they knew he worshipped her and they wished him well. He had given them no instructions and they were at a loss to know how he expected them to behave. Should they put on their best bonnets and pay a formal call on Mrs Taylor, or should they wait until John brought her to see them? They hesitated and were lost. John, who was aware that his mother would have done anything in the world to please him, was incensed by what he chose to consider a display of bad manners. By their failure to call, his mother and sisters had slighted the woman who was to be his wife, and he never forgave them.

Willie King and Jane Ferraboschi, who were not immediately available, fared better. "I am indeed very much to be congratulated", John wrote to Willie in April. He and Harriet proposed to marry towards the end of the month, after which, he thought, his mother would find the Kensington Square house too large. "I wonder you do not persuade [her] to live with you—She likes housekeeping, & to keep house for you seems to me the most sensible thing she could do."[7] This arrangement suited neither mother nor daughter and, when Mrs Mill left Kensington Square, she went with Clara and Harriet Isabella.

To Jane, Mill explained that he and Harriet intended to live a little way out of London. The large, rambling house which they discovered in Blackheath Park seemed ideal, and there, with Haji and Helen Taylor, they made their home. Herbert, who had taken charge of his father's business, remained in London and married soon afterwards. He was not on good terms with his mother, who was convinced that in any family dispute he sided with old Mrs Hardy and the Leys against her.

Not a single member of the Mill family was invited to the wedding. Harriet, with her younger children, had taken up temporary residence in Dorset, and the ceremony was performed at the registrar's office in Melcombe Regis, with Haji and Helen as witnesses. True to his principles and Harriet's that men and women were equal, Mill renounced the normal control of a husband over his wife and her belongings, and throughout their married life he wisely refused to interfere in any way with the disposal of her income. In a formal statement he said:

> Being about ... to enter into the marriage relation with the only women I have ever known, with whom I would have entered that state; & the whole character of the marriage relation as constituted by law being such as both she and I entirely and conscientiously disapprove, for this among other reasons, that it confers upon one of the parties to the contract, legal power & control independent of her own wishes and will; I, having no means of legally divesting myself of these odious powers ... feel it my duty to put on record a formal protest against the existing law of marriage, in so far as conferring such powers; and a solemn promise never in any case or under any circumstances to use them.

Harriet was to retain "absolute freedom of action" and complete control of her property; and, Mill added, "I absolutely disclaim & repudiate all pretence to have acquired *any* rights whatever by virtue of such marriage."[8]

Old Mrs Mill and her daughters were distressed, not only by their beloved John's failure to invite them to his wedding but also by his refusal to see them. Harriet Isabella ventured to call at the India House a few weeks later, but he refused to receive her. The newly married Mrs John Stuart Mill clearly found her husband's conduct unnecessarily severe and persuaded him to call on his mother. Husband and wife arrived unannounced and were received by a nervous Mrs Mill and her daughter Harriet Isabella. Clara had only just returned from visiting Jane in Paris, and, after a stormy crossing, felt unequal to the effort and remained upstairs in her room.

This first and last meeting between the two Harriet Mills—old Mrs Mill and the woman who had been her daughter-in-law in all but name for nearly twenty years—was disastrous. Mrs John Stuart Mill behaved graciously enough; she made conversation, she inquired after Willie King's little daughter Clara. Her husband, however, remained cold and remote. He may have felt ashamed of his humble, humdrum mother; but Harriet Isabella, though not his Harriet's intellectual peer, was an intelligent woman, if less polished than her sister-in-law.

Clara Mill, who was naturally anxious to give no further cause of offence, called on Harriet a few days later, bringing with her Clara King, who had heard all about Haji and Helen Taylor from her uncle George Mill. Harriet would have received them willingly; but her husband turned them away from the door.

When Mary Colman, John Mill's youngest sister, learned what he had done, she rounded on him fiercely. Mary, a strong-minded, somewhat tactless young woman of twenty-nine, was a devout—not to say a militant—Christian: she devoted all the energy she could spare from her husband and children to work in Bristol's ragged schools for the children of the poor (founded by the philanthropic Mary Carpenter). She now took it on herself to upbraid her brother for his callous treatment of his mother and sisters, and also for indifference towards herself. In so doing she exposed, as she saw it, the underlying reason for his inexcusable behaviour: he had never really cared for any of them. Shortly before her marriage in 1847, she reminded John, he had written to her in terms "which first made me aware that individually I was an object of no interest to you, that you had no affection for me". Until then he had been uniformly kind towards his family, but she knew now that this kindness proceeded merely from a wish not to cause unnecessary pain. The "agony" he had caused her was such that she had resolved "never again to love you or any human creature to such a degree as to cause me such grief". She had no wish to communicate with him, but his cruelty to the mother and sisters who loved him so dearly obliged her to confront him with the truth. What, she demanded, had they done to offend him? "I can find nothing except that my mother did not call on your wife the day after you announced your engagement." Had he expressed the slightest wish, his mother would have obeyed. There had followed "the farce" of the call he and Harriet had payed at Kensington, "and your evident dread lest any of your family should show the least affection to you" before Harriet. She, however, was in no way to blame. "Do not imagine that I attribute to the influence of your wife this conduct of yours. I have none but good feelings towards her, I was no liar when I told you I wished to know her." She ended by begging him, "by the only feeling that now seems remaining to you, 'your love for your wife' not to throw this from you as coming from one of a family now evidently hateful to you", but to consider whether his conduct would be conducive to his wife's peace of mind as well as wounding to his family. Even if, by her frank speaking, she was to bring the relationship to an end, she would at least have the satisfaction of knowing that she had not "shrunk from the duty of honesty"[9] towards him.

There was a reference in Mary Colman's letter to John's especial unkindness towards his youngest brother George, who was then in an advanced stage of tuberculosis and living in Madeira. Both John and Harriet Taylor had been fond of George, their sons' friend. George Mill, who liked and admired Harriet, with certain reservations, had told Alexander Bain that she was "a clever and remarkable woman, but nothing like what John took her to be".[10] It is, of course, possible that this remark had been relayed to John, possible also that George had gossiped with his sisters and that the gossip had spread beyond the confines of the family. This in itself would have been enough to arouse John's anger; but his coldness towards George was such that the poor young man wrote to him in 1850 that, "as I can write nothing which I should not fear you would continue to think impertinent, the less I write the better. I can only say that I would confidently give my letter into the hands of Mrs Taylor (the best umpire I could find) along with yours which preceded it, convinced that she would say, it did not warrant the terms used in your last letter...."[11]

At the time George Mill was still on affectionate terms with Harriet. After a visit to England that summer, he wrote to her on his journey back to Madeira inquiring after her health and apologizing for his own lack of eloquence: "Adieu dear Mrs Taylor—The only excuse I can give for writing so stupid a letter is that ... I would that I could waft you our soft Madeira breezes for the next few months."[12]

George Mill had revered his eldest brother as a great and a good man. John Mill showed his indifference when he wrote George a brief note about politics in April 1851 but made no mention of his approaching marriage. When George learned from his mother or one of his sisters that the wedding had actually taken place, he wrote to Harriet, complaining mildly that John must have thought him "either uninterested or undeserving to know". He asked after their future plans and, as usual, about Harriet's health. "If you feel in me any part of the interest which I feel in you all, you will not leave me in entire darkness.... Believe me/dear Mrs Taylor (I can't forget the old name) Yours affect^ly Geo G. Mill."[13]

To call Harriet "Mrs Taylor" was tactless enough; but George had offended still further, apparently by expressing surprise to Haji Taylor that his mother, with her advanced views, should have been willing to endure the bonds of matrimony for a second time. This brought down on his head the united wrath of his brother and his sister-in-law. What right had George to dare to hint that Harriet had been acting contrary to her avowed principles, demanded John. What imagined principles should have prevented two people who had known each other for so long a period, "during which her & Mr Taylor's house has been more a home to me than any other, and who agree perfectly in all their opinions, from marrying?" He had informed his mother and sisters of his approaching marriage, not because they had any right to be told, for their relations with him had "been always of too cool & distant a kind" to give them the right "to expect anything more than ordinary civility from me—& when I did tell them I did not receive ordinary civility in return".[14] Harriet, writing at the same time as her husband, accused George of a total lack "of truth modesty & justice to say little of good breeding or good nature". But, "As to want of the good breeding which is the result of good feeling that appears to be a family failing . . . ."[15]

These were the last letters George Mill received from John and Harriet. Two years later he died, taking his own life when he knew that he was dying. According to James Bentham Mill's old college friend the Rev. J. Crompton, he killed himself "with the object of saving trouble to the sister who attended him [Clara]". Questioned after John Mill's death, Crompton confessed that he had never met "the superior being Mrs Taylor". He had known John Mill slightly, but the acquaintanceship appeared "to some extent to have suffered in consequence of Mill's devotion to his wife". Although the interviewer questioned Crompton fairly closely, the results, he complained, were meagre, "owing to the discursive and erractic style of his conversation. One came away with the impression that there were large stores of information on which a visitor who interviewed Mr Crompton with the indecent persistence of a Special Correspondent might successfully draw: but then a Special Correspondent might also be kicked out of doors."[16]

In the meantime, old Mrs Mill had done her ineffectual best to heal the breach in the family. She was not invited to Blackheath and, if she wanted to see John, she had to call on him at the India House. After one of these useless errands she told her unmarried daughters that once more John had complained of their incivility towards his wife. The accusation goaded Clara into a letter of protest. She was, she said, unconscious of any offence, but, since it was plain that John considered his family deserving only of common civility and since "there are some of us, myself among the rest, whom you hold in the same estimation as my father did", there seemed no point in attempting to prolong a relationship which had become so painful. In any event, she could see no reason why Harriet should wish to seek the companionship of a family for whom he had so poor an opinion. "You are, to use George's words 'a great and good man' and you see farther than I do. I do not therefore pretend to judge you, I only cannot understand you . . . ."[17]

Clara, John replied, flattered herself if she imagined for a moment that Harriet would welcome any gesture of friendship. "My wife and I are one." Harriet was "accustomed not to seek but to be sought, neither she nor I desire the acquaintance of anybody who does not wish for ours".[18]

Harriet Isabella had also protested, for John now wrote to his mother that he had received from his sisters "two most silly notes . . . filled with vague accusations". He trusted, he concluded in his most offhand manner, that his mother was none the worse for her recent "journey to the I. H.".[19]

For the next two years the sisters remained aloof, but old Mrs Mill continued to write and to trail across London to the India House in a fruitless effort to bring about a reconciliation. By the spring of 1854 she was too ill to make the journey. With their unfailing instinct to diagnose the wrong disease, the doctors had assured her that it was only rheumatism; but it was soon apparent that the seat of the trouble was her liver. "I thought it was odd that my stomach should be so much affected from rheumatism", she wrote to John, who passed on the information to Harriet, in France with her daughter

Helen. "This looks very ill I fear",[20] he said.

Clara Mill and Mary Colman broke their long silence a few days later to inform John that their mother had a tumour on the liver. She was not, they thought, in any immediate danger but at her age any illness could be dangerous. Mary's letter, which must have cost her a great effort to write, showed that Mrs Mill was suffering agonies of mind as well as body:

> My mother is very unhappy because she thinks that she has not behaved well to your wife. She is constantly urging me to go to Blackheath and call on her, saying that it would please you very much and nothing will divert her mind from this one point. She is still very weak, unable to stand, and thinks evidently that you are very angry with her, and do not come to see her on that account ....
>
> Will you therefore either let me know what you think we had better do, or, for my mother's sake, write *her* a few lines to prevent her from wishing us to go, or in some way set her mind at ease.[21]

By way of setting his mother's mind at ease, John wrote to tell her that he had received "another of Mary's vulgar and insolent letters", so impertinent that it deserved no reply. For some reason or other Mary seemed to imagine "that I wish to see her. Will you tell her, that neither I nor my wife will keep up any acquaintance with her whatever." He hoped, he added, that his mother was well on the way to recovery and asked her to keep him informed of her progress. "I need not say", he concluded, now that it was far too late, "that we shall always be glad to see you."[22]

Mrs Mill did not pass on her son's intemperate message to Mary, who wrote again, asking if he realized that their mother was now gravely ill. "I know that she feels your not going to see her very much though she does not speak of it generally only thinks of it which makes her worse." Mrs Mill had never been really well since her son George's tragic death; now she was going downhill. "If you wrote to tell her you were going to see her it would I think be better as she is very weak. I was very sorry to hear that your wife was still obliged to be away from England. I hope you have good account of her."[23]

Old Mrs Mill, meanwhile, had answered John's letter with pathetic dignity. She had, she said, been able with assistance to come downstairs two or three times and hoped that she might grow stronger.

> I was very much surprised at the message you sent to Mary the last time you wrote, but I did not deliver it, as I was sure it would make her very unhappy, she has gone to the country.
>
> I did not know what she wrote to you, that could have given you cause to be so much displeased with her.
>
> We always hoped to be upon good terms with Mrs Mill and her family—your Marriage gave us all pleasure as you had chosen a Wife who was capable of entering into all your pursuits and appreciate your good

qualities.

I trust that I shall soon get strong and that Mrs Mill will do me the favour to come and take a family dinner with me. In the meantime my kind regards to her.[24]

The improvement in old Mrs Mill's health was short-lived; but, had it been possible for a family dinner to take place, it is certain that John would have refused the invitation on his wife's behalf. In any event, she was still in France, and John too was ill. By now the doctors had admitted that he had contracted the family disease—tuberculosis—and his condition was aggravated by a painful carbuncle, for which he was having constant treatment. He had intended meeting Harriet and Helen in Paris and escorting them back to England; but, as he wrote to Harriet, the carbuncle might well prove dangerous if left untreated and it would be some days before he was fit to travel. Could she and her daughter manage the journey on their own? "She alone can judge—but I am most anxious that she should not come if she is really dreading it much",[25] he wrote in his third-person style. Harriet and Helen, who were perfectly capable of crossing the Channel unattended, arrived home in mid-April.

Early in June, Mill heard from Harriet Isabella, whose words, as he had told his wife, were "always much less bad than Clara's though her conduct has been much the same",[26] that their mother's condition was deteriorating. He condescended to pay her a single visit, and followed it with a cool and formal letter which may , as Professor Hayek has pointed out, have been intended chiefly to convey information to his sisters, since his dying mother would have been incapable of reading it. He hoped, he said, that his mother was feeling better and would "continue free from pain". His object in writing was to inform her that on his doctor's express orders he was leaving at once for the Continent and, although he might shortly return, it would not be for long. He reminded her how important it was for her to have an executor to her will who was permanently domiciled in England, "either instead of me, which I shd prefer, or as well as myself". His wife, he added, "sends her kindest wishes & regrets that her weak health makes it difficult for her to come to see you as she would otherwise have done".[27]

Harriet would doubtless have called on her mother-in-law long before if her husband had given her the slightest encouragement. Now she was too ill, too ill in fact to accompany him on the trip which his doctors had ordered. A few days before his departure he received two letters from Harriet Isabella. In the first she told him that her doctor "recommends that my Mother's relations should know she is dying... It is a great blessing she suffers no pain."[28] In the second, written on 10 June, the following day, she explained that Mrs Mill was "in such a state of prostration" that it had not been possible to give her his letter. Two days earlier, however, Mrs Mill had signed a codicil to her will "appointing Clara jointly with you. She desired that your name should remain, but I suppose Clara could do all there will be to do, if she has your leave for so doing." She asked John to let her know where he could be found in case of need, adding, "I am very sorry to find your health is so much out of order and can only fervently hope that the air of the continent may restore it again."[29]

At some point during the past few weeks Mill had taken the trouble to call on Richard Quain, his mother's doctor. Dr Quain wrote to him on 11 June that, as "you were much concerned by the statement I had to make . . . I think it right to let you know that if Mrs Mill should continue a little longer unable to take more food than she now takes her life must soon terminate. She has for several weeks been gradually sinking."[30]

Mill did not receive this letter before he left England, but it seems more than likely that he was still at Blackheath when Harriet Isabella's letter of the 9th, with the doctor's warning that the end was very near, arrived (postal deliveries were then much faster than they are today, and it is probable that the letter arrived on the same day as that on which it was dispatched). By 11 June he was in Jersey on the first stage of his journey, writing to Harriet without so much as a mention of his mother's name. "Had a beautiful afternoon for my walk & . . . I shall walk again after putting in this letter. I am as well darling as I could expect to be, & in tolerably good cue for walking—perhaps by & by I shall be so for writing—but as yet I feel as if I should not wish to write a thing except letters to my dearest one."[31]

Old Mrs Mill died four days later. Mill was in Brittany when the news reached him, sent by his brother-in-law Charles Colman, who wrote at Clara's request to ask if, as his mother had wished, he would act as one of her executors. Seeming quite unmoved by the news of her death, Mill replied curtly, refusing to act. To Harriet he wrote that it was a comfort to learn that his mother had died without pain, but he added unfeelingly, "since it was to be, I am glad that I was not in England . . . , since what I must have done & gone through would have been very painful & wearing & would have done no good to anyone". He went on to discuss the terms of his mother's will, under which, if he remembered correctly, he stood to inherit a seventh part of her income, between £400 and £500. His salary was ample and when he retired he would receive the highest possible pension; so "I do not think we ought to take it—what do you think?" The money should go to his sisters, but, "considering how they behaved, it is a matter of pride more than anything else—but I have a very strong feeling about it". If he refused the legacy, the question arose of its division: should each of his sisters benefit, or should the money go to Willie, who was most in need, "or to Jane who alone of them all has behaved decently well?"[32]

Despite their travels abroad, Mill and Harriet had been living well within their income, for Harriet had her own money, which was more than sufficient for her wants. All the same, as Mill pointed out, they had to consider their health, make plans for the future, and decide whether after his retirement it would be advisable for them to settle permanently in a warm climate.

Harriet evidently thought it quixotic in John to contemplate the idea of relinquishing his legacy. He capitulated at once, writing that, "of course as your feeling is so directly contrary, mine is wrong, & I give it up entirely". The only reason why he had suggested it at all was that he was determined that his sisters "should not be able to say that I had taken away anything from their resources".[33]

Charles Colman had enclosed with his letter a sad little note from Mrs Mill to her son. It was dated 27 March 1854, when she must first have guessed that her illness was mortal.

> I did not mention the furniture in my will which you were so kind as to leave for my use, but as some of it is a great deal worn, I hope you will take the best of it, and do as I should have done if I had considered it my own, give the rest to your two unmarried sisters, Clara and Harriet. Your plate is being taken care of and will be restored to you by your sisters.
>
>   God bless you, my dear son, I sincerely hope that you and Mrs Mill will enjoy many many years of uninterrupted happiness.[34]

Old Mrs Mill, Charles Colman explained, had never been able to understand that the furniture had been an outright gift and was hers to dispose of. Clara and Harriet Isabella, standing on their dignity, turned down the offer of the shabbiest pieces of furniture. They were thinking of giving up housekeeping and had no wish for any of it. They wanted to know what they should do with the plate which belonged to their brother. John wrote from France to Harriet for advice: "Perhaps darling you will write to Rouen what you think should be said & in what manner, both about [the furniture] & the plate." Harriet decided that they needed neither the furniture nor the plate and was prepared to be more magnanimous than she had been over the money. "I shall write the letter to Colman exactly according to your pencil which seems to me perfectly right", replied her husband; "about the plate, there is nothing at all curious or which was presented to my father, & to us it would only be worth its value as old silver—I will therefore as you suggest tell him to deal with it as with the furniture".[35]

Charles Colman was duly instructed to sell the plate and the furniture and divide the proceeds equally among the sisters, who cannot have received very much from the sale.

If John Mill thought that this would put an end to his painful dealings with his sisters, he was very much mistaken. Willie, Clara and Harriet Isabella had retreated into silence, but four years later Mary, the battling Christian, returned to the attack. She would have written sooner, she told her brother, had she not thought that he would find any communication from her distasteful; yet

> No day passes without my thinking of you . . . , and I wish you to know the simple truth that nothing can alter my affection for you and that nothing

but the knowledge that you were a Christian could give me so much happiness as to know that you would be glad to see me again. Do you never think of the *last* of what is left of the children whom my father committed to your charge—

Have I injured *you* . . . irreparably or do you think me still a *Hypocrite* too vile and base for you to hold communication with.

My brother, you might forgive a merely personal injury and in the latter case you might enquire what my life has been and if you have misjudged me forgive at least an ill judged letter on my part. . . .

Should your feelings towards me have returned to what they were once you will now know how gladly I should hear it, how gladly I would take my children to their uncle.[36]

How dared this sister whom he never wished to see again insult him with pious hopes of his conversion? John Mill, smouldering with indignation, did not trouble to reply. Mary, never one to take silence for an answer, wrote again to know whether he had received her letter and to beg him to tell her in what way she had offended:

I would be very glad to hear that you were better and both Charles and myself should be very glad to receive you here, as well as Miss Taylor who is I presume with you, when you feel equal to leaving home.

Do not my dear John harden yourself against me we none of us know how long we will be here I would gladly go and see you at any time though at present I am forbidden to put my feet to the ground but I shall be strong in a week. If I only knew what I could do for you my dear brother . . . .[37]

There was nothing she could do for her dear brother except to leave him in peace. In a furious letter which opens simply "Mary", he told her that he could see no reason for her to reopen the correspondence after such a long interval if she could not "shew more good sense or good feeling. . . There is besides, a total want of modesty in supposing that I am likely to receive instruction from you on the subject of my strongest convictions, which were also those of your father."[38] There was nothing at all in her letters, quite apart from her reference to his supposed agnosticism, to make him wish to see or to communicate with her again.

In religious matters John had followed his father; but James Mill had not forbidden his daughters to receive any instruction. According to Harriet Isabella, their grandmother Harriet Burrow "was a truly excellent and religious woman and taught us to pray. I remember her giving me sixpence for learning my catechism! My father never interfered and as quite children we girls used to go to church."[39]

It is possible that the thick-skinned Mary would have accepted her congé had not the tragedy of Harriet Mill's death occurred later the same year—1858. All John Mill's sisters wrote to commiserate with him, forgetting the past in the knowledge of what the disaster must mean to him.

To Jane Ferraboschi, who had never offended, he replied, "you cannot know, nor can anything I could say enable you to conceive, the immensity of my loss".[40] He asked her when next she wrote to Harriet Isabella and Mary to thank them on his behalf for their sympathy.

As Mary had not heard at once from John she wrote again, as usual to know if her first letter had miscarried, and to tell him for the second time how much she felt for him in his grief:

> If ever you should feel that I could in any way do anything for you I trust you will believe the truth that I can never remember anything but your former kindness to me—but if it should be the will of God to separate us for ever here on earth, I have this one consolation that when the mists which obscure our earthly eyes here shall have vanished you *must* know that whatever my personal faults may have been my love to you has always been sincere and unselfish called forth by your qualities and not by your position.

She had, she said, grieved over their estrangement not only for herself, but also for the brother who had been impervious "to the suffering [he was] inflicting".[41]

Her brother made no concessions: "You always write as if you had some great reason to complain of me & as if some caprice of mine had been the cause of the estrangement as you call it ... your own conduct & manifestations of feeling were the sole cause of the existence of any estrangement & you have given no sign ... that your conduct and feelings had been in any way wrongly interpreted ...."[42]

Mary was as determined as ever to discover in precisely what way John considered her at fault. It was possible, she admitted numbly, that her unhappiness at the unnecessary suffering "of those who are now gone"—her mother and George—had impelled her to use strong language; but "I had not the slightest ill feeling towards you or any one connected with you. In the first place, nothing had happened to call out such a feeling, as you know, and in the second place it would have been impossible for me to have had such a feeling towards any one you loved ...."[43]

With weary disgust her brother assured her that he nourished no ill will towards her and was prepared to put "the best interpretation" on the events of the past, which, however, he did not choose to specify. But there was to be no question of any meeting: "I do not expect that I shall ever again wish to *see* any person (two or three excepted) unless on necessary business or for some public purpose. The melancholy life I have before me would be quite unsupportable if I could not be left alone with those who are fellow sufferers with me & who feel as I do."[44]

"May God comfort you my dear brother"[45] was Mary's parting shot.

Had it been feasible, Mill would have had no more to do with any of his sisters, excepting Jane. But in 1862 Harriet Isabella, since Clara's marriage at the age of fifty the only spinster, informed him of the death of their last surviving brother, James Bentham. His friend Crompton, who had seen nothing of him since his departure for India many years earlier, reported that he had returned "with a temper much impaired through a diseased liver which caused his death not long afterwards".[46] This was mere hearsay: James Bentham had died of some form of paraplegia, following a six months' illness.

"It seems to have been strange disease", wrote John to his sister. "It is frightful to think of the quantity of suffering which so often accompanies the process of going out of life." She had told him somewhat diffidently, for fear he would disapprove, that James Bentham had appointed her his sole executor and heir. John told her that he would not dream of contesting his brother's will or question his right to dispose of his property as he wished, "even if I did not think, as I do, that disposition to be a very proper one".[47]

John's widowed sister Willie King had died the previous year, apparently without any communication from him for a number of years. With Jane he remained on friendly, if distant, terms. He wrote to her in 1865 to thank her for her congratulations on his election to Parliament and to wish her many happy return of her birthday. "The cause of my not having called on you is that it is many years since I have passed more than a few hours at Paris." He was disappointed that when she visited England some time previously "my absence prevented me from seeing you".[48]

Eventually, not very long before his death, John Mill made handsome amends to Mary Colman, whose chief fault had been her infuriating tendency to preach. By 1871, Mary, once the centre of a happy family, was a sad, forlorn woman. She was separated from her husband and extremely badly off, and when he learned of this John made her a regular allowance. Two years later her favourite son, a sailor, was drowned at sea. A second son, Henry, was caught with his hand in his office till. "I did not think it possible that I could . . . suffer more than I have already done", wrote poor Mary to her brother, "but he has now confessed . . ."[49] Mill promptly advanced the money to pay off the debt on condition that suitable restitution to Henry's employer was made. He did more than that: his interest in women's education led him to offer to pay for Mary's daughter Marion — Minnie as she was called—to attend Bedford College, London, "the most suitable place for our purpose".[50] With Mary's glad consent, he arranged for Minnie's admission to Bedford with Miss Thomas, matron of the students' hostel.

Unfortunately, Minnie was unable to make the grade, although her uncle never knew it. Four months after his death Miss Thomas wrote to Helen Taylor for instructions. Mrs Colman, she said, had taken Minnie away, giving no indication as to whether or not she would return. To Miss Thomas, naturally concerned about the usual term's notice in lieu of fees, Helen replied haughtily that she had understood Miss Thomas had been aware that Minnie's abrupt departure had been "on account of her inability to undergo the fatigue of the course."[51]

Many years after Mill's death the letters and papers which he had bequeathed to Helen Taylor came into the hands of her niece Mary, daughter of Haji Taylor, who cared for her aunt Helen in her old age. Mary removed the family letters from the selection of Mill's correspondence which was published in 1910. These letters, she wrote in a foreword, "are too many of them painful though strangely interesting reading". She could hardly be accused of exaggeration when she continued: "He cannot by the most wounding reproaches shake [his family's] faith in him as a "great and good man". He seems to endeavour to do this, but fails. They recognise that he is cruel and insulting to them, and they suffer acutely, but their affection is as invincible as his resentment... As one reads one feels less anger with him than deep love and admiration for those brave women, who seem to consider in each scornful word only the wound from which it springs, and which they perpetually seek to find and heal."[52]

Mill would undoubtedly have felt aggrieved all over again by Mary Taylor's valedictory words. Yet his conduct towards his mother and sisters remains almost inexplicable. Of course they had discussed Harriet Taylor among themselves and with young George Mill, possibly even with their friends; of course they had failed to call on her immediately the marriage was announced; of course they were not her intellectual or social equals. But these facts in themselves were surely not sufficient excuse for such prolonged hostility. The only possible explanation is that, despite his seeming contentment and early display of affection, he had never really cared for any of them, but shared the contempt which his father had never troubled to hide.

Mary Taylor was right when she claimed that Mill's family bore him no malice. When he died in May 1873, Mary Colman, to whom he had eventually behaved so well, hastened to Avignon, his home in France, to comfort his stepdaughter Helen. Clara and Harriet Isabella both wrote to Helen with genuine, unforced sympathy. Harriet Isabella, who had rushed to her brother's defence over the press account of *The French Revolution* incident, wrote to Helen when she learned from the newspapers that he was critically ill: "My deep love and reverence for my brother has never changed. He is the person to whom I have owed the most during the early part of my life, and even after all these years of estrangement it is very bitter to me to think of his danger...."[53]

Mrs Digweed—Clara Mill—was even more generous. "No one could have known my poor brother without loving him", she wrote. "How vividly his early life and affection are before me!" For Helen she had a special word of sympathy: "We know your devotion to him and sympathise very sincerely with you on the loss of such a companion...."[54]

CHAPTER 13

On Liberty

The house in Blackheath Park, home of John and Harriet Mill for the seven years of their married life, was described by Charles Eliot Norton as square and plain, standing in its own grounds, "but with a characteristically English air and look in its seclusion behind a wall".[1] Haji Taylor, who stayed on after his mother's death until his own marriage in 1860, spoke of the green fields and farm land which surrounded it, making it an ideal retreat from a world which neither John nor Harriet desired. He described the interior, the imposing dining-room, its walls "encompassed with tall bookcases surmounted by plaster casts of classic celebrities, and a fine engraving of Raphael's Madonna della Seggiola over the mantelpiece".[2]

Norton did not see the house during Harriet's lifetime: like the rest of Mill's friends, with the exception of W. J. Fox and one or two others, he was not granted the privilege. Harriet's two children, Kate, the maid, and a series of pampered cats were company enough. Mill generally returned from the India House in time to make the tea, a domestic chore he much enjoyed; occasionally he stayed on in London for a meeting of the Political Economy Club, which his father had helped to found.

For the first year or so of their marriage, life for the Mills was happy and uneventful and their precarious health gave them less cause for anxiety than usual. Haji Taylor, when he came to write his memoirs in the 1890s, gave much thought to what he should say of their premarital relations and came to the conclusion that they were best relegated to a footnote. With a certain lack of candour he asserted that Mill was "the fast friend for many years of my father and mother, and equally esteemed by both". With more regard for the truth he continued, "During more than a score of years that I have seen them much together—including half-a-dozen continental journeys in which I have had the happiness of sharing, and innumerable English ones—I never knew him to utter a cross word or show impatience in her regard, nor to demur at any expressed wish on her part; and it must be added, she no less considered his wishes in all things."[3]

In the midst of the peace and contentment, the music, the readings aloud, the discussions, and the solitary country walks which Mill continued to take, there was a single element of doubt: Mill was suddenly troubled by the fear that the marriage was not valid. He had, he explained to Harriet, on the registrar's instructions, signed his full name to the official document instead of his usual signature, "J. S. Mill". This "cannot possibly affect the legality of our marriage . . . ; but so long as it is possible that any doubt could for a moment suggest itself . . . , I cannot feel at ease, and therefore, unpleasant as I know it must be to you, I do beg you to let us even now be married again".[4] Harriet must have assured her husband that he was talking nonsense, for there was no second ceremony.

After the initial idyllic period their married life was punctuated with partings. Harriet, as ever, sought to recover her health in travel; Mill, too, was forced to take more than one period of sick leave. When feasible they went abroad together, but there were times when one or other of them had to go alone. In 1853 Mill left Harriet in Sidmouth, Devon, to see whether the sea air would do her lungs good, and returned to Blackheath and his work at the India House. "My own dearest one!" he wrote on his return, "I sat in the room usually warmed by her presence, & in the usual place, & looked at her vacant chair, wishing for the time when it will be again filled . . . ." Letters helped to bridge the gap, and they wrote almost daily. "This is the first time since we were married my darling wife that we have been separated & I do not like it at all—but your letters are the greatest delight . . . ."[5]

As a trial run for the *Autobiography,* which he was already planning under Harriet's watchful eye, Mill kept a diary for an experimental period of three months. He realized that his father's name had fallen into oblivion in the seventeen years since his death; and it seemed vital to Mill that some record of his life with Harriet should survive, in addition to an account of his public service and of the books which he had written alone or in co-operation with her. Many of the diary entries reflect his adoration of his wife. In a typical entry he wrote,

What a sense of protection is given by the consciousness of being loved, and what an additional sense . . . by being near the one by whom one is and wishes to be loved the best. I have experience at present of both these things. . .

I feel . . . bitterly . . . how little I have yet done as the interpreter of the wisdom of one whose intellect is as much profounder than mine than the heart is nobler. If I ever recover my health, this shall be amended; and even if I do not, something may, I hope, be done towards it, provided a sufficient respite is allowed me . . . .[6]

To Harriet he spoke and wrote of the work in which her help was imperative. He hoped, he told her, that they would live long enough to complete everything they wished to produce, "to most of which your living is quite as essential as mine, for . . . my faculties at the best are not adequate to the highest subjects". She must not imagine that, should he survive her, he would abandon their plans. "But I *am not fit* to write on anything but the outskirts of the great questions of feeling & life without you to prompt me as well as to keep me right . . . ."[7]

While she lived, Harriet was more than ready to prompt and guide him and, as we have seen, to approve or amend the references to herself and others in the draft of Mill's *Autobiography*.

It was at about this time that Mill's tuberculosis revealed itself, although neither he nor his doctor was prepared to concede it. He wrote to Harriet of his cough, his feverish attacks, his expectoration, and his stomach disorders. He had noted "the decided & unmistakable appearance of blood in the expectoration", he informed her, but the doctor had assured him that he "was not in a consumption at present". Most of his ailments had a habit of disappearing of their own accord and the bleeding might be no exception. "Indeed if I had belief in presentiments I should feel quite assured on that point, for it appears to me so completely natural that while my darling lives I should live to keep her company."[8]

Harriet, with her invariable belief in mind over matter, told him briskly that she could not help thinking "that the practice of looking at the expectoration in the morning, is in itself a great measure the cause of there being any expectoration at all". If he tried, as she had, to avoid the habit, he would lose it "altogether as I have done".[9]

Over-optimistic about her own health, she was giving her husband sound advice. She had only four more years to live; he had nearly twenty, and he was not to die of tuberculosis.

It was during this year—1854—that Mill wrote the short essay, "Liberty", which provided the groundwork for his book *On Liberty*. Husband and wife, together or apart, worked on the book together, as they had on the *Principles of Political Economy,* but even more closely than before. As Mill stated, "None of my writings has been either so carefully composed, or so sedulously corrected as this. After it had been written as usual twice over, we kept it by us, bringing it out from time to time, and going through it *de novo,* reading, weighing, and criticizing every sentence . . . ." It was, he stated with perfect sincerity,

more directly and literally our joint production than anything else which bears my name, for there was not a sentence of it that was not several times gone through by us together and carefully weeded of any faults, either in thought or expression, that we detected in it. It is in consequence of this that, although it never underwent her final revision, it far surpasses, as a mere specimen of composition, anything which has proceeded from me either before or since. With regard to the thoughts, it is difficult to identify any particular part or element as being more hers than all the rest. The whole mode of thinking of which the book was the expression, was emphatically hers.[10]

Even Mill's early biographers, never prone to give Harriet a modicum of praise, conceded her share in its composition. "Liberty was planned by Mill and his wife in concert",[11] wrote W. L. Courtney; Bain spoke of the book as "the chief production of his married life", one in which Mrs Mill "bore a considerable part".[12] In recent years others, among them Professor Gertrude Himmelfarb, have strongly supported this theory. "That Mill should single out this particular quality of *On Liberty*", she writes, of Mill's claim that the book reflected Harriet's whole mode of thinking, "confirms not only the nature and extent of her influence but also the fact that *On Liberty* itself represented a distinctive mode of thought. If Mill regarded it as distinctive, we can do no less."[13]

In 1854 Mill had been contemplating the publication of a series of essays, among them "Liberty", but in January 1855, during the extended period of sick leave which had started shortly before his mother's death, the idea occurred to him that it merited a separate volume. He could not make up his mind without consulting Harriet, and so he wrote asking her to reread the essay and to tell him whether in her opinion "it will do as the foundation of one part of the volume in question—If she thinks so I will try to write & publish it in 1856 if my health permits as I hope it will." Before she had had time to reply, he wrote again, to the effect that "I think I shall be able & disposed to write a very good volume on Liberty, if we decide that that is to be the subject." Harriet agreed in principle, and Mill, whose health had improved in the heady atmosphere of Rome, promised to give the subject further thought, "since my darling approves". The more he thought it over, the more enthusiastic he became. It seemed to him that the book "will be read & make a sensation. The title itself with any known name to it would sell an edition. We must cram into it as much as possible of what we wish not to leave unsaid."[14]

Mill and Harriet were reunited in the summer of 1855 and so there are no letters to show exactly how the work was proceeding. The book was to have had a final revision during the winter of 1858-9, immediately following Mill's retirement from the India House; but in 1858 Harriet was critically ill, and so "that hope and every other were frustrated by the most unexpected and bitter calamity of her death".[15]

Mill had no heart for further revisions; the volume, as much hers as his, must appear as it stood. All he could bring himself to do was to write the dedication which moved Mrs Gaskell to apologize for the pain she had unwittingly caused him:

> To the beloved and deplored memory of her who was the inspirer, and in part the author, of all that is best in my writings—the friend and wife whose exalted sense of truth and right was my strongest incitement, and whose approbation was my chief reward—I dedicate this volume. Like all that I have written for many years, it belongs as much to her as to me; but the work as it stands has had, in a very insufficient degree, the inestimable

advantage of her revision; some of the most important portions having been reserved for a more careful re-examintion, which they are now never destined to receive. Were I but capable of interpreting to the world one half the great thoughts and noble feelings which are buried in her grave, I should be the medium of a greater benefit to it, than is ever likely to arise from anything I can write, unprompted and unassisted by her all but unrivalled wisdom.

On Liberty, published in 1859, carried the old conception of political freedom into the realms of everyday life. As Mill explained to his German translator, Theodor Gomperz, its theme is "moral, social, & intellectual liberty, asserted against the despotism of society whether exercised by governments or by public opinion".[16] No body, official or unofficial, had the right to interfere with the liberty of action of an individual unless that liberty constituted a danger to society. The "only purpose for which power can be rightfully exercised over any member of a civilized community, against his will, is to prevent harm to others.... In the part which merely concerns himself, his independence is, of right, absolute. Over himself, over his own body and mind, the individual is sovereign . . . ." This point was hammered home more than once: "the only freedom which deserves the name, is that of pursuing our own good in our own way, so long as we do not attempt to deprive others of theirs, or impede their efforts to obtain it".

Such a conception of liberty was, of course, rooted in Mill's and Harriet's defiance of convention; but the book itself is a balanced, rational argument against tyranny, whether by governments, groups of people or individuals; an eloquent and reasoned plea for the downtrodden to be accorded their just rights and privileges. Its terms are far-reaching, but, as one would expect from the partnership, great emphasis was placed on the wrongs of women and children. The obligation of the State to curb individual tyranny was "almost entirely disregarded in the case of family relations, a case, in its direct influence on human happiness, more important than all others taken together". All that was needed to curtail and control "the despotic power of husbands over wives" was to give wives the same rights as their husbands and allow them "the protection of law in the same manner, as all other persons". In the case of children, "misapplied notions of liberty are a real obstacle to the fulfilment by the State of its duties. One would almost think that a man's children were supposed to be literally, and not metaphorically, a part of himself, so jealous is opinion of the smallest interference of law with his absolute control over them."

One of the most revolutionary of the recommendations of *On Liberty* concerned education, a subject which thereafter was to occupy Mill increasingly. Here, Harriet's influence is especially apparent in the insistence that girls as well as boys deserved the best schooling the country could supply; and this at a time when, with very few exceptions, the education of girls lagged far behind that of their brothers. It was, husband and wife maintained, the duty of the State to ensure that every citizen was educated up to a certain standard. Conversely, it was the duty of every father to defray the cost of his children's schooling, provided he had the means to do so; but, since the vast majority of fathers wilfully disregarded this obligation, it was for the State to make sure that it was enforced:

> Were the duty of enforcing universal education once admitted, there would be an end to the difficulties about what the State should teach, and how it should teach, which now convert the subject into a mere battle field for sects and parties.... If the government would make up its mind to *require* for every child a good education, it might save itself the trouble of providing one. It might leave to parents to obtain the education where and how they pleased, and content itself with helping to pay the school fees of the poorer classes of children, and defraying the entire school expenses of those who have no one else to pay for them.

This did not imply that Mill and Harriet were in favour of State education. On the contrary:

> That the whole or any large part of the education of the people should be in State hands, I go as far as any one in deprecating.... A general State education is a mere contrivance for moulding people to be exactly like one another: and as the mould in which it casts them is that which pleases the predominant power in the government ..., it establishes a despotism over the mind, leading by natural tendency to one over the body. An education established and controlled by the State should only exist, if it exist at all, as one among many competing experiments, carried on for the purpose of example and stimulus, to keep the others up to a certain standard of excellence. Unless, indeed, when society in general is in so backward a state that it could not or would not provide for itself any proper institutions of education, unless the government undertook the task: then, indeed, the government may, as the less of two great evils, take upon itself the business of schools and universities.... But in general, if the country contains a sufficient number of persons qualified to provide education under government auspices, the same persons would be able and willing to give an equally good education on the voluntary principle, under the assurance of remuneration afforded by a law rendering education compulsory, combined with State aid to those unable to defray the expense.

Compulsory universal education should be securely underpinned by compulsory public examinations, "extending to all children, and beginning at an early age. An age might be fixed at which every child must be examined, to ascertain if he (or she) is able to read."

In demanding that examinations should be taken by girls as well as boys,

Mill and Harriet were marching beside the early reformers of girls' education. They went a good deal farther—too far, one might suggest—when they proposed that the parent of a child who failed a test might, "unless he has some sufficient ground of excuse . . . be subjected to a moderate fine, to be worked out, if necessary, by his labour, and the child might be put to school at his expense".

Examinations should be held annually, "with a gradually extending range of subjects, so as to make the universal acquisition and . . . retention of a certain minimum of general knowledge virtually compulsory". Above a minimum standard examinations should be continued on a voluntary basis, students wishing to do so working towards the acquirement of certificates of proficiency. Here, as elsewhere in the book, it is emphasized that the freedom of the individual must be safeguarded:

> To prevent the State from exercising . . . an improper influence over opinion, the knowledge required for passing an examination . . . should be confined to facts and positive science. The examinations on religion, politics, or other disputed topics, should not turn on the truth or falsehood of opinions, but on the matter of fact that such and such an opinion is held, on such grounds, by such authors, or schools or churches. . . . All attempts by the State to bias the conclusions of its citizens on disputed subjects are evil.[17]

When it appeared in print, *On Liberty* was widely reviewed. "There has been an amount of response to it far beyond what I expected", Mill told George Jacob Holyoake. To a friend who had written to condole with him on the loss of his wife and, at the same time, to congratulate him on the book, he replied, "I . . . only wish that you had known her who is gone sufficiently to know what a feeble and inadequate expression that dedication gives to what she was. While she lived, she never sought to be known beyond her small circle of intimates—but now it seems perfectly shocking that the world should be so utterly unaware of the treasure it has lost."[18] It would be a sacred duty to him, he wrote to another friend who admired the book, to try to make the world understand what Harriet had been and all she stood for.

On Liberty was an immediate success and most, though not all, of Mill's friends were suitably impressed. Moncure D. Conway, for example, called it a book "of wonderful truisms, of startling commonplaces". It should, he declared, be prescribed reading for students, even though "there is scarcely a State on earth that would not be revolutionised by a practical adoption of its principles".[19] To Mill's surprise and pleasure, Charles Kingsley, who might well have been highly critical, was extremely complimentary. He said, so Mill informed Alexander Bain, that the book had "made him 'a clearer headed & braver minded man upon the spot' ".[20]

A note of dissent came from Caroline Fox, once so admiring. "I am reading that terrible book of John Mill's on Liberty", she wrote to a friend, "so clear, and calm, and cold . . . He looks you through like a basilisk, relentless as Fate." She had, she said, known him well in the past, "and owe him much; I fear his remorseless logic has led him far since then".[21] Caroline Fox was evidently not one of the friends to be invited to Blackheath.

Mill himself considered that, of all his books, *On Liberty* was the most likely to survive. It went through many editions during his lifetime, but, unlike the *Political Economy,* it was never revised. He may well have considered emendations but rejected them, since Harriet was no longer alive for consultation and direction. Professor Himmelfarb has suggested that, having published the book as a memorial to Harriet, "and having given her credit for the major part of it, he could hardly alter it without desecrating her memory. One may even suspect that the lavish tributes and credit veiled an unconscious ambivalence towards the book, for the more he paid homage to her and the more he identified her with it, the less he himself was identified with it."[22] Mill was aware that the book, like any other book, had shortcomings, which he persuaded himself that Harriet alone could have corrected; but it is hard to believe that, consciously or unconsciously, he wished to disassociate himself from it.

Elsewhere, Professor Himmelfarb expresses the fear that the book's message, that the only freedom which deserves the name is freedom to pursue our own good in our own way, provided that in so doing you do not interfere with the liberty of others, might be misinterpreted as "an invitation to excess"; and argues that it is Mill's other writings, notably the *Principles of Political Economy* and the *Logic,* which "more truly deserve the title of 'liberal' ".[23] It is ironical that, if any of the students who read *On Liberty* today should, by any chance, be influenced by it towards anarchy, there would be as many liberated women among them as men. To the unbiased reader the book is likely to remain, as another authority, Mrs Mary Warnock, puts it, the "most moving"[24] of all Mill's works.

CHAPTER 14

Waiting in the Wings

In Harriet's peregrinations, both before and after her marriage to John Mill, her daughter Lily, as she called Helen, was her constant attendant. This child, who had inherited her mother's intelligence and force of character but little or nothing from her father, received a strange, unsettling upbringing. John Mill's influence over her was profound, as hers was to be over him during the last fourteen years of his life.

Helen would dearly have liked to go to school, but, with a mother who demanded her company wherever she went, this was out of the question. Harriet was her only teacher, as James Mill had been John's. She gave the girl few, if any, organized lessons; but Helen, conscientious and methodical, had the run of her mother's library and, beginning at one end of a bookshelf, ploughed straight through to the end, sometimes understanding what she read, often not. At fourteen she discovered the book which had so entranced Caroline Fox, Mill's *System of Logic*—or perhaps it was put in her way. She grasped very little of it; but it was a major part of her mother's system that her pupil should be encouraged to think for herself, to tackle difficult concepts which she could not fully grasp. As this suggests, Harriet, in her training of Helen, adopted James Mill's theory of education; though she did not adopt his slave-driving methods. According to Helen, who was fond of the father she so seldom saw, he and her mother were at one on this point. As she told a friend in the women's suffrage movement who, in later years, asked her advice about the education of her own children, her "dearest mother" had imbued her with the high principles, restraint, orderly habits, the "enthusiasm for virtue, & pleasure in reading" which were so important to her.

My father held with very great strength an opinion in which my mother quite agreed, that children shᵈ be left free to choose their opinions for themselves, with no other prejudice than the knowledge of the opinions their parents hold. I never heard in my childhool on any speculative subject, politics or religion, "This is the truth, this is the right opinion".

Nor was there any attempt to conceal that there were worthy people who thought quite differently. I was never told that I ought to think this or that, but I was blamed if I asked what I ought to think, & told it was my duty to think for myself, & to find out the truth. While I was still a child my parents often said to me "I have a right to think it so & so because I have studied the subject & thought much about it; *you* sh^ddo the same & not ask me what to think...."[1]

There is so much of this in Mill's *On Liberty,* and John Taylor had so little chance of guiding his daughter in any way, that it seems likely that Helen, out of filial loyalty, was giving him the credit for something she owed to her mother and stepfather. Loyalty to her father's memory was one of her finer traits. When in due course she edited Mill's *Autobiography* and came to a reference to her father, which she did not feel entitled to delete, as "a most upright, brave, and honourable man, of liberal opinions and good education, but without the intellectual or artistic tastes which would have made him a companion" for her mother, she appended to the manuscript, after the word "intellectual", a pencilled comment of her own: "not true".[2]

Helen certainly grew up to form her own opinions and use her own judgment—sometimes too freely, for restraint was not one of her virtues. But, while hers was a positive, dramatic personality, her brothers, in comparison, were weaklings.

Between Helen and her mother there existed a passionate love-hate relationship marked on both sides by emotional blackmail. During Helen's childhood Harriet naturally had the upper hand: "Be good & do what you know is right"; or "I cannot love you if you are not good."[3]

As an integral part of her education, Helen was taken by Harriet, on their European travels, to cathedrals, churches, picture galleries, plays and operas. Her knowledge of the arts was precocious, unless, in her written comments, she was merely adopting her mother's opinions. There are frequent mentions of the arts in the diary which she kept sporadically between 1842, when she was eleven, and 1847. There are also mentions of her attendance at mass, in England as well as in Europe, for Helen and her brother Haji had strong leanings towards the Roman Catholic Church. Harriet did nothing to discourage this tendency, realizing, perhaps, that Helen was more attracted by the ritual and the music than the liturgy. "I went this morning to a Catholic Chapel", noted Helen in a typical entry in 1846. "The service was nicely performed... with real sweet smelling flowers, and acolytes properly behaved and properly dressed." She went again the following Sunday, when the music was "beautiful, making a real impression if sacred". When Haji was available they went to mass together; when this was impossible, as it was when they stayed with their grandmother, they performed the ceremony themselves. In comparison with the Church of Rome the Church of England services, which she also attended, seemed dreary and uninspiring. She found the music "horrid, positively unpleasant to hear.... The sermon was . . . excessively pompous."

Haji's interest in Catholicism proved lasting, but Helen's faded. Helen's real love, far stronger than her love of any church, was the theatre. Her dream from the age of twelve was to go on the stage, a career which few 'respectable' women contemplated at that time; and she not only criticized the performances of professional actresses in the theatre but also learned the roles of Shakespeare's heroines and rehearsed them in the privacy of her mother's garden. The comments in her diary on the plays she saw, the concerts she attended, and the books she read may well have been inspired by Harriet, undoubtedly so in her criticism of the author of a book she read in 1845, who "declares women inferior to men. That is enough to 'do for her' with me."

Harriet may have imagined that Helen's passion for the theatre was another passing fancy: it was not. Her favourite roles were Portia and Lady Macbeth until a visit to *Measure for Measure* in 1846 turned her thoughts to Isabella. The heroine, she reported, "acted nicely but to me it seemed took too calm an idea of Isabella. Spirited bold independent and courageous it seems to me she ought to be", not, as depicted, "mild gentle and amiable".[4] Helen herself was to be spirited, hold, independent and courageous; so, too, one may be sure, was her private performance of Isabella.

The most significant indication of Harriet's domination over her daughter is the fact that the diary contains no mention of John Mill's name. There are entries to mark the visits to and from Papa, Grandmama, Grandpapa, Haji (or Hadji, as Helen called him) and, less frequently, Herby; there is even mention of a visit from young George Mill, a close friend of both the Taylor boys. But, as far as Helen's diary is concerned, John Mill, never far from Harriet's side, might not have existed at all.

As she grew older Helen began to chafe at her nomadic way of life and her perpetual attendance on her ailing mother. She longed and schemed to turn her dream into reality; yet, so emotionally dependent on one another were mother and daughter that she could not find the strength to break away. The situation was unchanged when Harriet married John Mill: Lily was still needed; Lily must stay at home. There was also some anxiety about her health. In 1855, when she was twenty-four, Helen showed signs of tuberculosis and Harriet took her to the Isle of Wight. "Lily continues very unwell and causes me the greatest anxiety", Harriet wrote to Mrs Hardy in one of the bickering letters they still occasionally exchanged. Quinine had been tried but had disagreed with her, and "the continuing fever and great weakness continue".[5] The doctor recommended sea bathing, and by October the danger was over, although Helen continued to suffer intermittently from heavy colds.

Harriet herself had never really recovered from her serious illness of 1853. Since then, so she wrote to her brother Arthur, she had had two surgical operations, the nature of which she did not specify. Mill, on the other hand, had returned form his six months' sick leave abroad "quite set up in health, but he is not strong tho' as busy as ever, & I am often anxious about him".[6]

By the autumn of 1856, however, Mill was in good health and Harriet as well as she was ever likely to be—well enough to give her daughter grudging permission to take the first steps towards an acting career. Helen's plans were already made. She wrote at once for advice to an experienced actress, Mrs Mary Ann (Fanny) Stirling. Fanny Stirling, who was noted for her kindness to members of the profession and to anyone else who asked her help, invited the girl to call at her London home in Brook Street. "I am sometimes induced to give lessons",[7] she replied, which was precisely what Helen wished her to say.

Helen was charmed with the warm-hearted actress, a woman eighteen years her senior, unpretentious and humble about her own very considerable attainments but thoroughly professional. She had made her name as Celia in *As You Like It,* played Cordelia to Macready's Lear, and was famous as Peg Woffington in Charles Reade's *Masks and Faces.* At forty she was much in demand, and in her later years she was to make a great hit as Mrs Malaprop and as the nurse in Irving's production of *Romeo and Juliet,* a role she was to play so often and with such verve and distinction that she earned the nickname "Nursie".

Mrs Stirling realized that Helen had a natural if untrained talent and promised to help her in every way she could. Helen was wildly enthusiastic. "I go very often to town to see Mrs Stirling", she told Haji, "and have been twice with Miss Stirling [Mrs Stirling's daughter Fanny, later Mrs Allen, who in 1860 began a very brief stage career] to see her act which she does gloriously. She spent a Sunday with us here once. We have talked of going to America together, but that plan will not come to anything yet a while if indeed it ever does, for I should not like to leave my precious darling for so long and be so far away from her."[8]

The "precious darling" would never have allowed her daughter to go so far afield; indeed, she was very much against her going away at all. But Helen, as obstinate as her mother, was discontented at home and showed it; and Mrs Stirling was persuasive, believing as she did that the girl should have her chance. She made friends with Helen, whose isolated life had prevented her from forming friendships with girls of her own age. Towards Harriet, her near-contemporary, she was wide-eyed with admiration. Harriet, who became fond of Mrs Stirling, accepted the admiration as no more than her rightful due, the more so because it was accompanied by a suitable degree of reverence for John Stuart Mill. (Harriet may never have learned it, but Mrs Stirling, who had made a most unhappy marriage and lived apart from her husband, was devoted to Sir Charles Hutton Gregory, consulting engineer to the Crown Agents for the Colonies. She married him in 1894, shortly after her husband's death, when she was eighty-one and Sir Charles eighty. The two old people, whose mutual devotion was of long standing, had only one year of married life before Fanny's death.)

After putting her through a brief period of training, Mrs Stirling decided that Helen needed a period of practice with a provincial repertory company. Harriet, like others of her time, considered the majority of actors as inferior beings and repertory actors as beneath contempt. She gave her consent only on condition that Helen would never appear on the stage under her own name. "Miss Trevor" was finally chosen, near enough to "Taylor" but not too near to be recognizable. To Harriet, with her dread of tittle-tattle, it was imperative that Helen's whereabouts should be kept secret, to avoid gossip. Helen therefore undertook to send letters to her mother care of John Mill at the India House and to provide him with a supply of addressed envelopes for Harriet's replies. Mill was perfectly ready to act as postman: it was enough for him to be able to do something to relieve Harriet's maternal anxiety.

Thus prepared, Helen set off for Newcastle in November 1856 accompanied by Haji, who had agreed that, if questioned, he would say that his name was the same as his sister's. Haji, then unemployed, had made an ill-starred attempt at farming, a career which his mother had deplored. He had also travelled—and was to travel again—in Italy, staying in monasteries and observing the monastic life; but Mill guessed correctly when he maintained that the young man would never become a monk.

Mill must have been thankful when his stepchildren departed, leaving him alone with his wife. He was exceedingly fond of Helen, but Haji, who was apt to sit around with his head in his hands, was something of a trial.

Severing the umbilical cord was an agonizing experience to mother and daughter. Helen's first letter was scribbled in the cab on the way to Euston Station. The second, posted at Peterborough, showed obvious signs of remorse: "My darling, we are well off so far.... O my darling it makes me so wretched to think of you unhappy, so dearest tell me how you are & try for me to be well.... Adieu my dear darling precious Mama."9

Despite Mrs Stirling's intervention with the manager, there were at first no parts for Helen to play, and she began to feel both homesick and guilty: "It is so sad to be without my precious Mama, I miss her all day long to turn to, to look at, and to hear that dear voice....... Being away makes me feel if possible more than ever how precious you are to me. The day seems so dull and prosaic without you my beautiful darling...."10

This letter, far from arousing Harriet's sympathy, irritated her intensely. Helen had sulked until she got her own way: what else did she want? Harriet's reply was stiff with resentment: "I do not wish to say anything about my feelings or state because I wish you to be wholly uninfluenced by me in all your future proceedings. I would rather die than go through again your reproaches for spoiling your life. Whatever happens let your mode of life be your own free choice henceforth...."11

This certainly brought Helen to heel: "O my darling," wrote the repentant daughter, "I feel as though I could not endure it and if you ... still miss me I will come back and never leave you another day for all the happiness in the world." She went on to make a startling suggestion, one which neither Mill nor her mother would contemplate for a moment—that, instead of returning home, Harriet should join her. "Nothing can disappoint or tire or vex me that is associated with the theatre and if you were with me too I should have everything I could wish for on earth. . . . Will you think of this darling, and whether you could leave Mr Mill for some time . . . ."[12]

Harriet, slightly mollified, thanked her dearest girl "for all the sweet & loving things" she had said, but she was not prepared to welcome her home at this juncture nor to abandon her husband: "I am better today. I shall calm down by degrees—I feel this clearly . . . that deeply as I feel and thank you for the offer of sacrifice you make your happiness only must be considered and if you are happy I shall I hope become so in time. I must be with you sometimes, I hope often, but generally or always as you propose that I could not do—I could not leave alone my one generous firm unchanging friend and that when his health is not strong, for any other motive than your health."[13]

For the moment—but only for the moment—Helen stopped pestering her mother to join her. She was practising Lady Macbeth, and had pressed Haji into service "to stand up for Macbeth that I may be in the habit of seizing hold of some one and addressing myself to an actual person".[14] Unfortunately, when the great day came, the manager, who had promised her an audition, explained to her that the part was beyond her at present. At twenty-five, Helen was slim, tall and beautiful. Fanny Stirling had taught her to move with grace and elegance, but, although she had dignity, she was far too inexperienced to play one of Shakespeare's major heroines.

With no immediate prospect of a part, Helen offered to come home for a few days. Harriet refused: she was well aware that he daughter would be worried in case an opportunity arose in her absence. If she came home at all it must be when she knew she would be free "to stay a good time. The only way I can share in your enjoyment . . . is to wish you all possible happiness which I do with all my heart . . . ."[15] She was also helping her daughter financially; and Helen, worried because she and her hungry brother ate more than a pound of meat a day and were paying £1 a week for their lodgings, was doing her best to economize. "I always feel that all we have is in common", wrote her mother, "and you are to have and use whatever you like—we always have been perfectly one about that darling."[16]

Touched by this display of generosity, Helen, never the most percipient of women, made another effort to persuade her mother to come north for the next six months. If not—and, however affectionate her letters, Harriet never failed to mention the misery the separation was causing her—Helen offered to make the supreme sacrifice:

> If you suffer so much by my being away I will come home. I beg I pray I implore you do not think me unkind, do not suffer from that cause. I love you with my whole heart and soul and will do anything to prove it to you. . . . I wish I knew how much of what you suffer is from our separation. [But] you and Mr Mill were willing to seperate [sic] for six months for the sake of his health, would you be so again to give me a chance of

happiness? ... I do not think that the sacrifice of home would be to you so great as that of the theatre is to me, but you must judge of that and whether you love me enough to make it.[17]

Helen should have been prepared for coals of fire. "Do not talk of the sacrifice of your happiness for me", wrote her mother, "that would never make me happy—no, you must have your own course & I must fit myself to it in the best way I can for both & for all." Helen had not merely suggested that Harriet should leave her husband for six months, but also—and this was unpardonable to Mill, the buffer state between them—endanger her health by travelling from one provincial town to another and staying in uncomfortable lodgings. Helen would not need her as a chaperone, for, when Haji left, Fanny Stirling would arrange for a respectable woman to look after her. But, continued her mother, she must not be "unhappy or pained about me—we love each other most dearly and together can be independent of all enemies".[18] By enemies, Harriet meant, as usual, old Mrs Hardy, the Leys and her own son Herbert.

Daily the letters flew backwards and forwards between the two loving, jealous women, Helen agonizing over the details of her mother's illnesses, which Harriet never sought to suppress. "Do not think dearest that you have said anything to give me pain ... except that you are not well", moaned Helen. "I cryed [sic] before, my darling, to think that you were ill and I not able to say one word of comfort."[19] Sometimes she was overcome with homesickness. "I miss you terribly, especially in the evenings.... I like to think that at about nine o'clock that you are talking with him. I feel very unhappy at three because you are at dinner and I am not there to help you. I grow impatient at five because he has not come in but at six it is pleasant to think that he is making tea and that you have got my letter.... Tell Mr Mill how much I am obliged to him to putting so many nice letters in the post."[20]

Without the constant encouragement of Fanny Stirling, who wrote practical motherly letters of advice almost daily, Helen would probably have given up the struggle and returned home. Mrs Stirling wrote to her about theatrical lodgings, the vagaries of landladies, dressers and, above all, with advice on the best way of handling theatrical managers. Helen should do her best to obtain a good part for her debut: after that, as a sop to the manager, she should be prepared to accept anything she was offered, however insignificant. "I am disappointed for you not in you.... Do not be discouraged, try to get some parts of any sort ...."[21]

Mrs Stirling thought the most suitable part for her debut (it was to be in Sunderland) would be the heroine of Nicholas Rowe's popular tragedy *Jane Shore*, written in imitation of Shakespeare's style, according to the author, and based on the story of Edward IV's mistress Mrs Shore the goldsmith's wife, who, after her royal lover's death, was accused by his successor of sorcery and forced to do public penance. Helen reported triumphantly that she had secured the role; and she was determined that Jane, even in her adversity,

should look her best. "If my own notion is right she should wear black",
Helen wrote to her mother, "and by the bye with blk velvet dress and blk satin
shoes should the stockings be white or black?"[22] Harriet replied that, since
Jane was in mourning for the king when the play opened, the stockings
should be black. "It is a very *theatrical* part", wrote Helen proudly. "I have got
to scream to faint to die or the stage."[23] This was indeed a challenge, but she
felt sure she was equal to it. On the opening night, "I wore the velvet gown
low at the neck and with short sleeves. The jet coronet with the large black
veil, my hair as I wear it best at home; the jet girdle, the little ruby cross you
gave me at Boulogne, the Genoa gold bracelet on one arm and the garnet
bracelet on the other. The garnet bracelet excited great admiration."[24]

Seldom can a recently bereaved mistress have looked more opulent on a
provincial stage! She was not in the least nervous, she assured her mother,
and had been surprised that the members of the caste had gone out of their
way to tell her not to be frightened and that the manager himself had
enquired after her nerves as she stood waiting in the wings for her first
entrance.

"I am sure you must have looked most beautiful", replied Harriet fondly.
The behaviour of the caste was, however, only what she would have expected:
"That notion they all have that you must of course be frightened shows what
a low class they generally are connected with theatres, as no well bred young
lady would show any, or feel much trepidation on such an occasion and I was
sure you would not."[25]

As Jane Shore, "Miss Trevor" had been given star billing on the poster
which advertised the performance, but she had to share the limelight with
"Dancing by the Viennoise Sisters". She herself was conscious that her
performance was far from perfect, although she was applauded not only on
her entrance but at several points in the course of the play. "In the last scene
which is very difficult I did not act well at all, I was terribly disappointed with
myself."[26]

A glance at the last scene shows just how difficult it was. Before she dies
the penitent, in a long tirade, complains,

> My feeble jaws forget their common office,
> My tasteless tongue cleaves to the clammy root,
> And now a general loathing grows upon me,
> Oh! I am sick at heart![27]

The local newspaper was far from complimentary; and Haji wrote
guardedly home to his mother, "The earlier acts, in regard to their effect on
the audience, were tolerably successful... During the last act, however, the
audience exhibited some signs of impatience, caused apparently by the length
& monotory of Jane Shore's part..., for she has to lie on the ground nearly all
the time, bewailing her misery, & this the audience seemed to get tired of,
especially as it was difficult to hear." He thought, however, that Lily showed

considerable confidence, spoke several of her speeches well and mimed to good effect, but, while her fainting and dying were realistic enough, her voice was monotonous, her gestures stiff. All the same, for a first appearance, her performance "appeared to me very successful".[28]

Fanny Stirling was sensible and consoling. "I am so glad my dear girl that the first step is made. I would rather hear you say that you felt monotonous and cold than that you were perfectly satisfied with yourself... Good parts will come to you as soon as you have once begun in earnest to act."[29]

Helen, aware that she lacked experience, told her mother that she would "be glad to take *any* parts if I could but act often".[30]

Harriet had thought of spending a few days with her daughter in December 1856, despite her many ailments—among them swollen hands and pains in the side and chest; but her husband was suffering from severe pains in the head and on no account could she leave him. Instead, Helen, whose future prospects were uncertain, came south to join them for Christmas at Brighton. Harriet sent her detailed instructions about breaking the journey in London. Helen, who was to travel alone, replied that she quite understood. At Brighton station she was "to look out for Mr Mill, and if I do not see him to go first to the Albion [Hotel], then to the Queens, then to the Old Ship."[31]

After Christmas Helen went north again, this time to Doncaster, where the manager "wanted me to play a singing fairy in the pantomine.... But the fairy sings and I do not so that put a stop to that...."[32] Later on, he told her, she could have the principal women's part in a translation of the French melodrama *Memoirs of the Devil;* meanwhile, since she refused to be a singing fairy, he had nothing for her.

While Helen was waiting in Doncaster for a suitable part, one of several altercations over money broke out between mother and daughter. Harriet may have said that "all we have is in common", but there were moments when she did not feel it. During Christmas, Helen reminded her, she had gained the impression that Harriet thought she was extravagant and had asked for too much:

> But I had always been in the habit, "childishly" as you said it is true but also I am sure with the love and confidence of a child. Had I not done so I should six years ago have endeavoured to earn and save money as a governess untill [*sic*] I had got a little to begin with to go on the stage which by economy might last me till I could get a small salary. I never thought of doing anything of the sort because I never supposed that I should want money while you had plenty, & thought you would rather have me with you than away to earn a hundred pounds. When at Brighton you seemed to speak of this trusting to you as presumptuous selfish and mean....

Yet, a day or so later, Harriet had spoken to her lovingly and kindly, "and pressed me to take more".[33]

Harriet was ready to increase Helen's allowance but she was not above making her feel uncomfortable at having to accept it. Unfortunately for Helen, *Memoirs of the Devil*, on which she had been relying, proved a complete fiasco, for Miss Trevor and one of the actors were the only members of the company who took the trouble to learn their parts. "You know I am not given to too much laughing", Helen wrote ruefully, "but I *literally* several times could not keep my countenance on the stage, and that in spite of my vexation."[34]

There was little or no humour in Helen's or Harriet's serious approach to life. They lacked the playfulness which Mill possessed and his friends found so endearing.

Sober-minded Helen soon found additional cause for wry laughter. After performing in the Doncaster pantomime as "Fame"—presumably a non-singing role—she was rewarded with the offer of Juliet. "I am absorbed in Juliet. I have literally been repeating her words all day."[35] Alas for her hopes, when the great day dawned she had a cold! "I shall do it badly but still it is such a pleasure...my first Shakespearian part..."[36] Unfortunately the performance "was full of extreme absurdities, one of which was the littleness of my Romeo [the manager's wife] who was at least a head shorter than myself which made the effect of our farewell embraces extremely funny."[37]

At this time, although she did not offer to go home, Helen was more than usually worried about Harriet, who had told her of a new and unusual symptom. "How unhappy I am to hear of my darling having the earache so bad, and of that dear beautiful little ear being swollen with it."[38]

Fanny Stirling had arranged for her to go north from Doncaster, to Glasgow, where she would receive "a pound a week to begin with & more directly if [the theatre manager] finds you are what I assured him he will find you".[39]

By the end of January, however, the swelling in Harriet's ear had subsided and she felt well enough to suggest spending a week or two with her daughter. "I cannot tell you how glad I am", wrote Helen. "Now I shall always be looking forward to it.'[40] She had been given only a few minor parts to play and was bitterly disappointed that there would be nothing spectacular for her mother to see.

Harriet was ready with consolation: "Do not feel disappointed dear one—you are tired and overdone, it will take a turn and go better before long no doubt... All day I have kept repeating Oh my dearest girl you must not be disappointed. Keep up your spirits my darling for my sake, you cannot be more interested in succeeding than I am for you. There is *nothing* I would not do to help you."[41]

Mill, worried at the thought of his wife travelling alone, arranged to escort her as far as York and see her into the Glasgow train before returning to London. Harriet proposed to spend a fortnight with Helen in Glasgow, meeting her husband again on the homeward journey. She had asked Helen to arrange accommodation, and Helen had suggested that she should share her rooms. "I think we could keep warm when once here, and in the depth of such a dark winter one place is scarcely darker or gloomier than another."[42] The prospect was scarcely inviting, but Harriet was less concerned about the cold than the need to keep their relationship a secret. No one must know that she was Mrs Mill and Miss Trevor's mother. Helen must be sure to explain to the landlady that her mother was "only a *friend* or a *lady*."[43]

The subterfuge would have been difficult to sustain and so Helen looked elsewhere and discovered two vacant rooms, a large living-room and a small bedroom. They were not ideal. "The W. C. is far off but the woman said of herself that ladies never went there, that the servant was very attentive." There was an additional problem: the rooms were in the street in which the manager and his wife lived, and "I fear this may be an objection."[44] It was an insuperable objection to Harriet, who decided to spend the first few days in an hotel and then look for lodgings herself.

Shortly before her mother's arrival Helen was called on at very short notice to deputize as Lady Capulet. Fanny Stirling, with her commonsense and eye to the main chance, thought this an excellent omen: "Don't be in despair dear, either with yourself or the practice ... You are now at your *worst* both of business & salary, for once having had such & such parts & such a salary you never go into another theatre for less—always up—up—exelcior [*sic*]!!!"[45]

John Mill, plagued with his usual headaches, had been advised to take a few days sick leave, which he spent with Harriet in York and Edinburgh. "I enjoy excessively the feeling of those three days", he wrote when they had parted, "and shall enjoy the remembrance of them & be very happy till you come & a great deal happier afterwards, so be cheerful darling & keep loving me as you so sweetly do. Bless you my own only darling love..."[46]

Harriet found Glasgow both cold and uncomfortable, and she saw very little of Helen, who was busy with rehearsals. The ever-anxious Mill was annoyed with Helen for persuading her mother to join her. He offered to come north himself; but Harriet refused, fearing that her famous husband would be recognized and her own relationship with Miss Trevor disclosed. Then she fell ill and, evading the proximity of her daughter, travelled alone to Edinburgh, where Mill met her. He was so alarmed at her condition that he insisted on taking her straight home and, when she was a little better, sent her to Brighton to recuperate.

Helen, too, had been ill. She was also feeling guilty and, abandoning the company, hurried home.

In the autumn, while Mill toured the Lake District and Derbyshire on foot, Harriet and Helen spent a holiday together before Miss Trevor departed to resume her career in repertory. It was the last time these two emotion-torn women were alone together.

CHAPTER 15

"Her Great and Loving Heart..."

Harriet might well have brought pressure to bear on Helen to return home had it not been for the optimism and affection of Fanny Stirling. Mrs Stirling, one of the few friends to visit Blackheath Park, saw Harriet whenever her own work permitted; her letters brim with devotion to the mother, affectionate concern for the daughter. Her disarming admiration of Harriet was the reason why no friction or jealousy over Helen existed between them, although Fanny had feared that Harriet might resent her influence.

In the spring of 1858, when Helen had been away from home for more than a year, Fanny spent a few days at Blackheath during one of John Mill's temporary absences. When she left she took with her a despondent note from her hostess, to which she hastened to reply: "*You* done living, my dear Mrs Mill! I think I never felt more than at this moment... in how very small a circle—hole—or tub—*I* have been living. No, we are not likely to meet on any common ground of interest, for you with your active mind & heart have enlarged thoughts & interests of & about others. I have shut myself up in my own shell... & the small doings & events of my own four walls. My activity—my dear Mrs Mill is all in my legs & body—I've none in my head or heart."

She went on to speak of Helen, of the possibility of a successful career on the stage, and of Harriet's natural feelings: "Helen—who should be the object of interest between us, & whom I believe we both love tho' differently—*is* I fancy rather a stumbling block, for I am always fancying you may feel that but for me this passion of hers might die a natural death—or merge into something else—this feeling too leads me to speak of it to her as little as possible—I cannot talk to her of it hopefully & cheerfully when I know that every word could be like a blow to you." Helen, like Desdemona, felt a " 'divided duty'—she loves you too well to leave you"; and yet, as they both knew, "She... longs with all her strength for what she dreams is an artistic & a happy life! So we are all constrained together some of us pleasing the other because what pleases her I feel must give you pain...."[1]

In the face of letters such as this Harriet had not the heart to tell her friend to cease her encouragement of Helen. Nor could she resist Fanny

Stirling's artless flattery, so reminiscent of Eliza Flower's: "In holding out
your hand to me, you have done more good than you can possibly guess. In
opening your doors to me, giving me a glimpse of a home where all is good &
honest & true you have given me—oh! so much . . . ."[2]

Fanny's awe-stricken reverence for John Mill was the surest way to
Harriet's heart. If she saw his name mentioned in a newspaper she wrote at
once to tell her friend: "It has been a pleasure to see Mr Mill so spoken of
lately, I have felt how your eyes would brighten—the sight of his name always
carries me to a certain home at Blackheath that seems to me to combine oh! so
much! strength elegance—poetry—comfort (not too poetical to stuff your
ducks!!)—Can God understand that I look at what seems such happiness with
envy!"[3]

By the autumn of 1858 Mill had completed his work at the India House.
He had been appointed Chief Examiner in 1856, but retired following the
transfer of the government of India to the Crown. His pension was on the
highest scale; Harriet had her own money; they were free now to write and to
travel as they wished.

Old Mrs Hardy, despite her lasting feud with her daughter, never lost her
admiration for Mill. She hoped, she now wrote to Harriet, that his health was
not "seriously impaired" and invited him to visit her, if "change of air were
needful to him . . . Pray give my love to him and tell him so." Harriet was not
included in the invitation. "I know it would be in vain to ask you—you have
not enough interest in me to visit me."[4]

Needless to say, Mill had no intention of visiting his mother-in-law: he
and Harriet were planning to winter in the south of France, possibly even to
live permanently abroad. Haji had returned to Italy, following a nomadic
course from one monastery to another. Recently, so he wrote to Helen, he
had visited the Santo Scala in Rome and, with other penitents, had climbed
the twenty-eight marble steps on his knees, "which is very sore work".[5] Haji
was disposed of, at least for the time being, but Harriet was worried about her
dearest Lily. Fanny Stirling now offered Helen a temporary home in Brook
Street. "You must not & shall not go away feeling wretched & miserable
about her", she wrote to Harriet. During the Mills' prolonged absence did
Mrs Mill think that Helen "could be well and happy with me?"[6]

This seemed the best possible solution. Helen came to London to discuss
the arrangement with Fanny, who was rehearsing at the Olympic Theatre for
Wilkie Collins' melodrama The Red Vial. At Fanny's request she added a
special message to one of her letters to her mother. Helen was to tell Harriet
that she must not think of writing to her friend, but that "when she is away I
shall feel sad if she forgets me". It would be a privilege if, instead, she might
be allowed to see some of Harriet's letters to her daughter. "Tell her she has
brought this most impudent request upon herself & made me hers for ever by
the sweet way in which she once passed a letter from Mr Mill over to me—tell
her I loved her for it. . . . Tell her I love her for trusting you to me . . . ."[7]

Mrs Stirling, a real professional, was in an acute state of nerves before the opening night, unlike Helen, who was never in the least degree nervous. Helen was to see her mother and stepfather off at the station before going to the theatre. They would meet after the play, Fanny told her, when "my work will be over & you will see me have a good cry most likely".[8] When she had recovered her composure they would sit down and eat supper together.

The moment they parted, Harriet and Helen resumed their over-emotional correspondence. Harriet, who had begged her daughter not to wait until the train moved off, experienced a pang when she saw "the dear bonnet walking away".[9] In her first letter, written the day after Fanny's opening night, Helen spoke of her mother's appearance at the carriage window. It was "so sweet to feel the love that gave me the very last sight of that beautiful and loving face".[10]

The Red Vial had a shocking press and was saved from immediate disaster only by Mrs Stirling's acting. As soon as Fanny had recovered from what Helen described as an unusually bad attack of the eye, she promised to arrange for her protégée to join a repertory company in Aberdeen.

Meanwhile, the Mills were *en route* for Hyères by way of Avignon and Montpellier. They had been detained for several days at Dijon owing to Harriet's extreme exhaustion, but were "now going on to Lyons, which as it is only four hours ought not to be so very fatiguing". The trouble was that Mill was as incompetent as a travelling companion as he was in all other practical matters of life: "the fact is we always get the last seats in the railway carriage, as I cannot run on quick, & if he goes on he never succeeds." Toiling behind her husband, "I always find him running up and down & looking lost in astonishment, so I have given up trying to get any seats but those that are left."[11]

The Mills reached Lyons on 19 October, the day Helen left for Aberdeen. At Carlisle she posted a letter which she knew would give her mother pleasure, enclosing a cutting from the *Illustrated News of the World* for 17 October:

> We learn with regret that ... Mr John Stuart Mill [has] retired from the examinership of the India House, which he has held ... with such great benefit to the public service; as did his father ... before him. We understand that it is his intention to seek an improvement in his health by settling down for the winter in a warmer climate. He retires ... with the affection and respect not only of the officials of that great department ... but of every one high or low, rich or poor, who has been brought into contact with him.

Helen apologized because she had not been able to buy a copy of *The Times* or any of the other newspapers which carried appreciations of Mill. She inquired most anxiously about her mother, who never sought to minimize her symptoms, and was intensely relieved to hear from her stepfather a day or so later that she seemed considerably better. Harriet, too, was optimistic.

"O my dearest girl I really am better today", she wrote. "I think of you all day & night my darling & cry a great deal, but next time I write I shall be a great deal better I hope, bless you."[12]

Mother and daughter could seldom agree when together; parted they behaved like a pair of star-crossed lovers. If Mill found this excess of emotion trying, he never showed it. "My darling precious one," cried Helen, "if you are not better I must come to you. Tell me *exactly* how you are and remember that I could soon hear through the electric telegraph if you were ill . . . ."[13] She would relinquish everything, even her beloved career, if she thought that her mother really needed her, "and never leave you a day again".[14]

When the Mills reached Avignon Harriet was exceedingly ill. On 1 November Mill telegraphed to Helen to say that she was worse and also to inform her that he had asked Dr Gurney, who had saved her life once before, to come from Nice to the Hotel de l'Europe, where they were staying. His telegram crossed with one from Helen to the effect that, if she heard nothing by the following morning, she would leave Aberdeen immediately. She did so; but neither she nor the doctor arrived in time: Harriet died in the hotel on 3 November.

"O dear Hadji it is all over", wrote Helen to her younger brother in Rome, "but I was too late too late too late. He cannot write he suffers so dreadfully—he was twenty-four hours alone [with the body]—I must try to take care of him now . . . ."[15]

Neither Haji nor Herbert had been summoned to visit their dying mother, perhaps because Mill was aware that it was only her dearest Lily she would have wished to see. Nor were they present at the funeral, which, owing to the climate, could not be delayed. In any event, Mill and Helen wanted to be alone with their dead.

Mill's anquish resounds through his letters. To W. T. Thornton, a former colleague of his at the India House, he wrote, "My wife, the companion of all my feelings, the prompter of all my best thoughts, the guide of all my actions, is gone! . . It is doubtful if I shall ever be fit for anything public or private, again. The spring of my life is broken. But I shall best fulfil her wishes by not giving up the attempt to do something useful, and I am not quite alone. I have with me her daughter, the one person besides myself who most loved her & whom she most loved, & we help each other to bear what is inevitable . . . ."[16]

He could best fulfil Harriet's wishes by arranging for the publication of their book *On Liberty,* and this, so he told George Grote, he would do. As though to make some amends for his previous coldness to Mrs Grote, he sent her a message of thanks for her sympathy in his loss.

To Arthur Hardy, the brother for whom Harriet had always felt affection, he wrote, "She is buried in the cemetery of the town of Avignon & with her all our earthly happiness; we have henceforth no interest in life but to fulfil her wishes in all we can, & to return continually to her grave."[17] They had bought a small house not far from the cemetery, he explained, to enable them to spend as much time there as possible.

Only to the sisters with whom he had quarrelled were Mill's letters cold and formal.

Mill, of course, received a due measure of sympathy. Fanny Stirling, whose awestruck admiration would in any case have prevented her from writing to him, thought most of Helen. "Is there no way dear in which you can use me or mine to your comfort or help, use me in some way my child, if 'tis only to lean upon and weep." She understood, none better, Helen's exaggerated feelings of guilt and now did her best to assuage them. Helen had the support "of a higher nature than any I could presume to offer—coming from him who loved & appreciated her as she deserved it must be doubly precious to you ... & soften this terrible blow it must show you that *he* (who is well able to judge) sees that you have no cause for self reproach ..., I feel as tho' I never could shake off the feeling that *I* have in some way or other been to blame in this ...."[18]

Only the most generous-minded of women would have attempted to exonerate Helen at her own expense. Naturally, however, Helen was overwhelmed with remorse, even though, with her mother happily married, there was no reason why she should not have tried to make a career for herself. The expiation of guilt was one of the reasons why she now decided to devote herself to Mill for the remainder of his life. She was also undoubtedly moved by another emotion: like the daughters of many brilliant mothers she wanted to prove herself Harriet's equal.

On the day of Harriet Mill's death "Miss Trevor" also died, never to be resurrected. Many years later, when Helen herself was dead, her niece Mary Taylor asked Miss Elizabeth Lee (sister of the editor Sir Sidney Lee) who was writing an obituary for the *Dictionary of National Biography*, not to forget Helen's stage career. Although she had

her ups and downs on the stage ... like most beginners, yet I think she was getting on excellently when the blow came of her mother's death. True, she was still a provincial actress, but actresses usually learnt their business on the provincial stage. She had *leading* parts to act, which surely meant a great deal for her talents. She had only been about two years—less if I remember rightly—on the stage [and] after two years many people are only in the crowd.... I am anxious that she should not be ... represented as a failure ...."[19]

Helen played other leading parts during her lifetime, and Miss Lee chose to ignore Miss Trevor's existence.

John Mill, who was quite incapable of looking after himself, seems to have been unmoved by the demise of Miss Trevor, unaware that Helen was making any sacrifice. It is possible that she herself realized that she had no future as an actress, but it is impossible to imagine how Mill could have continued to live and work without her. Theirs was to be a mutually rewarding partnership, for, with Mill's help, Helen now embarked on a career which made her one of the most remarkable women of her generation.

As Mill had explained to Arthur Hardy, before returning to England he had bought an unpretentious little house and garden near the cemetery of the suburb of St Véran, where Harriet was buried. There he was to spend part of every remaining year of his life, haunting the cemetery, spending hours meditating and communing with the memory of his "dear one". Harriet's was no ordinary grave: a marble tomb with an imposing inscription was to be erected over her remains.

When all was ready, Helen, whose grief had appeared scarcely less than Mill's, summoned Haji to attend: "I—am I think I may say *we*—shall be extremely disappointed if you are not here at the time . . . We have looked forward to it as quite an epoch, and we feel strongly that we ought to be all present on the occasion. . . . As to expense I hope you will not consider that. . . . When you consider the immense expense that the whole thing has been and will be, only for the sake of showing a sentiment and a feeling, what is this comparatively small addition, to show that you share the feeling with us?"[20] There is no record of any invitation to Herbert Taylor to be present or to contribute towards the expense: as far as Helen was concerned, Herbert had behaved badly to her adored mother and was beyond the pale.

After much thought and many revisions Mill had composed yet another of those dedications which his friends found so ludicrous and which did Harriet's posthumous reputation more harm than good:

HER GREAT AND LOVING HEART
HER NOBLE SOUL
HER CLEAR POWERFUL ORIGINAL AND
COMPREHENSIVE INTELLECT
MADE HER THE GUIDE AND SUPPORT·
THE INSTRUCTOR IN WISDOM
AND THE EXAMPLE IN GOODNESS
AS SHE WAS THE SOLE EARTHLY DELIGHT
TO THOSE WHO HAD THE HAPPINESS TO BELONG TO HER
AS EARNEST FOR THE PUBLIC GOOD
AS SHE WAS GENEROUS AND DEVOTED
TO ALL WHO SURROUNDED HER
HER INFLUENCE HAS BEEN FELT
IN MANY OF THE GREATEST
IMPROVEMENTS OF THE AGE
AND WILL BE IN THOSE STILL TO COME
WERE THERE BUT A FEW HEARTS AND INTELLECTS
LIKE HERS
THIS EARTH WOULD ALREADY BECOME
THE HOPED-FOR HEAVEN[21]

The tomb became one of the sights of Avignon, a kind of shrine, as Mill must have hoped. When he was in residence visitors were expected to pay their respects to Harriet before calling on him. Visitors were few, for at Avignon Mill liked to preserve his solitude; and no one who had not responded suitably to the inscription would have dared to call. Among those who visited the cemetery in Mill's absence in England was John Stuart-Glennie, friend of the historian Henry Thomas Buckle, whose works Helen was to edit. Stuart-Glennie was genuinely moved by the inscription. "I do not know when I ever read anything that, by virtue of the intense and noble feeling expressed, made a deeper impression on me than this epitaph", he wrote. To those who had accused Harriet of being no more than Mill's mouthpiece, giving back to him his views in her own words, he replied that, if she had done no more than this, her facility "certainly implies in a woman, quite exceptional sympathies and faculties".[22]

There were not many people to mourn Harriet, apart from her sorrowing husband and daughter and, to a lesser extent, her son Haji. Fanny Stirling grieved for her; so, too, did W. J. Fox, made desolate by the loss of his beloved Eliza. "Mrs Mill gone! so lovely once! so superb ever!" he wrote to Mrs Peter Taylor, who had ignored the scandal which surrounded him. The next day he wrote to his daughter, who, like Harriet, was an upholder of women's rights: "Mrs Mill died . . . at Avignon. She would not have objected to being buried there, in the ground to which Petrarch has given a world-wide fame; of which it might (if she remains) be said, A greater than Laura is here."[23]

John Mill never ceased to mourn; yet Harriet triumphed in death as she had in life. He sublimated his grief in work, offering her the books and the public service of the future. One who understood this was Henry Solly, who had been befriended by Mill after their first meeting at Mickleham in 1830. The two men met again after Harriet's death, and Solly, then a Unitarian minister, felt that a few words of sympathy were required—not an easy task, since Mill was not a practising Christian. He did his best, then added "that there was no consolation for private grief like public usefulness; and though I cannot recall his words I can see his grateful, pleasant smile and acquiescence".[24]

CHAPTER 16

Petticoat Government

To begin with, Helen acted a triple role, as John Stuart Mill's housekeeper, secretary and catalyst. She organized the households at Blackheath and Avignon; she wrote his letters; she listened endlessly to his reminiscences of her mother, perhaps capping them occasionally with reminiscences of her own. In physical strength she was Harriet's superior, accompanying Mill on some of his strenuous walking and botanizing expeditions when they travelled abroad together. She suffered from numerous unspecified complaints; but the early tuberculosis scare was never repeated and she lived into a healthy old age.

She was as dedicated and conscientious as a secretary as she had once been as an actress; and Fanny Stirling, who loved her "dear girl" as fondly as ever, was anxious that she should not become a slave. Mrs Stirling, who retired temporarily from the stage in 1868, wrote to Helen at about that time, "I shall be sitting (most likely) literally doing nothing till *June* — & *you* killing yourself with work — I *wish* you would let me be *your* secretary — you are Mr Mill's — I should be so happy to feel I was doing *something*".[1]

What help Helen needed Mill gave her himself. As her influence over him increased it became a commonplace for his letters to open, "My daughter asks me to say". He referred to her almost always as his daughter, not his stepdaughter; but to the end of his life, on the rare occasions when they were apart, she addressed him respectfully in letters as "Dear Mr Mill". It would be tempting to think that "dearest Lily" was in fact his child, since she resembled him in industry and ability far more closely than she resembled her own father; but there is no evidence to give the faintest substance to such a charge. Sometimes she behaved towards him more like a governess than a daughter. On these occasions he responded meekly. He had adored being dominated by Harriet; he enjoyed being dominated by Helen. Naturally there were no protestations of love in his letters to his stepdaughter, only of trust and affection, but in other respects they differed very little from his letters to his wife. They showed a similar reliance on her judgement and practical ability, the same certainty that she would be interested in every detail concerning his ever-fluctuating health. He asked her advice on the content and wording of difficult letters and accepted it as an indication of what his darling would have said in the same circumstances. There were moments when he was uneasily aware that she might become too dependent on their present existence. She must not think that "I should always continue to be the only one, as I must necessarily fail you some day & I can never be at ease unless . . . you have some other resource besides me, and I am sure my own darling would feel as I do."[2]

When, however, a possible "resource" presented himself, neither Mill nor Helen took him seriously. He was Mill's disciple and German translator Theodor Gomperz, one of the elect who had been welcome at Blackheath during Harriet's lifetime. In the summer of 1862, returning from a holiday in Greece, Mill and Helen spent a few days in Vienna with Gomperz as their guide to the city; and in Vienna Gomperz fell in love with Mill's slender, striking-looking companion. When they left Vienna Mill continued, as usual, to write Gomperz warm and friendly letters, which Gomperz mistakenly construed as encouragement. He came to London during the winter with the intention of asking Helen to marry him, but, before he could pluck up the necessary courage, she left England with her stepfather for France. Might he pay them a visit at Avignon, Gomperz now inquired.

It seems difficult to believe that Helen, at least, had not realized the situation or that Mill had not guessed the reason for so unprecedented a suggestion. "Come by all means if you like," answered Mill indifferently, "though I should not for a moment have thought of proposing it to you." It was only on the rarest occasions that he invited a friend to Avignon, since he and Helen were very much occupied. When they were not writing they were out walking, regaining in the peace and solitude of the mountains the strength and mental energy to resume their busy lives in England. If, however, Gomperz was still determined to visit France, "I shall be glad to see what I can of you". He would not have been so forthcoming had not Gomperz mentioned that his motive "was chiefly to see us & I sh^d very much regret that you sh^d either be disappointed or think us unfriendly in case you sh^d see less of us than you expect".[3]

This rejection was the cause of a nervous breakdown. When Gomperz came to England in June accompanied by a friend, he was suffering from delusions of persecution. Mill, realizing that he had been both discourteous and unkind, invited the two men to dinner. The invitation was accepted, but there is no record of any visit. Instead, Gomperz wrote to Mill of ill-wishers who were maligning him. Mill replied that he was quite unaware of any such thing; neither he nor Helen had heard a word to his detriment. But, he added, there was something disturbing in Gomperz's letter: "If I rightly understand the wishes you speak of—which I sincerely hope I do not—, it does not rest with me to say anything, but that I should never willingly be the smallest obstacle to them. But you seem to ask my opinion, and if I give it sincerely, I have no choice but to say—painful as it is to say it—that I do not think you have any chance . . . ."[4]

Mill must have written the letter with Helen's connivance; and at this stage of his life Gomperz would have made an unsuitable husband. Yet, had circumstances been different and Helen had felt something more than friendship for Gomperz, she would probably have refused him. She was an ambitious young woman who had hitched her wagon to a very considerable star: she was invaluable to Mr Mill and knew it; in her eyes no man could stand comparison with him.

For some years after the débâcle they heard nothing from Theodor Gomperz. The nervous breakdown passed, as Mill's breakdowns had passed, and in 1869 they learned that he had married. "Pray accept our warm congratulations on that auspicious event", wrote Mill in evident relief, "& every possible wish for the happiness present & future of yourself & the lady who has joined her destiny to yours . . . ."[5]

Mill had emphasized to Gomperz his need for solitude, the happiness of tramping the hills of southern France alone or with Helen. But Helen understood him very well: she knew that, after the years of solitude with Harriet, he also needed company. Harriet had isolated him from his world; Helen proceeded to draw him into it again.

Mill had never quarrelled with "the Historian", as Harriet Grote dubbed her husband, as though no other historian worth his salt existed; but he had cast Mrs Grote into outer darkness. Now, after the years of enmity, this quasi-mother was received back into favour. She responded warmly and meetings of the four were frequent. Mrs Grote, never one to check her facts, described thirty-year-old Helen as "a nice, clever girl of twenty".[6] In a typical letter to Helen she wrote, "The 21st is a long way off! Nevertheless if I am alive when it arrives, to Blackheath I repair. Meanwhile, as I want to see you & the Philosopher, I propose that you sh^d dine here on Wed^y 10th. A moon will light you home, and we shall have 'good talk' . . . ."[7]

It was through the Grotes that they came to make some new friends, the young Amberleys. Viscount Amberley was the eldest son of Lord John (later Earl) Russell, twice Prime Minister; Kate, his wife, was the fourth daughter of Lord Stanley of Alderley. They were just twenty-two at the time of their marriage in 1864, a delightful, impressionable couple, both destined to die young.

Lord Amberley met Mill at dinner with the Grotes shortly before his marriage. He had been "greatly interested" in the prospect, but found, to his surprise, that the philosopher spoke very quietly, "and is not in appearance like a great man". Soon afterwards, passing through Avignon, Amberley paid a duty call at the cemetery and noted that the inscription on Harriet's monument, while "striking & most characteristic of Mill", contained "not a word of a distinctly religious character". He went on up to the house and found Mill gardening. Courteously, Mill invited him into his study for a talk. "Conversation interesting but not satisfactory, as . . . I felt as if I was detaining him from more agreeable pursuits . . . ."[8]

It seems clear that, in writing so coldly to Theodor Gomperz, Mill had not intended any slight but had merely been excessively tackless. He *was* preoccupied, and self-invited visitors were not welcome. Amberley, however, ingratiated himself with Mill next day by returning to the cemetery to copy the inscription on Harriet's tomb.

The next meeting was more propitious. The Amberleys, now married, were invited to meet Mill and Helen for a weekend at the Grotes' new house in Surrey. Mill was one of Kate Amberley's heroes. At eighteen, against her mother's will, she had read *On Liberty,* without taking much of it in; she re-read it a year later with greater understanding. The weekend talk ranged over the book, on which Kate felt qualified to express a modest opinion; on the education of the poor, in which Mill had a particular interest; on Christianity, and the undeniable fact that so few professing Christians acted according to the tenets of their faith.

Kate took an instant liking to Helen, her senior by eleven years. Mill came up to her highest expectations, and she was touched by his solicitude for her husband, who had recently been defeated in a Parliamentary by-election for the City of Westminster. Mill went out of his way to praise one of Amberley's election speeches which had been damned in the press and urged him to stand again. The chief fault the newspapers had found in her husband, Kate explained to Helen, "is not having made up his mind decidedly & finally on all the great questions of legislation . . . in detail. I should think a man who had done so, at twenty-two, must either be a humbug or unreflective . . . ."[9]

Her meeting with Mill, so she wrote in her journal, had been the greatest pleasure, "so edifying & made one feel so hopeful & strong of the use one could be in the world".[10] She was overjoyed, too, to think that the great man appreciated her husband's qualities: Mill's commendation was of more value than praise from any other quarter.

Harriet Grote was delighted with her weekend's work. The Amberleys, she told Helen, "were *enchanted* wi *their* visit & Lady A quite 'cottoned' wi *you.* I am glad you both were pleased wi your stay here. *I* enjoyed it very completely in spite of the *bad* weather. 'Historian' gone to London . . . ."[11]

It was to the Amberleys that Mrs Grote had described John Mill's mother as a stupid housemaid of a woman. They had not, of course, met either his mother or his wife, but now they had their first glimpse of Mill's adoration, of Helen's sense of guilt. "I am such a bad interpreter of my mother, I hardly like speaking of her", Helen confessed when she and Mill were alone with their new friends. Thereupon Mill "stood up & said with tears in his eyes 'No, no one could interpret her, she was above every one & inspired every one.' "[12]

As a token of friendship Kate Amberley gave Helen a little dog, which must have succeeded in fraternizing with the reigning Blackheath cat. She was never quite sure how her invitations would be received. When, for example, she arranged a picnic luncheon in Richmond Park for the Russells, Harriet Grote and other friends, she wrote rather timidly to Helen, "It seems a foolish thing I am going to ask you (who are a hermit) to do—but nevertheless I like to give you the option."[13]

Whether or not Mill could find the time or inclination to attend a picnic, however sophisticated, we do not know; but there were other occasions on which he was glad to accept the Amberleys' hospitality, more especially when he had recruited them into the women's suffrage movement.

Helen was exceedingly good at arranging congenial parties. In June 1866, for instance, she wrote to Elizabeth Garrett (later Mrs Garrett Anderson) inviting her to meet the Amberleys. "Lady Amberley...takes so much interest in your plans for opening out the medical profession for women, that I think you would like to explain them to her yourself and would find her an intelligent and zealous co-operator."[14]

Kate Amberley had already been taken by Helen and Frances Power Cobbe, the plump and genial suffragist and anti-vivisectionist, to hear Elizabeth Garrett lecture on physiology. "Every one cared more for it than I did", she confessed in her journal; but she was far from pleased when Helen, obviously convinced that she had not understood a word, "wrote me a letter...pointing out the points as if I had been too stupid to seize them". Nevertheless, she was eager to meet Miss Garrett, whose fight to enter the medical profession was an inspiration to them all. She and Amberley went by train from Charing Cross to Blackheath, where Mill met them with his India House friend W. T. Thornton. They were to have gone for a walk, but it rained, and so they sat in the drawing-room until dinner at six o'clock. There were other guests present, "Mr Herbert Spencer (the philosopher) and Mr Hill, (an editor of the Daily News) and Miss Garrett.... She and I had been asked on purpose to meet one another, as I wanted to know her... delightful general talk, it was most pleasant." At the end of the evening John Mill and Helen sent the Amberleys and Elizabeth Garrett, still talking animatedly, back to London in their carriage.

On another visit to Blackheath the talk centred on politics. Mill spoke with warmth about the Jamaica problem, and they also discussed the Irish question. The conversation then turned to the idealistic young couple's dislike of luxury and ostentation; and when, Kate noted, "I said we had been called strange people for not liking it, [Mill] said 'it is much better to establish a character for strangeness, there is nothing like it, then one can do what one likes'."[15]

The Amberleys gave the ultimate proof of their affection for Mill and his stepdaughter in 1872, after the birth of their third child. Kate wrote to Helen "Do you mind god-mothering my little boy. I had always somehow counted on a girl to be called 'Cordelia Helen' but as it has turned out a 'Bertrand William' and a girl may never come will you give him your blessing and guidance? We hesitated to ask such a favour of Mr Mill otherwise I wish he too cd. have been godfather—for there is no one in whose steps I would rather see a boy of mine following in ever such a humble way, than in Mr Mill's."[16]

Helen replied that she would be pleased to be the baby's godmother and would take as much interest in him as she would in a girl, "for one of the sweet and attractive things about children is that one finds just as much earnestness and sweetness and purity about the boys as energy and courage about the girls, till alas! they fall under the influence of the vulgar world". She was interested in all Kate's children, she said, and only hoped her frequent absences from England would not prove an obstacle to "accepting the Godmothership". She had discussed the question with her stepfather, whose views on orthodox religion had made Kate hesitate. "Mr Mill says if you wish it he does not think that it would conflict with his opinions to enter into that relation ...."[17]

Kate and her husband, who had eschewed religion themselves, had no wish for a conforming godfather, and Kate wrote delightedly to Helen, "Many thanks to you & Mr Mill for your kindness about my little Bertrand whom I henceforth associate with you both with a devout wish that in years to come he may prove worthy of the sponsors by following their example & acting up to their high ideal of life."[18] Mill would have been vastly pleased had he lived to learn of his godson's intellectual distinction and courage, though he might well have been perturbed by some of the details of his personal life.

Frances Power Cobbe, like Kate Amberley, was one of Mill's female devotees. She found his behaviour towards Helen "beautiful to witness, and a fine exemplification of his own theories of the rightful position of women". She loved his courtly manners and his playful sense of fun, which resembled her own. He urged her to speak more on the subject of women's rights, and "used jestingly to say that my laugh was worth—I forget how much! to the cause'. One evening at dinner with their mutual friends the Peter Taylors she sat next to him, and, although she was embarrassed by his perpetual nervous twitchings, "I never enjoyed my dinner-neighbourhood more". They laughed heartily at one another's "little jokes" and he came to her rescue in a dinner-table argument. As the only Tory among radicals, she was slightly out of her element. "Ah, Miss Cobbe is a bitter Conservative", Mrs Taylor declared. " 'Not a *bitter* one', said Mr Mill. 'Miss Cobbe is a Conservative. I am sorry for it; but Miss Cobbe is never bitter.' "[19] Could gallantry or little jokes go further?

There were some people—Charles Eliot Norton was one—who found Helen's presence as hostess overpowering. Towards her opinions, "which are decidedly pronounced", Mill "exhibits a deference which suggests an element of weakness".[20] Norton would have been shocked to realize that Mill enjoyed being dominated by Helen, for whose views he had immense, almost obsequious, respect. His submissiveness seemed to Norton, as to certain others, to emphasize the womanish side of his character. The quality of his voice added to this impression: it was distinguished, so a visiting American journalist noted, by "the delicate and almost womanly gentleness of its tones".[21]

Norton was by no means alone in his resentment of Helen's influence. She was not over-sensitive and she revelled in her power; but she never sought, as her mother had sought, to detach Mill from his friends. One to whom Harriet had shown particular animosity was W. T. Thornton, who had kindly agreed to act as a trustee of her much-debated marriage settlement. In 1854 Thornton had published a volume of verse and dedicated one of the poems to Mill. Harriet wrote her husband a scathing report on the book and its author, who, so she inferred, was simply seeking to promote his own interests by dedicating an inferior poem to a distinguished man. Mill, as always, bowed to her opinion, this time with a hint of reservation:

> I do not think what you say too severe—he has suddenly plumped down to the place of a quite common person in my estimation, when I thought he was a good deal better. . . . His misjudgment of me is so far less than you supposed, as he has not put in any flattery *proprement dit,* but the fact itself is a piece of flattery which he must have thought would be agreeable or he would not have taken so impertinent a liberty. There are so few people of whom one can think even as well as I did of him, that I feel this a loss, & am like you angry with him for it . . . .[22]

Released from Harriet's view of Thornton, Mill reverted to his earlier good opinion and, under Helen's rule, his India House friend was invited both to Blackheath and to Avignon. Mill, who had written Thornton one of the most affecting of letters when Harriet died, now described him as "a person I particularly respect and like. In perfect candour, sincerity, and singleness of mind, few men come near him . . . ."[23] In 1869, when the Avignon house was being modernized and enlarged under Helen's direction, Mill wrote to tell him of the improvements she was making: these included a bathroom, a covered walk for exercise in bad weather, and a herbarium for his botanical specimens. "Helen says *your* room is not finished yet, because as she is an architect & master mason all in one, she is carrying on the improvements very slowly, not letting the attention to them interfere too much with her other work. . . . You will not be surprised to learn that among the other additions there is a Puss-House. Altogether we are very comfortable, & only wish everybody could be as comfortable as we are . . . ."[24]

The years between her mother's death and her stepfather's were certainly the happiest of Helen's life.

CHAPTER 17

A Victorian Scandal

At Avignon, Mill and his stepdaughter worked with energy and diligence. Helen wrote many of Mill's letters for him, in a clear, emphatic style reminiscent of his own. Mill himself was editing his *Dissertations and Discussions* and preparing new works, of which three are relevant here: *Considerations on Representative Government, The Subjection of Women,* and the posthumously published *Autobiography.*

The Subjection, the large-scale work which Mill had planned with Harriet, was actually written in 1861, the year in which his *Considerations* appeared, but it was not published until 1869. In the *Considerations* he linked together the political theories he had expressed at different times in his life and, among other things, confirmed his support of his friend Thomas Hare's system of proportional representation. In his argument for universal suffrage he claimed that the question of sex was irrelevant: every human being had the same need for, and interest in, good government, an equal right to exercise the vote. If anything, women needed the vote more than men: as members of the weaker sex they were more dependent than men on the laws of society: "No arrangement of the suffrage ... can be permanently satisfactory, in which any person or class is peremptorily excluded; in which the electoral privilege is not open to all persons of full age who desire to obtain it." He would not, however, allow any one to vote who could not read, write, "or perform the common operations of arithmetic". It would, he thought, be a simple matter to arrange for every potential voter, on arrival at the polling station, to be required in the presence of the registrar to "copy a sentence from an English book, and perform a sum in the rule of three; and to secure, by fixed rules and complete publicity, the honest application of so very simple a test".[1] In the interests of the registrar and his staff, if not of the voters, it seems fortunate that this demand was never implemented!

In 1865 Mill was asked to edit the literary remains of Henry Thomas Buckle. This was the year of his election to Parliament and so he passed the task to his stepdaughter, with total confidence in her ability. Three years earlier the forty-year-old historian, who was travelling in the Middle East collecting material for his monumental *The History of Civilisation,* had died of typhus in Damascus. Only two of the projected series of volumes had yet been published, the first in 1857, the second in 1861; but he had left behind a formidable array of papers and notes.

Buckle had been accompanied on his tour by his friend Stuart-Glennie, the man who was so impressed with the inscription on Harriet Mill's tomb; also by two boys, aged fifteen and twelve at the time of his death, Edward and Alfred Huth, the sons of close friends. It was an educational tour for the Huth boys, who were sent back to England when their mentor died.

Among Buckle's friends and admirers were two of the pioneers of girls' schools, Miss Emily Shirreff and her younger sister Mrs Maria Grey. (With Kate Amberley's mother, the Dowager Lady Stanley of Alderley, and Miss Mary Garney, they founded the Girls' Public Day School Company (later, Trust), which launched thirty-eight schools. When the future of the twenty which still existed as Direct Grant schools was threatened by the Labour Government's educational policy in 1976 the schools became independent.) Emily Shirreff, a dutiful daughter to a demanding widowed father, was nearly forty when he died, leaving her free to pursue her own interests. Buckle, who was seven years her junior, encouraged her to study and to write the book which made her name in educational circles, *The Intellectual Education of Women*. Emily Shirreff hero-worshipped Buckle, who was very attractive to women, and she was deeply distressed by his premature death. She and his other friends were anxious to see the publication of as much as possible of his remaining works.

Longmans Green agreed to publish; Buckle's friends and some of his relations were ready with information, although his sister, Mrs Allatt, registered disapproval of the project. A preface and biographical sketch were necessary and these were entrusted to Emily Shirreff. She was delighted to accept the commission, so Helen told Mrs Huth, despite "the very low terms offered by Mr Longman".[2] Since she was unaccustomed to work of this kind, Mill and Helen offered to assist her in any way they could.

Miss Shirreff's reaction had been optimistic, but, during the summer of 1869, she became oddly evasive. She had been unwell the previous winter, she explained, and unable to write and was not at all sure when she would be able to proceed. "We must be patient until she feels able to work satisfactorily",[3] wrote Helen to their mutual friend.

Some more evasive letters followed before Emily Shirreff delievered her ultimatum. "You will have heard . . . that she has resigned the plan of writing a biographical sketch", Helen told Mrs Huth in October. The work had apparently proved too exhausting, and "the materials are insufficient".[4]

Like many of her long-lived contemporaries, Emily Shirreff was frequently ill, but neither Mill nor Helen believed that she was being entirely frank. After some cautious questioning, she admitted that her researches had placed her in a dilemma: "I trust that nothing in your own experience may enable you to measure the suffering I have gone through before coming to this conclusion. Many a cherished recollection is embittered, many a letter, once a treasured possession, never can bear the same meaning again."[5] She hoped most earnestly that none of Buckle's friends, Mrs Huth in particular, need ever learn the results of her perusal of his journals.

This hint stimulated Helen to ask for some elucidation. Miss Shirreff wrote again, in the strictest confidence, offering a strangely inadequate reason. In the spring of 1858 Buckle had delivered a brilliant and much applauded lecture, "The Influence of Women", at the Royal Institution; this, so his friends understood, was spoken extempore. He had undertaken to reproduce the lecture as an article for *Fraser's Magazine* and, as though to underline its spontaneity, had asked Miss Shirreff and her sister to take notes. Miss Shirreff now realized that Buckle had not spoken extempore: he had learnt the lecture off by heart and had prepared it beforehand, in part if not in whole, for the press. "The pitiful vanity that could care for such a triumph sinks to insignificance beside the want of Truth, and yet that one so gifted, one seemingly so great should have stooped so far to win applause is sorrowful enough."[6] This seemed no great crime to Mill, whom Helen consulted. He assured her that many a lecture written in advance might still be said to have been spoken extempore, because of the differences introduced during the actual delivery.

Buckle had, of course, been guilty of some duplicity, in asking his friends to take notes, but this in itself did not seem sufficient reason for abandoning the project. Emily Shirreff was now obliged to reveal the whole truth. When Buckle had agreed to take the Huths' young sons to the Middle East, she wrote to Helen, he had told a friend "that he intended having a Nubian mistress when he got to Egypt & insisted on it, against his friend's earnest remonstration". Miss Shirreff's informant did not know if Buckle had carried out this threat, but "related another dark fact". This was that he had invited a woman who lived in England, "so often referred to in the journals (the name is generally erased)", to join him, "which she refused to do". Mrs Grey had pursued the inquiry on her unmarried sister's behalf and had discovered that this was all too true: Buckle had indeed had a mistress. This was naturally intensely shocking to two Victorian ladies of the utmost rectitude and integrity, especially so to Emily Shirreff, who had been romantically attached to him. She had finally decided to relinquish her task, she confessed, because if this charge were ever levelled against him, "I no longer dared to contradict anything".[7] She would have been in no position to contradict such an allegation. Buckle's biographer quotes a letter, which Mrs Grey almost certainly saw, to a young widow, Elizabeth Faunch, explaining that he might remain in the Middle East for several years: "Would you, dear, come out to me if I were to stay here? In such case I should of course make myself responsible for ... every ... expense you incurred, either directly or indirectly... With the best love of your very affectionate Harry."[8]

Mill and Helen had been hoping to persuade Miss Shirreff to change her mind. They had heard a rumour, so Helen told her, in a letter drafted by Mill, that Buckle had intended to take the Huth boys to Vienna to meet their mother; and that, had he proposed setting up house with a woman, he would not have done so until he had parted with the boys. She did not think, however, that Mrs Huth should be kept in ignorance of his intentions. As Mrs Huth "is bringing up her sons in a strong reverence for Mr Buckle", she added, "it seems only right that she should know something that concerns herself and them".[9]

Miss Shirreff replied with dignity that she saw no reason why Mrs Huth should be told: "I feel it to be needless pain". The boys themselves (one of them was later to write a life of Buckle) knew nothing of any plans he might have made. They had already written their own recollection of the journey, "& it is utterly insignificant".[10] For her own part, she could not—would not—write a biography. Instead, she agreed to give Helen a personal sketch of Buckle as she remembered him, for use as background material, and to allow her to see some of his letters. She asked her to mention as few names as possible, particularly of women, "for it is one of the things he has always been tormented with, that none but women valued him".[11] She had more letters in her possession, written during their years of friendship, but these, she insisted, were strictly personal and contained nothing of general interest.

Helen dealt as expeditiously as possible with a project which eventually burgeoned into three stout volumes. (*The Miscellaneous and Posthumous Works of Henry Thomas Buckle*, ed. with a biographical introduction by Helen Taylor, Longmans Green, 1872). She submitted her biographical introduction to Miss Shirreff, who was touched by a reference to the help which she and her sister had given him, but saddened by a mention of the notorious Royal Institution lecture, "which has clouded for ever my recollections of a bright and joyous time".[12]

Emily Shirreff was too sensible a woman to allow memories, however painful, to cloud the rest of her busy, useful life. Buckle's biographer has suggested that, when they knew one another, she "was too busy improving the minds of young ladies to find time for romance, but if [he] had lived longer he might have married her".[13] There was undoubtedly some understanding between them. During a brief period when she acted as Mistress of the women's college Hitchen (later Girton), one of the students remembered that she had told her that they were engaged. It seems a pity that she ever had to learn to her distress of the existence of Mrs Faunch. In 1872, aware of Mill's sympathetic interest in the education of girls, she sent Helen a copy of the prospectus of the National Union for Improving the Education of Women of All Classes, with news of the first of the Girls' Public Day Schools, which was opened in Chelsea the following year.

By that time Helen's work on Buckle's papers was completed. She had endured a brief period of panic and alarm in 1870, during the Franco-Prussian War. With her stepfather she was staying with the Amberleys at their country house when she learned that the French Government of National Defence had postponed the forthcoming elections. This action, Mill thought, might prolong the war and, in the event, troops might be billeted in the vacant house in Avignon. Helen spent a sleepless night imagining her precious manuscript at the mercy of careless soldiers, and, after talking the matter over, persuaded Mill that they should leave England the following day. They could travel via Switzerland, and Mill, who, so Helen feared, might be mistaken for a Prussian spy, should remain in Geneva while she and the personal maid who had accompanied her to England proceeded to St Véran alone. This important matter settled, the whole party went for a long walk. After dinner, Kate Amberley recorded, "Mr Mill read us Shelley's Ode to Liberty & he got quite excited & moved over it rocking backwards & forwards & nearly choking with emotion; he said himself: 'it is almost too much for one' Miss Taylor read the Hymn to Intellectual Beauty but in rather a theatrical voice not as pleasant as Mill's . . . ."[14] Helen could never forget that she had once been "Miss Trevor".

The rescue operation was successful. Helen retrieved her bulky manuscript intact, collected Mill in Geneva, and together they returned in triumph to England.

CHAPTER 18

Mill for Westminster

The overriding reason for Mill's decision to entrust Helen with Buckle's papers was the invitation which reached him in March 1865. "To be the representative of West[minste]r is an honour to which no one can be insensible", he wrote in the course of a letter to a radical politician, James Beal, who had invited him on behalf of his fellow liberals to stand for Parliament. (The radical members of the House of Commons never formed a distinct party but subsequently became the advanced section of the Liberal Party.) He accepted on certain conditions which, had he not been so highly respected, would have sent James Beal in search of another candidate. If he could be of use, "it could only be by devoting myself . . . to the same subjects which have employed my habitual thoughts out of Parl^t. I therefore could not undertake the charge of any of your local business": he would not stoop to canvass, address the usual spate of meetings or spend any money on his campaign. His views were well known; "& until I am convinced that they are wrong, these & no others are the opinions that I must act on".[1]

Mill's conditions were accepted and the invitation renewed. He signified consent, and at once an election committee was formed and a fund was raised to defray his expenses. Whether he was elected or not, he was pleased to discover that something had immediately been gained: "what are thought the most out-of-the-way of all my opinions, have been, and are, discussed and canvassed from one end of the country to the other, and some of them (especially women's voting) are obtaining many unexpected adhesions".[2] Several years earlier—in 1859—Mill had written to the same friend—the social reformer Edwin Chadwick—that "one of the most conservative as well as most liberal provisions in a reform bill would be to give the franchise to all women who fulfil the rating or other conditions required of men".[3] In local elections—though not in the cities—women taxpayers were by this time entitled to vote, but not, of course, in Parliamentary elections.

Among Mill's most fervent supporters was a group of women who were already compaigning for their rights. Frances Power Cobbe was one: in 1862, with her paper "University Degrees for Women", which she read at a congress of the National Association for the Promotion of Social Science, she

145

had fired the opening shot in the fight for higher education for women. Mill had been so impressed with this paper that he had written to a friend, the future Postmaster-General Professor Henry Fawcett, that the admission of women to university degrees was now "almost une *cause gagnée*".[4] (He was wrong. In 1878 London University became the first to open its degrees to women; Oxford accorded them full membership and degrees in 1920; Cambridge not until 1948.)

The most militant educationist was Emily Davies, a demure-looking woman whose appearance belied her strong, resilient character. Miss Davies waged a successful campaign to enable girls to compete with boys in the university local examinations, a vital step towards the establishment of Girton College, with which she was to be so closely associated. Mill was enthusiastic. If, he told a correspondent, the examinations "are useful and necessary means of rendering education efficient in the case of men, they must be equally so in the case of women".[5] When a Schools' Inquiry Commission was set up in 1864 to consider middle-class education, the wily Emily Davies managed to insinuate girls' schools into its terms of reference simply because the authorities had not expressly stipulated that they should be omitted. If Mill was elected to Parliament—or even if he was not—he would be an important witness when, as he promised, he gave evidence before the Commission.

Barbara Leigh Smith (Madame Bodichon), a keen suffragist and one of the founders of Girton College, was another of Mill's most ardent helpers. So, too, was Bessie Rayner Parkes (Madame Louis Belloc), mother of two famous children, Hilaire Belloc and the novelist Marie Belloc Lowndes, and the founder and editor of the *English Woman's Journal* (from 1866, the *Englishwoman's Review*). In 1860 she had written of their hero,

> There is no name in England which carries so much weight, whether it be at Oxford or Cambridge, or in the two Houses of Legislature, as that of John Stuart Mill. Among all classes of thinking men all over the country there is no one whose opinion of the right or wrong of a political measure is so much respected... His books can never be popular, yet no man's works have affected the people more deeply. His profound treatises and essays... affect indirectly every individual, however ignorant.... What he has written is founded on reason, and stands like a solid rock amidst the shifting sands of public opinion....[6]

Whether or not they could understand them, she advised all serious-minded young women at least to make an effort to read Mill's books.

These women and some fifty others had formed the Kensington Society, which met regularly at the house of Mrs Manning (later first Mistress of Girton). Most of them had already been involved in the agitation for the introduction of a Married Women's Property Bill to relieve married women property-owners from the necessity of allowing their husbands complete control of their belongings. Helen Taylor was now invited by Emily Davies, secretary of the Kensington Society, to join the exclusive circle. "None but intellectual women are admitted", she was informed, "and therefore it is not likely to become a merely puerile or gossipping Society."[7]

The society which Helen now joined had no incentive for idle gossip. Among its members were the pioneers of medical training for women, Elizabeth Garrett and Sophia Jex-Blake; the pioneer headmistresses Frances Mary Buss and Dorothea Beale; Jessie Boucherett, advocate of women's right to employment; and a writer, Isa Craig (Mrs Knox), whose appointment in 1860 as assistant secretary to the Association for the Promotion of Social Science was a landmark in feminine history. Henry Fawcett "thinks it is a great thing", wrote Mill to Helen, "and so indeed it is. He says it was done by the most strenuous canvass by Miss Parkes and others & that now everybody is glad of it, as the duties are done most admirably." Professor Fawcett persuaded him "to attach more importance than I did to what Miss Parkes & her set are doing. He says the E[nglish] W[oman]'s Journal increases in sale & has got into places where it was scouted at first...."[8]

At the second meeting of the Kensington Society, held in 1865 soon after Mill's acceptance of the invitation to stand for Parliament, Barbara Bodichon read a paper advocating the extension of the suffrage to women. It was so well received that she wanted to go ahead at once and found a women's suffrage society. Emily Davies, always cautious, held her back: the time, she thought, was not yet ripe.

These were the women who were eager to see their champion in Parliament. They were anything but passive supporters. Emily Davies, Barbara Bodichon, Bessie Rayner Parkes and Isa Craig drove round Westminster in a hired carriage plastered with placards soliciting votes for Mill. "We called it giving Mr Mill our moral support", remarked Emily Davies, "but there was some suspicion that we might rather be doing him harm, as one of our friends told us he had heard him described as 'the man who wants to have girls in Parliament'."[9]

Mill remained aloof from the political arena: he did not come to London until polling day was little more than a week ahead. "I do wish they would bring him in without his stirring from his own house",[10] wrote Kate Amberley to Helen Taylor. Helen was pessimistic about the outcome: "I do not think it possible that he can really be returned for Westminster (in spite of the efforts of kind friends, among whom you can count in the first rank) but I am sure that he did right not to decline to stand for we receive every day proofs that his mere candidature is producing a good effect on people's minds...."[11]

With no great expectation of success, Mill was gratified by the publicity given to his views and the consequent increase in the sale of his books. As he wrote to Thomas Hare, whose system of proportional representation was, of course, aimed at fair play for minority groups: "my Westminster supporters are all busy finding what they can say to defend their candidate on the points of representation of minorities and women's suffrage. Certainly this election affair is a better *propaganda* for all my political opinions than I might have obtained for many years...."[12]

When at length he condescended to visit the constituency, Mill made a total of two speeches. To the electors of Westminster he said, "I am not here because I propose myself but because others propose me; & I hope you do not suppose that I think all the fine things about myself which have been said & written about me with so much exaggeration but with a strength and depth of kind feeling for which I can never be sufficiently grateful". He stood before them as "the candidate of advanced Liberalism". He had issued no election address but was willing to answer questions, although not about his religious beliefs, which were personal to himself. In fact, he answered questions which had not been put to him. "What obliged me to say anything about women's voting, or about representation of minorities? Would any of you have thought of questioning me on these points? Not one"; but it "did not suit with my idea of plain dealing to keep any of them back".[13]

This was frank speaking, but the electors accepted it in the right spirit. The second meeting consisted of working-class men, who were not yet enfranchised. (Working men in towns received the Parliamentary franchise under the Reform Bill of 1867.) Helen, whose views were becoming more left-wing than Mill's, was very much in favour of such a meeting. "I like him to address the working men", she wrote to Kate Amberley, "and I think his doing so will produce impression on them that will be of use in the future...."[14] In her enthusiasm she had overlooked some words he had written in 1859 in his *Thoughts on Parliamentary Reform:* "Of the few points on which the English as a people are entitled to the moral pre-eminence with which they are accustomed to compliment themselves at the expense of other nations the one of greatest importance is that the higher classes do not lie; and the lower, though mostly habitual liars, are ashamed of lying." Mill and Harriet together had planned the *Thoughts,* and, had she lived to see it completed, Harriet would undoubtedly have blue-pencilled this emotive, reactionary sentence. Mill was now asked if it was true that he had written it. He paused for a moment, his nervous twitch much in evidence, then answered calmly, "I did." Instead of the expected catcalls and abuse, his words were greeted with a burst of spontaneous applause. When the noise had died down, the trade union leader George Odger rose to his feet. He said without equivocation that "the working classes had no desire not to be told of their faults; they wanted friends, not flatterers.... And to this the meeting heartily responded."[15] Mill was, perhaps, the only man in the country whose reputation would have remained untarnished in such circumstances.

Great was the rejoicing, especially among his women supporters, when he was elected. "I must write one line to say how very delighted I am, more so I dare say than you are", wrote Kate Amberley to Helen, who was secretly dreading the additional time they would have to spend in England. All Mill's admirers "must feel pleased at such a triumph & acquisition to the H. of

Commons." Amberley had been beaten again at the polls, but "you should have seen how delighted [he] was, much more pleased than if *he* had been elected for this he said was of national importance".[16]

The press, too, was laudatory. "Nothing could be more creditable to a body of electors than the aspiration to be represented by the greatest English scientific politician of our age", declared *The Times,* a paper which was to give him a distinctly unflattering obituary. The *Morning Star* was sure that it would be difficult "to name any Englishman, living or dead, who could justly be called Mr Mill's superior".[17] Clearly, the editors did not appreciate how tenaciously Mill would hold to his chosen course.

It was an unnerving experience to hear and watch Mill speak. He twitched, paused and hesitated, weighing every sentence, and, although he improved with experience, he never became a compelling speaker: it was the content, not the delivery, of his speeches which made its mark. Kate Amberley learned that his first speech (it was on the Cattle Diseases Bill, not the most inspiring of topics) was ill-prepared, inaudible and boring. But when she herself listened to him for the first time from the seclusion of the ladies' gallery she heard every word. He spoke on Gladstone's Reform Bill, enumerating its many possibilities, and when he sat down he was cheered.

He was waiting for a suitable opportunity to introduce the subject of women's suffrage. It came after a speech by Disraeli in the House of Commons on 27 April 1866: "Where you allow women to form part of the other estate of the realm—peeresses in their own right, for example—where you allow a woman not only to hold land, but to be a lady of the manor and hold legal courts—where a woman by law may be a churchwarden and overseer of the poor—I do not see . . . on what reasons, if you come to right, she has not a right to vote."

Unfortunately, by the time he came to office in 1867, Disraeli had retreated from his advanced position; but, to Mill, to some of his colleagues, and to the Kensington Society, it had been a call to action. First, however, they had to formulate their aims. Should they ask for the franchise for women on exactly the same terms as men or with certain reservations? The Society, on Emily Davies's advice, thought their demands should be limited. Barbara Bodichon therefore wrote to Helen Taylor to know if she thought her stepfather would be prepared to present a petition in Parliament. She did not suggest that all women would have the vote—only women house- or property-owners. "I should not like to start a petition or make any movement without knowing what you think and Mr J. S. Mill thought expedient at this time. . . Could you draft a petition?"[18]

Helen, who wrote many of the letters which her stepfather signed, was perfectly capable of drafting a petition, but thought that this one should be a joint affair. With a Reform Bill under discussion, petitions would flow in. John Bright, for example, was already agitating for an extension of the franchise, though not to women; and Mill himself thought that a women's petition would help.

A few days earlier, Helen, who enjoyed telling Mill's correspondents exactly what he thought of them, had written on his behalf to a Mrs Caroline Liddell, who had confessed that, while she supported the idea of women's suffrage, she was not strong-minded enough to contemplate taking an active part in electoral proceedings. Helen, in Mill's name, suggested that if she wanted to help the movement she should draw up a petition, obtain as many signatures as she could, and send it him for presentation in Parliament. She then proceeded to administer a severe trouncing:

> I am glad to be able to say that I know several members of Parliament who wish to grant the franchise without distinction of sex, but I know many more who would be ashamed to refuse it if it were quietly and steadily demanded by women themselves. I am sorry to find that you disclaim being strong-minded, because I believe strength of mind to be one of the noblest gifts that any rational creature ... can possess, and the best measure of our efficiency for working in the cause of truth. But such mental powers and energies as we any of us do possess, ought to be employed in striving to remove the evils with which circumstances have made us acquainted; and a woman who is a taxpayer is the most natural and most suitable advocate of the political enfranchisement of women ....[19]

Mill, of course, put his signature to this letter.

Helen now replied in her own name to Barbara Bodichon: "I think, that while a Reform Bill is under discussion and petitions are being presented to parliament from various classes asking for representation or protesting against disenfranchisement, it is very desirable that women who wish for political enfranchisement should say so ...." She was well aware that they would have no chance of success; but that was no reason why they "should not ask for what they will never obtain till they have asked for it very long". The most important thing,

> is to commence the first humble beginnings of an agitation for which reasons can be given that are in harmony with the political ideas of English people in general. No idea is so universally accepted and acceptable in England as that taxation & representation ought to go together, and people in general will be much more willing to listen to the assertion that single women & widows of property have been unjustly overlooked and left out from the privileges to which their property entitles them, than to the much more startling general proposition that sex is not a proper ground for distinction in political rights. It seems to me therefore that a petition asking for the admission to the franchise of all women holding the requisite property qualification would be highly desirable now, quite independently of any immediate results to follow

from it ... If a tolerably voluminously signed petition can be got up my father will gladly undertake to present it ....[20]

So far so good. The crux of the problem was whether "all women holding the requisite property qualification" should be taken to mean only widows and spinsters whose property was under their control, or should be seen as including married women, who were entitled to their money and property even if they were not allowed to dispose of it, since it legally belonged to their husbands. Emily Davies, quite apart from her natural propensity to advance with prudence, was anxious not to embroil herself in anything which might jeopardize her schemes for women's education: she therefore continued to counsel a limited demand. After a great deal of cogitation and correspondence, a form of words was devised in such general terms that they might be taken to apply to all or only to a section of the women concerned.

Mill had told Madam Bodichon that he could make do with a hundred signatures, but she was determined to get a great many more. She set up a small committee, composed of herself, Emily Davies, Elizabeth Garrett, Jessie Boucherett and Rosamond Hill, the sister of the housing reformer Octavia Hill. The committee, which met in Elizabeth Garrett's house, collected the signatures of nearly 1,500 women: among them, Harriet Martineau; Josephine Butler, whose own crusade was to rock the women's movement; Mary Somerville, the scientific writer who gave her name to Somerville College, Oxford; Emily Shirreff and her sister Maria Grey; and Mrs Peter Taylor, who had remained staunch to W. J. Fox and Eliza Flower in their hour of need. Elizabeth Garrett's sister Millicent, the future suffragist leader, was too young to sign. She was only nineteen and in December 1866 became engaged to Mill's friend Henry Fawcett, who, although blind, was an active member of Parliament. "So we may now rely upon his being kept in the path of duty",[21] wrote Emily Davies to Helen.

The document was to be presented as the Petition of "Barbara L. S. Bodichon and others"; it was to be taken by Madame Bodichon and Miss Davies by hired cab to Westminster and solemnly handed over to John Stuart Mill. But the hard work and the excitement had proved too much for Barbara Bodichon, who was ill on the fateful day—7 June 1866—and so Elizabeth Garrett took her place. Westminster Hall was filled with a crowd of chattering men but there was no sign of their quarry. Henry Fawcett appeared and, when they approached him, sent his secretary in search of Mill. The young women, embarrassed by the curious stares at their cumbersome burden, carried the petition roll to the only other women in sight, who was selling apples near the entrance. She obligingly concealed the roll under her stall, then asked what was in it. When they explained she took it out and added her own signature before returning it to its hiding place. At that moment Mill came hurrying in, and the petition was produced for his inspection. "Ah, this I can brandish with effect",[22] he cried.

Mill presented the petition the day the House went into committee on the

Representation of the People Bill. He followed it up with a motion for a return "showing the number of freeholders and householders in England and Wales who, fulfilling the conditions of property or rental prescribed by law as the qualifications for the electoral franchise, are excluded from the franchise by reason of their sex". The wording was purposely vague; but members took it to refer only to widows and spinsters.

The House received both the petition and the motion with mild interest: petitions and motions were common enough; they did not necessarily demand immediate action. With the press it was different: they made a considerable stir. The *Law Times* found both petition and motion eminently reasonable: "The claim is merely that single women who are independent householders and have the same qualification as other electors should be permitted to vote.... And wherefore should they not? Having given to the question much thought... we are unable to suggest a single sound objection.... We heartily wish success to the endeavour of Mr Mill."

The *Saturday Review,* however, shed crocodile tears:

> We have no right to bamboozle any one—least of all... women—by pretending to give them a sugar plum and really giving them a dose of physic. What does voting imply? It implies solicitation, dunning, reproaching, humbugging, and cajolery. Why are respectable women, because they happen to be spinsters or widows, and live in houses of their own, to be exposed to the impertinent intrusion of agents, canvassers, and candidates; to be besieged alternately by the adulation of fools, and by the insolence of bullies; to be subjected to the domiciliary visits of... rowdies.... Let any man who knows the history of contested elections... ask himself whether he would voluntarily consign them to such humiliations....

An anonymous woman contributor to *Blackwood's Magazine* was positively vituperative: "If Mr Mill perseveres in his foolish delusion—if he drags our names, which are spotless, and not for vulgar mouthing, into schedules and statistics—if his uncalled championship continues to expose us to the smartness of newspaper articles, and the gibes of honourable members ... not even certain sacred words of true love and reverence which he was uttered in his lifetime ... will deliver him from our indignation and resentment."[23]

All the same, any publicity was better than none; and Helen Taylor, striking while the iron of the petition was hot, wrote an article, "The Claim of Englishwomen to the Suffrage Constitutionally Considered", for the *Westminster Review.*

The members of the petition comittee felt that they had worked to good effect. "It is very encouraging", wrote Emily Davies to Helen. "No doubt we owe [the petition's reception] to the admirable manner in which the case was stated. But still, some time ago, it would have provoked laughter I suppose, however stated." She was uneasy about the lack of precision used in defining the categories of women: a decision on this point was essential, for further petitions were to be drawn up and submitted as soon as sufficient signatures had been obtained. "The case of married women complicates things very much. Ought we not to come to some decision about the line to take about it? Do you think it better to leave it open, as in Mr Mill's motion & in our own Petition, or in future, to limit our demand to unmarried women and widows? The limitation seems to strengthen our position so very much with most people, that one feels tempted to adopt it, if it could be done honestly & without embarrassing future action." She wondered if it would be better for the petitions to be signed by women alone or by men as well as women. What did Helen and her stepfather think? Miss Davies wanted to thank Mr Mill "deeply and warmly" for all he was doing. "One feels an almost irrepressible impulse to try to tell him & then we are held back by feeling that it would be an impertinence." To Helen, too, she was deeply grateful. "I think you are perhaps scarcely aware how much your steady sympathy & your prompting helps to sustain those who have to carry out the details. I speak now of the past, before you had begun to take part in the actual work. The advantage of making your personal acquaintance will count for still more in one's life work."[24]

What Emily Davies did not know was that Mill and Helen had been putting their heads together on the married-women issue and had arrived at the decision that, whatever the effect on their case, it must be made abundantly clear that all women property-owners—married women as well as spinsters and widows—must be included. Miss Davies received a dusty answer and replied meekly enough that she had no wish to say anything which would specifically exclude married women. To do so would be dishonest, because it would misrepresent their real opinions. "To avoid touching upon the position of married women and not in any way to mix up the marriage laws with the question of the franchise is exactly what I wish. The difficulty is how to do it . . . ."[25]

She consulted Mrs Manning and her stepdaughter Adelaide, who was later to become the first secretary of the Froebel Society. She would be glad, she said, to have their opinion as to whether "unmarried women and widows" should be specifically named in the disputed clause. Miss Taylor "decidedly refuses to put them in". Helen had indeed uttered a dire threat, as Miss Davies explained: "If we insist on inserting these words definitely limiting the claim, Mr Mill and Miss Taylor will give us no help in getting signatures, and it is possible that Mr Mill may refuse to present the petition . . . ." To Helen she sent another plea, although she can have had little hope of a favourable result. Did Miss Taylor not think that to demand the vote for all women house- and property-owners "on the same condition as men" was a little too specific? "Commonplace people, women as well as men, have a horror of what they call "women wanting to be on an equality with men". And I should be glad to avoid anything that might possibly suggest that unpleasant phrase."

Helen would not be moved and replied firmly that all eligible women must be included and the demand must be for complete equality. She herself could not sign any petition which stipulated different qualifications for men and women. "Signatures will be the argument".[26] sighed Emily Davies in a plaintive letter to Barbara Bodichon. She wrote to Helen conceding defeat; but behind the scenes she was still doing a little propaganda. When they first met at dinner at Blackheath she had been charmed both by Mill and by Helen, impressed by what she called their simple goodness. Now her admiration for Helen was waning: she found her obstinate and overbearing.

Others thought so too. Charles Eliot Norton, for one, considered that she was having a deleterious influence over Mill, whose involvement in the suffrage issue was of no great value to him as a thinker. "It has a tendency to develop the sentimental part of his intelligence, which is of immense force, and has only been kept in due subjection by his respect for his own reason." Helen, who was driving him—so Norton thought—into greater activity than was either necessary or desirable, he characterized as

> an admirable person doubtless, but [she] is what, were she of the sex that she regards as inferior, would be called decidedly priggish. Her self-confidence, which embraces her confidence in Mill, is tremendous, and Mill is overpowered by it. Her words have an oracular value for him—something more than their just weight; and her unconscious flattery, joined with the very direct flattery of many other prominent leaders of the great female army, have a not unnatural effect on his tender, susceptible and sympathetic nature . . . .[27]

Mill relished the flattery of the great female army, which he undoubtedly deserved. He was their champion, the hope of the future. Helen was also a champion, but towards her the army's opinions were mixed. Mill could be reasonable; Helen was stubborn and intractable.

In London and elsewhere suffrage petitions were being framed, signatures collected and committees organized. First in the field with a fully-fledged committee was Manchester. In January 1867 the solemn, earnest Lydia Becker had dragooned her friends and sympathizers into the creation of a women's suffrage committee: it came into existence at a meeting presided over by Manchester's radical member of Parliament, John Bright's brother Jacob. The Manchester committee, with Lydia Becker as its energetic secretary, took pride of place; but the London petition committee, which had been disbanded, soon came to life again in the shape of a provisional committee of thirteen, with Emily Davies as secretary, Mrs Peter Taylor (Clementia—or Mentia to her friends) as treasurer. "The more I see of Miss Davies the more strongly I am impressed with her judicial way of getting things done", Barbara Bodichon told Helen, "and I believe she can work Education and franchise together . . . ."[28] Emily Davies, though dubious, allowed herself to be persuaded into giving both tasks a trial.

Quite apart from her enthusiasm for the cause and her status as the wife of a member who would support it in the House, Clementia Taylor had a most valuable asset. She and her husband lived in a large and beautiful seventeenth-century house, Aubrey House on Campden Hill, Kensington. It was there that the women's petition, which had overflowed Elizabeth Garrett's dining-room, had been assembled.

Helen Taylor, who had been advising the members of the embryo committee at every turn, told Mrs Peter Taylor that she rejoiced to learn that it had been established "on so good a footing ... and that by it work can now be undertaken which no individuals can so fitly take charge, and from which therefore I shall now gladly retire".[29] She could, had she wished, have become an official and a leader, but she infinitely preferred wire-pulling behind the scenes.

The provisional London committee (it called itself the London Society for Obtaining Political Rights for Women) was collecting signatures for a new petition of women householders. Manchester, in the lead as usual, was organizing two, one to be signed by women householders, the other by men and women of all classes. Signatures were also being collected in Edinburgh and, in the early months of 1867, several petitions were presented in Parliament, one by Mill himself. These petitions were to be followed by others: they were, in effect, the prelude to a speech on the franchise which Mill was to deliver in May.

In preparation for this important speech Mill had delved deeply into the anomalous position of women. He knew more about their lack of domestic rights than any living man, and so he paid particular attention to the inequalities of education. He had already, as he had promised Emily Davies, given evidence before the Schools Inquiry Commission. On 6 August 1866, he had been questioned on the uses of educational endowments in schools, though not with specific reference to the education of girls. He said, as he had said before, that parents who could afford it should finance their children's schooling but that those who could not should receive adequate help. Endowments were all too often frittered away, but this was one of a number of ways in which they could be used with profit. Another was the award of exhibitions to enable the intelligent children of the poor to proceed to secondary education: this suggestion seemed to him "to be of a highly moral and improving character, and I would give it my warmest support". Among other recommendations, he was in favour of establishing teacher-training schools in which students "should learn, not only the things they will have to teach, but how to teach them".[30]

Although Mill was thinking of girls as well as boys, he had not realized at the time the existence of a glaring piece of sex discrimination in the use of educational endowments. He was still preparing his speech when he made some inquiries on this point. "I understood you to say", he wrote to Thomas Hare, "that the majority of the old deeds of endowment of schools included girls as well as boys, but that this part of the original design has been allowed to fall into desuetude. Am I right as to the fact?"[31]

Hare informed him that he was indeed right; and so he inserted an impressive passage into his speech. In it, he inveighed against the lack of good schools, universities and training colleges for women, and against fathers who sent their sons to public school and university but attached no importance at all to the education of their daughters. Then he referred to the endowed schools: "What has become of the endowments which the bounty of our ancestors destined for the education, not of one sex only, but of both indiscriminately? I am told by one of the highest authorities on the subject, that in the majority of the endowments the provision is not for boys, but for education generally: in one great endowment, Christ's Hospital, it is expressly for both: that institution now maintains and educates 1100 boys, and exactly 26 girls...."[32]

Had Mill consulted the women educationists he would have received the same information, for they too were campaigning for the restoration of endowments intended for girls' schools. In due course Mill followed up his speech with an article in the *Fortnightly Review* of April 1869; and yet, despite their combined efforts, coupled with the work of an Endowed Schools' Commission, girls numbered less than a quarter of the total number of pupils in endowed schools at the end of the century.

It was only natural that Mill should include medical education in his campaign for equal opportunities. He had already crossed swords with the redoubtable Florence Nightingale, who, it seemed to him, was actively discouraging women from attempting to enter the medical profession. In her *Notes on Nursing* she had written,

> I would earnestly ask my sisters to keep clear of both the jargons now current everywhere...; of the jargon...about the "rights" of women, which urges women to do all that men do, including the medical and other professions, merely because men do it, and without regard to whether this *is* the best that women can do; and the jargon which urges women to do nothing that men do, merely because they are women, and because... "this is women's work," and "that is men's"...Surely woman should bring the best she has, *whatever* that is, to the work of God's will, without attending to either of these cries....[33]

It is hardly surprising that Mill found this passage ambiguous, and, in reply to a query, Miss Nightingale told him that she would be glad to revise it if he considered it open to misinterpretation. He answered, reasonably enough, that he was pleased to know that she had not intended "to convey impressions which I still think the words...are calculated to give." Advocates of women's rights were, in his opinion, ready to concede too much "as to the comparative unfitness of women for some occupations", and he did not think, therefore, that they could "justly be accused of jargon, nor of contending that women ought to do certain things merely because men do them".[34]

Florence Nightingale was, in fact, opposed to the entry of ill-trained men as well as ill-trained women to the medical profession, and she had a poor opinion of the prevailing state of medical training. One of her friends was British-born Elizabeth Blackwell, who had become the first woman to obtain an American medical degree (in 1849) and was later to found the London School of Medicine for Women. Despite her friendship for Dr Blackwell, Miss Nightingale told Mill that the doctor and her world talked jargon; and, she added, "female M. D.s have taken up the worst part of a male M.D. ship of 50 years ago.... The women have made no improvement, they have only tried to be 'men' and they have succeeded only in being third-rate men ...."[35]

To this letter Mill replied that his own "opinion of the medical profession is not, I dare say, higher than yours", but too much must not be expected of inadequately trained doctors, and "the first two or three women who take up medicine" could not be expected to "be more than ... third rate".[36] They were in agreement that the medical profession itself was in need of a thorough overhaul.

Mill knew and admired the patient persistence of Elizabeth Garrett, Mrs Fawcett's elder sister, who was finally to obtain her medical degree in Paris in 1870 after a long and fruitless struggle to gain recognition in her own country. In 1865, to the annoyance of the British medical profession, she was permitted to take the examination of the Society of Apothecaries, and, having passed it successfully, opened a dispensary for women and children in Marylebone, London, which later became the New Hospital for Women. She was also trying to gain admission for women students to the Royal Free Hospital, but, as she explained to Helen in April, 1867, "the majority of the medical staff now say that our proposal is not one upon which argument is needed, as it is 'opposed by all the higher instincts of mankind' ".[37]

In the speech which Mill was preparing he referred to Elizabeth Garrett by name:

A young lady, Miss Garrett, from no pressure of necessity, but from an honourable desire to employ her activity in alleviating human suffering, studied the medical profession. Having duly qualified herself, she, with an energy and perseverance which cannot be too highly praised, knocked successively at all the doors through which, by law, access is obtained into the medical profession. Having found all other doors fast shut, she fortunately discovered one which had accidentally been left ajar. The Society of Apothecaries, it seems, had forgotten to shut out those who they never thought would attempt to come in, and through this narrow entrance this young lady found her way into this profession. But so objectionable did it appear to this learned body that women would be the medical attendants even of women, that the narrow wicket through which Miss Garrett entered has been closed after her, and no second Miss

Garrett will be allowed to pass through it.[38]

Elizabeth Garrett had been rightly indignant that an examination which she had passed with ease should at once have been closed to women, and was grateful to Mill for drawing Parliamentary attention to the Society's action. "I shrink from thanking Mr Mill as if in my own name for the help & encouragement which I rejoice to know his words gave—& were intended to give—to all women", she wrote to Helen, "but I hope I may say that I am not without a sense of very hearty gratitude for all the help he gives us."[39]

CHAPTER 19

'We Do Not Live in Arcadia'

On 20 May 1867, Mill rose to move an amendment to the Reform Bill to substitute the word "person" for the word "man", an amendment which, if accepted, would automatically admit to the suffrage "all women who, as house-holders or otherwise, possessed the qualification required of male electors". This action, said Mill, "was by far the most important, perhaps the only really important, public service I performed in the capacity of a Member of Parliament".[1] No one—certainly not Mill himself—anticipated success, and some of his antagonists, looking forward to a good evening's entertainment and a crushing defeat, gave up their dinner engagements in order to be present in the House.

The weakness of Mill's voice, the lengthy pauses and nervous twitchings were in evidence as always; but he had prepared his speech with the greatest care and his integrity and uncompromising honesty made themselves powerfully felt, even among those members who had come prepared to jeer. His plea for equality in education has already been mentioned. His chief claim for equal rights, he said, was founded on justice and the principles of the British constitution. Turning to the basic humanity of this claim he continued,

> I know there is an obscure feeling—a feeling which is ashamed to express itself openly—as if women had no right to care about anything except how they may be the most useful and devoted servants of some man.... This claim to confiscate the whole existence of one half of the species for the supposed convenience of the other appears to me, independently of its injustice, particularly silly. For who that has had ordinary experience of human affairs, and ordinary capacity of profiting by that experience, fancies that those do their own work best who understand nothing else? ... Is it good for a man to live in complete communion of thoughts and feelings with one who is studiously kept inferior to himself, whose earthly interests are forcibly confined within four walls, and who cultivates, as a grace of character, ignorance and indifference about the most inspiring subjects, those among which his highest duties are

cast? ... It is said that women do not need direct power, having so much indirect, through their influence over their male relatives and connections. I should like to carry this argument a little further. Is this a reason for refusing them votes? ... Sir, it is true that women have great power; ... but they have it under the worst possible conditions, because it is indirect, and therefore irresponsible power. ... But at least it will be said, women do not suffer any practical inconvenience ... by not having a vote. The interests of all women are safe in the hands of their husbands, and brothers, who have the same interest with them. ... Sir, this is exactly what is said of all unrepresented classes. The operatives for instance: are they not virtually represented by the representation of their employers? ... Is not the farmer equally interested with the labourer in the prosperity of agriculture? And generally, have not employers and employed a common interest against all outsiders, just as husband and wife have against all outside the family? And what is more, are not all employers good, kind, benevolent men, who love their workpeople, and always desire to do what is most for their good? All these assertions are as true, and as much to the purpose, as the corresponding assertions respecting men and women. Sir, we do not live in Arcadia ... and workmen need other protection than that of their employers, and women other protection than that of their men.

Harriet must have been very much alive in his mind during his preparation of the speech; but never more so than when, in the remembrance of those articles and letters to the press "very little of [which were] mine", he said,

I should like to have a return laid before this House of the number of women who are annually beaten to death, kicked to death, or trampled to death by their male protectors; and, in an opposite column, the amount of the sentences passed, in those cases where the dastardly criminals did not get off altogether. I should also like to have, in a third column, the amount of property the unlawful taking of which was, at the same sessions or assizes by the same judge, thought worthy of the same amount of punishment. We should then have an arithmetical estimate of the value set by a male legislature and male tribunals on the murder of a woman ... which, if there is any shame in us, would make us hang our heads ....[2]

The implications of this speech, the demand for the righting of wrongs of which many people were scarcely aware, brought some previously antagonistic members to Mill's side. In the debate which followed the speech several extraneous hares were raised; and in his summing up Mill declared that nothing had pleased him more than to hear his opponents argue against measures which were not in fact before the House at all. When the question was finally put—that the word "man" stand part of the clause in question—there were 196 ayes and 73 noes, a majority of 123 against the amendment.

This was better than Mill had expected. "The minority of 73 (which would have been near 100 if the division had not taken place unexpectedly at a bad time in the evening) is most encouraging, and has put its members and many other supporters in great spirits",[3] he told the political economist Professor John Elliot Cairnes. His greatest triumph, he said, was to have secured the vote of John Bright, who claimed the suffrage for men only and until very recently had been one of his strongest opponents.

Lady Amberley, who was in the ladies' gallery, noted that, although the attendance was thin, and although Mill paused for nearly two minutes near the beginning of his speech, his eyebrows working fearsomely, he was listened to with patience and respect. The press was divided in its opinions. The *Daily News* agreed with Kate Amberley that the speeches of his opponents were wide of the mark. The fact that Mill had obtained as many as 73 votes was "probably due almost as much to the incredible weakness, and in some cases, the positive silliness of [their] speeches . . . , as to the rare power and merit of his own". The *Morning Star* found Mill's speech "a composition of remarkable ability [which] will be long remembered"; the *Morning Herald*, on the other hand, thought it "as feeble and halting, as his proposal was abhorrent to the almost universal instinct of mankind"; while *The Times* considered that it would "gain few fresh converts" among those who, after due thought, had found "the arguments in favour of the political rights of women . . . unconvincing".[4]

Helen Taylor was also in the ladies' gallery. Elizabeth Garrett joined her sister Millicent in time for the division and told Helen afterwards that "the comparative success far exceeded my anticipations".[5] "So we are beat, as you always said we would be", said Jessie Boucherett to Helen. "Our gratitude is not the less due to Mr Mill for the good fight he made . . . ."[6] Harriet Grote was also "full of grateful admira^n at John Mill's courageous and masterly speech".[7]

Some of the women were over-optimistic, believing themselves to be in sight of the promised land. One of these was Miss Caroline Lindley, a friend of Professor Cairnes and his wife and of Helen, with whom she carried on a voluminous and—on her side—often incoherent correspondence for nearly twenty years. Now she wrote ecstatically, "Truly my whole heart responds to every word in . . . the excellent speech of dear Mr Mill. To have sat beside you and listened would indeed have been a heart luxury to me . . . I believe the good time for man is coming. . . . How much to you and Mr Mill do we all owe . . . ."[8]

Mill, aware that the good time was not just around the corner, decided that the results of his speech at least warranted placing the provisional London suffrage committee on a permanent footing. He and Helen therefore arranged to meet the members in June. The meeting was far from harmonious: it "leaves one with a melancholy feeling behind it",[9] Emily

Davies confided to Adelaide Manning. The chief bone of contention was Mill's and Helen's argument that, while it would be suitable to recruit men to a general committee, the executive must consist entirely of women: they thought that it would be most undesirable to create the impression that women were incapable of managing important matters without the assistance of men. Emily Davies and Barbara Bodichon thought otherwise, as did some members of the provisional committee who were not present. "I know Mrs Peter Taylor is strong for men on the Committee", Madame Bodichon said, "and so are *all* the other ladies . . . ."[10] Helen was adament. "Miss Taylor was perfectly unpersuadable", grumbled Emily Davies, 'and I believe we might all have talked for a week without making the least impression on her. It seems that Mr Mill is very strong in favour of excluding men from the Manchester Committee, and Mrs Knox went over to the enemy . . . Mrs Bodichon and I were obliged to give in . . . ."[11]

Mill and Helen were ready to the join the general committee. Helen, who was eligible to serve on the executive, refused on the grounds of her other commitments and frequent absence from England. Mill, whose goodwill was essential, now proceeded to invite a number of influential friends to join the general committee, among them Lord Houghton (the former Richard Monckton Milnes); Herbert Spencer; Lord Brougham, the former Lord Chancellor; and Lord Romilly. As he explained, "Business will be conducted by the Executive Committee of ladies, and the members of the General Committee are responsible for nothing except approval of the object and an annual subscription of a guinea . . . ."[12] When he wrote to Professor Cairnes, who, with Mrs Cairnes and W. T. Thornton, had already agreed to join the general committee, he was able to report that it "now considerably exceeds 100 in number, including two peers (Lords Romilly and Houghton) [and] thirty members of the House of Commons",[13] not all of them radicals. Despite his determination that the executive committee should be an all-woman affair, it was not long before men, who had already been elected to the Manchester committee, were also elected to London and the other branches of the movement. Much to his chagrin, the women had discovered that they could not manage alone.

Emily Davies, whose appointment as secretary of the London committee had been confirmed, soon found that she could not combine her work for education and the suffrage and returned to her first love. After a brief interregnum following the untimely death of her successor, Mrs Smith, one of the Garrett sisters, Mrs Peter Taylor agreed to combine the posts of treasurer and secretary. She enlisted a friend, Miss Caroline Ashurst Biggs, member of a radical family from Leicester (Peter Taylor's constituency), to deal with the bulk of the secretarial work. Miss Biggs proved highly efficient, so Mrs Taylor decided to hand over the secretaryship altogether, herself remaining available for consultation whenever required. Before the transfer took place she mentioned the matter to Helen, "because though not one of the [Executive] Committee, which I have always regretted—you & Mr Mill have been almost the founders of the Society—and have magnificently aided it—and in any step of importance I think it but just to consult with you". Miss Biggs, she added, "has clear judgment—is very clever & a good writer—and most thoroughly interested in our cause".[14]

Caroline Biggs was then only a name to them; but she was soon to be the proverbial red rag to a bull.

In the meantime, Clementia Taylor had another crisis—or, rather, two crises—on her hands. The first arose from a dispute over a suitable title for the London committee; the second was the old dispute over the inclusion of married women among the widows and spinsters for whom the vote was to be demanded in a further series of petitions.

Frances Power Cobbe, a member of the executive, suggested a name—the "London National Society for Woman Suffrage". Mill could hardly believe his ears. Ten years earlier he had stormed at George Jacob Holyoake for prostituting Harriet's "Enfranchisement of Women" with the use of the hated Americanism "woman suffrage", and here was his good friend attempting to repeat the solecism on a far wider scale! Miss Cobbe, Clementia explained in a letter to Helen, was under "a strong impression that Mr Mill suggested 'Woman', tho' I thought not". She enclosed a note from the offender maintaining (and with good reason) that "woman" suffrage sounded so much "better than such a horrid hissing as Wome*n's Suf*frage".[15]

How dared she think anything of the sort, demanded Helen. The name decided on was the "London National Society for Women's Suffrage": no other name would do. "I must beg you most urgently to represent to Miss Cobbe that Mr Mill & I consider her as pledged to the name to which she gave her consent when she was here. We wrote down the name at once. . . . We also understood that you expressly formed the Society on the ground of not excluding married women—not mentioning them in any way. It would be impossible for Mr Mill or myself to form part of a new Committee that does so." She was under the impression that both points had been agreed on "*before* we joined so that there might not arise any possible occasion for us to retire afterwards". It was with great pain that they realized there was still some uncertainty. "I must therefore with all friendly urgency repeat that we consider you and Miss Cobbe as pledged . . . ."[16]

The Manchester committee, as Jessie Boucherett had reminded Helen, was getting up a petition which did not exclude married women; but the London petition, if allowed to go through, "sets married women against us by affronting them. They do not like to be placed in an inferior position to single women in respect to votes and therefore oppose us altogether . . . ."[17]

Clementia Taylor could do nothing but yield to the dreadful threat of resignation. "Of course your and Mr Mill's withdrawal from the Society would be *destructive* . . . ."[18] Notices had already been printed with the abhorrent heading, the "London National Society for Woman Suffrage", but, despite Miss Cobbe's dislike of sibilants, these would be scrapped and a new set, using the words "Women's Suffrage", would be substituted. "I am pleased

to tell you [the executive] all agreed unimously to adopt Mr Mill's title. . . ."[19]
To this Mill replied that the choice of title, which he heartily approved, had
been Helen's, not his.

Mrs Taylor also caved in over the wording of the petition. Miss Cobbe
would be informed that "I could not again consent to the insertion of 'widows
and unmarried women' or any words implying restriction . . . ."[20]

Peace now descended on the London National Society for Women's
Suffrage, but not for long: compared with what was to come, the argument
about the title of the movement and the wording of the petition was no more
than a storm in a teacup.

Mill always claimed that the suffrage movement owed its existence
entirely to Helen. Following his speech in the House of Commons, "The time
appeared to my daughter, Miss Helen Taylor, to have come for forming a
Society for the extension of the suffrage to women. The existence of the
Society is due to my daughter's initiative; its constitution was planned
entirely by her, and she was the soul of the movement during its first years,
though delicate health and superabundant occupation made her decline to be
a member of the Executive Committee . . . ."[21]

He was guilty of exaggeration, but, if he was being unjust to such women
as Emily Davies, Barbara Bodichon and Lydia Becker, they were equally
unjust to her. They shared the planning of the movement between them, yet
Helen's name is barely mentioned in the early histories and autobiographies.
It is true that she refused to take an active part in running the movement, but
she was consulted at every turn, not simply as Mill's stepdaughter but in her
own right as one of the movement's founders. After their first, rapturous
visits to Blackheath the women found her tactless and overbearing. Mill they
continued to idolize, but they knew that, as leader, Helen would have proved a
hard taskmaster.

Letters between Helen and the other pioneers flowed backwards and
forwards almost daily. Lydia Becker, the senior member in office, met her for
the first time in July 1867: she was on her way from Manchester to Colchester
to collect signatures for a petition and, if possible, to form a new branch of the
movement. They arranged to meet at Euston station. "I shall wear a violet
serge dress & jacket, black hat & spectacles", wrote Miss Becker, who was
excessively plain, "so I think we shall easily find each other. I shall be very
glad to have the opportunity of consulting with you as to the course of action
to be taken by our committee."[22] She wanted Helen to help her amend the
wording of Manchester's petitions after the passage of the Reform Bill, for
example; to vet the Manchester society's rules; to comment on articles she
was writing for the press. After her first visit to Blackheath she wrote that
she wished she "could express to you something of the feeling with which I
appreciated the privilege you and Mr Mill conferred on me". The visit would
remain in her memory "a thing to cherish all my life".[23]

The visit to Colchester was a qualified success; but Miss Becker collected
twenty-nine signatures for a petition to the local member of Parliament,

distributed many copies of Mill's speech, and felt "sure they will bear fruit".[24] When she returned home she reported to Helen on Manchester's current activities. Efforts were being made to prove that, as the law stood, women were legally enfranchised already. Historical researches showed that in feudal days the power of appointing representatives to Parliament had apparently been governed not by sex but by property; and, if women freeholders had possessed that privilege then, they had surely retained it through the centuries. Miss Becker and her friends collected the signatures of more than 5,000 women householders who declared their willingness to appeal before the courts for their names to be added to the voting register. A test case was brought on the women's behalf by a prominent member of the Manchester society, Mrs Max Kyllmann, and was heard before the Court of Common Pleas in November 1868. One of the counsel representing the women householders was Dr Richard Marsden Pankhurst, who later married the suffragette leader Emmeline Goulden

Manchester had asked London for financial help towards the legal expenses. Mill and Helen, always generous with money, made personal contributions, but Helen sent Miss Becker a stiff letter on behalf of the London committee. "We do not understand how it happens that the Manchester Committee, with as rich or richer members than we have in London", should, after economizing on the organization of petitions in order to finance the test case, be in such straits "as to have to apply to the London Committee for help.... If the London Committee is to take upon itself the burdens of another Committee I imagine it will wish also to have the weight and influence of one...."[25]

Since London as well as Manchester would have benefitted had the test case been successful, it does not seem unreasonable that the London committee should have been asked to help. The case was, of course, doomed to failure, but at least the women felt they had made their point.

Shortly before the hearing, the name of a Manchester woman, Mrs Lily Maxwell, had appeared by accident on the Parliamentary register. A by-election was in progress and Mrs Maxwell, egged on by the resolute Miss Becker, who escorted her to the polling station, recorded her vote for Jacob Bright. "We could not have had a better representative", Miss Becker wrote to Helen. "She is a poor working woman, maintaining herself by her own trade with no man to influence, or be influenced by, paying her rates and taxes out of her own earnings, and with very decided political sentiments of her own...."[26]

Another Manchester woman, Miss Jessie Goodwin, appeared at the polls during the municipal election in December 1867. Miss Becker sent Helen a newspaper cutting describing the event. "The appearance of a lady ... created an amusing scene. There was a cry of 'Hats off!' and when it became known that the voter ... had given her vote and the poll clerk had duly entered it, her name being on the roll of citizens, the event was greeted with much cheering...." This incident, commented Lydia Becker with pardonable pride, "coming after the other will go far to show that Manchester women, at least, desire the franchise."[27]

Her "at least" was hardly fair to London or to Edinburgh, which now had its own suffrage society; but it underlined a proposal which Mill and Helen had made some time before, that the societies should band together under one umbrella—a national society. Miss Becker thought her executive would be willing if Mill and Helen would draw up a form of proposal "and accompany it by a letter stating the advantages you expect may accrue from adopting it".[28] This they did, and sent her a document which "exactly meets my wishes".[29]

A majority of London's executive favoured union on condition, so Clementia Taylor informed Helen, that each society should continue to frame and keep its own rules and act independently of the others, "thus being responsible for its own actions only". This was not the kind of union Mill and Helen had envisaged, but, as the women had not yet learned to pull together, it was the only one possible in present circumstances and duly came into being. Even so, it sounded far too restrictive to Frances Power Cobbe, who, with two other members, resigned from the London executive. Mrs Taylor enclosed Miss Cobbe's resignation with her letter to Helen: "Miss Taylor urges the utility of a common list of Members to show the whole force of the movement.... We are of the opinion that it would be impossible thus to *benefit* by the other Societies without also sharing any *disadvantages* which the inadvised acts of any of them might produce...."[30]

It was essential that a union weakened by its branches' insistence on acting independently should be strengthened with new blood. Among those now enticed into the movement were a slightly apprehensive Charles Kingsley and his definitely apprehensive wife. For this purpose they were invited to Blackheath, an invitation to which Kingsley responded with enthusiasm:

> To pass a night under your roof will be an honour which I shall most gratefully accept... I wish to speak with you on the whole question of woman.... I beg you... to [look] on me, though (I trust) a Christian and a clergyman, as completely emancipated from those prejudices which have been engrained into the public mind by the traditions of the monastic cannon law about women, and open to any teaching which has for its purpose the doing woman justice in every respect....

He confessed, however, that his wife's opinion had "long been that this movement must be furthered rather by men than by women." With his persuasive charm, Mill brought the reluctant Mrs Kingsley to his side. He also persuaded Kingsley to speak at a suffrage meeting, provided there were no reporters present, for Kingsley felt "a chivalrous dislike of letting this subject be lowered in print".[31]

Letters of invitation to join the movement were signed by Mill, but many of them—according to Mill, all the best—were in fact written by Helen. Her greatest success was the enrolment of two famous but hitherto highly elusive women. The first was Mary Colman's heroine, the philanthropist and prison reformer Mary Carpenter, who had opened the first of her ragged schools for the children of the poor in the slums of Bristol in 1846. The second was Florence Nightingale.

The correspondence of which Helen took so large a share was not, however, confined to the suffrage movement in Britain. Mill, as we have seen, was particularly optimistic of the success of the American movement, and it was always a red-letter day when he learned that Harriet's "Enfranchisement of Women" was having the desired effect. He believed, as he told the secretary of the Universal Suffrage Association in 1868, "that your country is destined to lead the way in this great question, as it has already done in so many others".[32] And, to an American journalist who called on him at Avignon the same year, he said that he thought he might "live to see the day when the elective franchise would be as fully enjoyed in Great Britain as in the United States".[33] He was, of course, being unduly optimistic.

CHAPTER 20

Women's Rights

One of Mill's final efforts in Parliament was the presentation in June 1868 of a petition in support of an amendment to the laws which gave husbands control of their wives' money and property. The Bill passed its second reading by a single vote, but, to his intense disappointment, was later withdrawn without a debate. To Mill, as to others, such an amendment was as much part of the struggle for women's rights as the grant of the franchise. Some ten years earlier he had written

> Suppose that there were a question before the Legislature specially affecting women; as to whether women should be allowed to graduate at Universities; whether the mild penalties inflicted on ruffians who beat their wives daily almost to death's door, should be exchanged for something more effectual; or suppose that any one should propose in the British Parliament, what one State after another in America is enacting ... that married women should have a right to their own property. Are not a man's wife and daughters entitled to know whether he votes for or against a candidate who will support these propositions? It is precisely this indirect influence of those who have not the suffrage over those who have which ... softens the transition to every fresh extension of the franchise, and is the means by which ... the extension is peacefully brought about ....[1]

Such was Mill's prestige that, had he remained in Parliament, it is possible that the suffrage and other issues would have been resolved during his lifetime, although it is far from certain that the majority of women would, at that time, have been sufficiently interested to exercise the vote, if given it.

Mill agreed to stand again for Westminster in the general election held in November 1868. His chances of success were doubtful: many of his constituents were opposed to women's rights; and, when his supporters and friends learned that he had contributed towards the election expenses of the notorious atheist and advocate of birth control Charles Bradlaugh, they were sure that he had done himself a great deal of harm. Mill himself made light of their fears. "I think it is a mistake to suppose that my support of Bradlaugh at all diminishes my weight", he wrote to Edwin Chadwick a month before the election. "The sort of people with whom it does so have had to put up with my Women's Suffrage ... and other 'crotchets', and have probably long ago given me up, or more properly speaking, have never taken me up at all." His views on birth control and religion had been canvassed in the 1865 election, his unfortunate remark that the working classes were habitual liars had been thrown in his teeth without affecting the issue. He was aware that his support of Bradlaugh would lose him some votes, but believed that it would gain him many more, "although this had nothing whatever to do with my doing it".[2]

It was too much to hope that his opponents would not make capital out of the donation of Bradlaugh's funds. He was accused of being an atheist himself, a charge which he denied, defending his right, as he had defended it in 1865, to answer no questions concerning his religious beliefs. Bradlaugh, as he truthfully argued, was a supporter of women's suffrage and Parliamentary reform, and was popular with working people: for these reasons, if for no other, he deserved support. Mill gave this explanation in different forms and with varying emphasis. Close friends, Harriet Grote and Kate Amberley among them, considered it a piece of gratuitous folly to contribute towards Bradlaugh's expenses while refusing to contribute towards his own. They were horrified to read in the press the text of a letter he had sent one of his Westminster supporters, Frederick Bates, giving him permission to use it in any way he pleased:

I suppose the persons who call me an Atheist are the same who are impudently asserting that Mr Galdstone is a Roman Catholic. I shᵈ think my friends in W[estminster] must by this time be aware that Tories, in election times, stick at nothing. An attempt was made to raise the same cry against me at my first election, & the defence which I did not choose to make for myself was made for me by several eminent dignitaries of the C[hurch] of England. At that time I declared my deliberate determination, on principle, not to answer any questions whatever respecting my religious creed, because I acknowledge no right in any one to ask them, and because I owe it to future candidates & to the interest of future constituencies not to encourage a practice, the effect of which would be that when no objection can be found to a candidate's character or political opinions, attempts would be made to extract from himself materials for raising a religious prejudice against him, which is often easiest stirred up against the best men. I think I shall act most rightly, & most in conformity to my principles by adhering to this declaration. If any one again tells you that I am an atheist, I would advise you to ask him, how he knows and in what page of my numerous writings he finds anything to bear out the assertion. You will find that he has nothing at all to say. If he talks about my subscription for Mr Bradlaugh, he shᵈ be asked whether he

thinks that the working men of Northampton who adopted Mr B as their
candidate, or the members of the Reform League who elected him one of
their Council, are all atheists....[3]

The most horrified of all Mill's friends was Helen, who had remained in
Avignon while he went to London. After reading the letter, which Bates had
given to the *Daily News*, she sent Mill a reprimand worthy of her mother at
her most authoritative:

It seems to me utterly unworthy of you, to speak mildly of it; and not to
speak of its imprudence. That you could write such a letter shows how this
electioneering hurry and excitement unfits you for writing and it seems to
me the height of folly to go on varying your replies on such a topic instead
of keeping as nearly as possible to one set form for everyone. I do not
know which I dislike most—the assertion that to be called an Atheist is
calumny, that you are as much one as Gladstone is a Catholic, or that
dignitaries of the Ch. of England have spoken for you!!! Surely to use such
arguments is to sacrifice all that it is worth while to be elected for. Then
you go on to say that you are no more an Atheist than all the working men
of Northampton who support Bradlaugh; and you defy him to find
anything in your writings to justify the assertion. I cannot tell you how
ashamed I feel. And you actually invite publication of this letter which
makes me literally blush for you and must lower the opinion entertained
of you by everyone who knows you and sees it. I beg and entreat of you,
refuse utterly to say one word on this topic except what you have already
said. Copy as literally as you can the letter I dictated (which I enclose)
about Bradlaugh; and what you yourself said at the former election, about
yourself. Do not disgrace yourself as an open truthful man; do not shut
the door to all future power of usefulness on religious liberty by such
mean and wretched subterfuges as this letter. Do not be drawn into saying
one fresh thing great or small. That is what your opponents want you to
do....[4]

Nothing could show more clearly the power Helen had gained over her
stepfather than his meek acceptance of her imperious rebuke and his
willingness to adopt her form of words in future correspondence on the
subject. However, his letter (it has not survived) elicited from her an almost
apologetic response. Realizing that she had gone too far—that Mill, with the
election only a few days off, was in need of comfort, not advice or
admonition—she wrote, "Do not allow vexation about the letter to depress
your spirits and therefore health; all this bitterness roused [by the publication
of his letter] ... shows how much work there still is to do in favour of free
thought and free speaking; if you are elected you must do it in parliament; if
not you can do it better by writing...."
She hoped that, if he lost the election, he would retire permanently from

Parliamentary life. But, she added, "I look upon this as a question which you ought to decide for yourself, and I do not wish to influence you one way or another. As a mere spectator it seems to me imprudent to risk the extremely probable chance of another failure; but if you are inclined to try, and if you think there is a good chance anywhere, I am heartily willing, and think you should follow your own inclination and judgment...."[5]

On the eve of the election Helen heard from the fond, faithful Fanny Stirling, who had seen Mill's letter in the *Daily News* and been shocked by the abuse with which it had been received: "I have watched & can see how Mr Mill has been bothered & bullied & badgered & altho' he would not feel it personally—would treat it with the contempt it merits—yet it must all have given you work & worry thro' him ... I can't let tonight pass without hoping that the result of tomorrow may be whatever you wish it to be...."[6]

Mill was defeated at Westminster, the Conservative candidate winning by a large majority. He wrote at once to Bradlaugh, who had also been defeated, to assure him that, while his support might have lost him some votes, other factors had contributed towards his defeat, and he would probably have lost if their names had not been associated. He was by no means the only advocate of women's suffrage to lose his seat. "The result of the new elections ... appears to be on the whole unfavourable to the cause', wrote Helen over his signature to a friend on the Manchester suffrage committee. "The new members in favour of it are but few." Despite their natural disappointment, supporters of the movement should continue to organize petitions. "It would show but little perseverance ... if they cannot go on year after year asking for this change of the law...."[7] And to Mrs Duncan McLaren, sister of John and Jacob Bright and president of the Edinburgh suffrage society, she wrote (also in Mill's name), "It remains for the intelligent women of the country to give their moral support to the men who are engaged in urging their claims, & to open the minds of the less intelligent to the fact that political freedom is the only effectual remedy for the evils ... that women suffer." Whatever authority he possessed to further the cause outside Parliament, "I shall not fail to exert to my utmost".[8]

Helen had been unable to conceal her delight and relief at the prospect of having "Mr Mill" to herself at Avignon. When she heard the news of his defeat she rushed off a wifely letter:

How I wish you were not obliged to spend all those tedious days at Blackheath! I want you to be here that we may enjoy together the strange feeling of liberty and repose; instead of which you are surrounded by circumstances which bring forward all the disagreeable side of the Westminster failure... If I thought you would feel the result as a disappointment on the whole, I should so wish to be with you; only then I think you would laugh at me, not for sympathising with you, but for supposing you could dislike the result!... How I wish you were here! I shall be so impatient till you arrive....[9]

Mill wrote to assure her that he was far from disappointed for himself. "Your letter . . . is a great comfort to me", she replied. When she awoke that morning, "I asked myself what had happened that made me feel so well & happy; and yet I had gone to sleep feeling it a disappointment!"[10]

To his personal friends in the suffrage movement his defeat was, of course, a devastating blow, but they could appreciate his relief at being free to live and write as he wished. Elizabeth Garrett, who told Helen she could understand that his friends might "almost rejoice", did not consider herself near enough "to feel this & I must think of the loss it is to everyone who cares how public things go on for the next few years. I lament it too very much as an indication of the terrible preponderance of stupid people."[11]

"We must have Mr Mill in Parliament again—to raise the tone of the debates",[12] wrote Clementia Taylor. Fanny Stirling, whose fear that Helen was being overworked had impelled her to offer her services as temporary secretary, wrote now of the new life she would experience, "relieved from this pressure of work which has been quite too much for any strong man much less for you. All is *indeed* for the best . . . ."[13]

Caroline Lindley, Helen's most verbose and eccentric friend, could always be relied on for something original: "How anxiously we have looked in the papers for words from our Friend and when found how sure they were to lift us to his own pure Atmosphere—say then dear one what has truth and justice lost where it was so much wanting in the practice of our so called leaders! . . ."[14]

The "dear one" sent her friend a few words of explanation, to which the emotional Miss Lindley hastened to reply, "But own Helen, you seek to help us, and you *shall,* for *if* for *you* and *Mr Mill* personally it is *better* that we thus suffer, surely we will *rather rejoice* with you, and . . . will follow our Friend on his glad way to you, & as you wind up your to be very often read letter by saying 'write sometimes' it shall be my *rest* when weary as the most earnest are *full oft,* to pour out as privileged, burning thoughts to thee, and dear, kind, indulgent Mr Mill . . . ."[15] Caroline took ample advantage of the privilege, and her burning thoughts continued to descend relentlessly on Avignon.

Several friends stressed the Darby and Joan atmosphere, as though Mill and Helen were an old married couple. "I don't think I will ever work in any election again", wrote Mrs Brewer, one of Mill's campaigners, to Helen. But "the other side of the picture pleases me. You and Mr Mill quietly and happily enjoying your sunny home . . . ."[16]

"I am in clover", wrote Mill to Thornton a few weeks after his arrival in Avignon, "and you may imagine with what scorn I think of the H. of C. . . . ."[17]

If they were contented they were also extremely busy. In addition to their books and letters, the suffrage issue was still very much alive, and Mill, as he had promised, was ready to work for it outside Parliament. To the women's suffrage workers he remained their hero, their ideal leader; but he was now leader emeritus. They had to look elsewhere for a Parliamentary leader and found him in Jacob Bright. This put Manchester once again ahead of London in the suffrage stakes. The workers were optimistic when, in May 1870, Bright introduced in the House the first separate Women's Suffrage Bill, which had been drafted by Richard Pankhurst. After a sensible debate, devoid of flippancy, the Bill passed its second reading by a majority of thirty-three. Clementia Taylor telegraphed the news to Helen in Avignon. "Hurrah!" she cried in a follow-up letter. "Of course I was in the House—it was a time of great excitement... The cheers that rang through the House when the paper was given to Mr Jacob Bright to read the numbers was sweeter than any music.... I know you and Mr Mill are rejoicing—to *him* we owe this success...."[18]

Success was almost as far away as ever. One week later Gladstone mustered enough opposition in committee to have the Bill thrown out by 126 votes. Mill was not cast down. "What immense progress the cause of Women's Suffrage has made since 1867",[19] he wrote to Thomas Hare. But 1870 was the beginning of a long series of frustrations. It is true that the extension of the municipal franchise to women ratepayers the previous year was a step in the right direction. So, too, was the passage of the Education Act of 1870, which enabled women to serve on the newly appointed school boards. Mill wrote to the American philanthropist Charles Loring Brace, "The right of women to a voice in the management of education has been asserted by the triumphant return of two ladies as members of the London School Board & of several others in different parts of the country...."[20] He was referring to Emily Davies and Elizabeth Garrett (she became Mrs Garrett Anderson the same year), who had been elected for London, and, among others, Lydia Becker for Manchester. Emily Shirreff's sister Maria Grey had been persuaded to stand for Chelsea, but lost by a narrow margin.

These measures proved to those who had doubted it that women were capable of taking responsibility, but, as they did not bring the goal of the Parliamentary vote any nearer, it was decided to step up a scheme which had already been launched in a small way—the organisation of suffrage meetings, to be addressed by women speakers as well as men, all over the country.

This put the women into a flutter. Whereas the first meetings had been unobtrusive drawing-room affairs with audiences composed of friends and well-wishers, it was now necessary for them to prepare themselves to speak in public. One or two of them had read their own papers at meetings of the Social Science Association. The first time Emily Davies wrote a paper she got someone else to read it for her; but Barbara Bodichon read her own—"Objections to the Franchise Considered"—at the Manchester congress of 1866. Helen Taylor considered that it was "drawn up ... with much ability [and] has already done immense good".[21] But reading a prepared paper was one thing; making an ostensibly extempore speech, even if it had been learned by heart and rehearsed *ad nauseam,* was quite another. Still, it had to be done. The only woman among them who did not suffer from nerves was Helen Taylor: she had the experience of the late Miss Trevor to guide her.

Mill, of course, was in great demand. He spoke at the first important meeting, arranged by the indefatigable Lydia Becker in the Trade Hall, Manchester, in 1868, with the Mayor of Salford in the chair, and Jacob Bright and Richard Pankhurst among the speakers. A startling innovation was a short speech by Miss Becker, who moved the resolution and admitted afterwards that she had felt completely unnerved.

There was another innovation at the first public meeting on women's suffrage to be held in London, in 1869 in the Gallery of the Architectural Society in Conduit Street: this was the presence of a woman—Clementia Taylor—in the chair. The imposing list of speakers included Mill, Charles Kingsley, John (later Viscount) Morley, then editor of the *Fortnightly Review,* and three members of Parliament, Sir Charles Dilke, Henry Fawcett and James Stansfeld. There was also a woman, Henry Fawcett's twenty-two-year-old wife Millicent. Though nervous, this composed and thoughtful young woman spoke simply and well. Even so, there were some disparaging remarks in the press about women appearing on the same platform as men.

Mill was delighted with the effect. "Nous venons d'avoir un *meeting* très important de la Société pour le suffrage des femmes", he wrote to the Italian statesman and historian Pasquale Villari, one of the very few friends invited to Blackheath during Harriet's lifetime. "Cette réunion a été admirablement présidé par une dame et il y [a] eu d'excellents discours...."[22]

Mill spoke for the Edinburgh suffrage society in January 1871. He was given a hero's welcome, the audience "rising and waving their hats and hankerchiefs", and greeting his speech with "loud and prolonged cheering".

The whole movement of modern society, he said in the course of his speech, "points in the direction of the political enfranchisement of women.... I do not know how long a time it may require to get rid of women's disabilities.... But of one thing I am certain—that when once they have been got rid of... they will appear in the retrospect so devoid of any rational foundation... that the difficulty which will be felt will be to conceive how they can ever have been defended, and by what possible arguments they can ever have been made to appear plausible."[23]

The suffrage movement certainly appeared to be gathering strength. Neither Mill nor Fawcett nor Peter Taylor had been at all put out when one of their opponents had referred in Parliament to the fact that at the London meeting the wives of two of his colleagues (he could not bring himself to mention them by name) had disgraced themselves by speaking in public. Mill was anxious for both women to continue speaking. He promised to ask Millicent Fawcett if she would speak at Stoke-on-Trent at a meeting organized by a working-man friend, William Wood, who had already organized a petition. "Either she or Mrs Taylor would speak well.... It is just possible that my friend Professor Fawcett might be able himself to go..., and the cause of Women's Suffrage has no more active, judicious and useful friends than Mr and Mrs Fawcett."[24]

On this occasion neither woman was free to go to Stoke; both had speaking engagements elsewhere. They knew Mill was right when he advised them to make themselves "visible to the public, their very appearance being a refutation of the vulgar nonsense talked about 'women's rights women,' and their manner of looking, moving, and speaking being sure to make a favourable impression from the purely feminine as well as from the human point of view."[25] He was especially impressed with Mrs Fawcett, who had published an article, "The Medical and General Education of Women", in the *Fortnightly*, and had worked it up into a lecture. The article was "a guarantee for its being excellent both in matter and stile [*sic*], and her person and manner will dispel prejudice and attract adherents wherever she delivers it",[26] he told her husband.

One or two of Mill's more puritanical friends thought he was putting too much emphasis on the womanly approach. To George Croom Robertson, Professor of Mental Philosophy and Logic at University College, London, a member of the executive of the London suffrage society, he wrote, "You seem to us to underrate the value of 'a pretty face' in a lecturer on women's rights. As my daughter says, it is not for the sake of effect on men that it is important, but for the influence it has on the younger women." It would show them that the movement was open to all women of good will, regardless of any special qualifications they might possess. "This is an advantage which outweighs even some inferiority in lecturing powers." It was women more than men they needed to enrol, "for when the majority of them think the change right, it will come".[27]

An exceedingly pretty face and a good intelligence had by now been enrolled in the person of Kate Amberley, who was in favour not only of women's suffrage but of equal rights and opportunities for women in every profession and occupation. She made her first appearance at a suffrage meeting, though not as a speaker, at the Hanover Square Rooms, London, in March 1870. The date had been fixed to coincide with Mill's presence at Blackheath. "We cannot hold a meeting without him", wrote the chairman, Clementia Taylor, to Helen; "it would be the play of Hamlet with Hamlet omitted".[28] Mill, Amberley, Jacob Bright, Dilke and Cairnes all spoke that night. So too did Mrs Grote, Millicent Fawcett, Helen, and Katharine, daughter of Thomas Hare. Katharine Hare was becoming quite a practised speaker. She had been terrified at first, but Helen had refused to let her off: all she had to do was to make up her mind beforehand exactly what she wanted to say and learn it by heart. "I am unfortunately so very nervous I can hardly trust myself to speak calmly or coolly", the poor girl had confessed the first time she had to speak; but "your presence and I am sure influence will help me to get through it. You and Mrs Taylor seem to have no doubt about its being a useful thing to do . . . ."[29]

If Katharine Hare still had a little trouble with her nerves, Helen was supremely confident. Tall, dignified and clear-voiced, she mustered the arguments she had used with Mary Carpenter and Florence Nightingale. "That women . . . have some reasonable ground for complaint, **very few** people will be found to dispute", she said. Give them the vote and the disabilities they suffered would soon vanish. "Therefore it is", she ended on a rousing note, "that we are bound to claim the suffrage that it may help us to force statesmen and lawgivers to come quickly to the rescue of these, the weakest and most neglected of mankind".[30]

Kate Amberley, seated on the platform between her husband and Helen, was slightly bored. "Miss Taylor made a long & much studied speech; it was good but too like acting."[31] Fanny Stirling, on the other hand, was full of praise. She had heard on all sides, even from people who had no idea they were friends, that Helen's "was in every way *the* speech of the evening—both as to matter & delivery—& everything".[32]

Mill made much of a point which feminists were apt fo confuse: "Those of us who claim for women complete equality have always said that this is a totally different question from the suffrage. The suffrage is a thing apart; no woman by claiming it, is in the smallest degree committed to the larger demand; but the addition of women to the electoral body would almost certainly infuse into the legislature a stronger determination to grapple with the great practical evils of society . . . ."

Harriet Grote opened her speech with unusual humility. "It is an act that savours more of temerity than of courage when a person of advanced age and infirm health appears to offer a few observations; but the cause is worthy of an effort." Then, warming to her theme, she went on, "I never was engaged in any cause in which my feelings were more completely seconded by my reason. . . . I have always felt that the arguments against were so feeble and limited, that the wonder is that they were ever put forth . . . ."[33]

Kate Amberley found Mrs Grote's speech refreshingly short and natural. Mrs Fawcett's she thought "uninteresting & Mrs Pet Taylor (Chairman) was inaudible fr sore throat. It went off very well", she added, surprisingly in the circumstances, "& was a great success." Afterwards her mother-in-law, Lady Russell, wrote to Amberley, "I congrat yr wife on not havg made a speech."[34] She had spoken too soon: Kate's opportunity was coming. "I wish I cd speak but I should get frightened I know", she had protested to Helen, "& I am no good in the writing way either for I tried an article about women a little time ago & Amberley says I have no style & want force so I must relinquish hopes of being useful in any apparent way . . . ."[35]

This was not a valid excuse to Helen. If she had her way—and few could resist her tactics however much they might resent them—Kate must both write and speak; she should not be discouraged by her husband's criticism:

It is an excellent thing to have a severe critic at home; I am a *very* severe critic on Mr Mill . . . My dearest mother was a severe critic of everything I did and constantly stimulated me to go on trying to do well without in the least hiding from me the defects of what I had already done. From this I have gained the advantage that I do not grudge any quantity of trouble. . . . The faintest kind of disapprobation from Mr Mill (when I am lucky enough to get it) suffices to make me cancel a whole article... But believe me it is far pleasanter to have some one on whose sternness one can rely for anticipating what hostile critics may say, than to be thrown entirely on one's own judgment....

Will you let me see the article you have written and shall I suggest improvements in it? Mr Mill tells me I alter other people's writings particularly well and should make a good editor... I have a great deal of practice in doing this, beginning with Mr Mill's writings which I go over five or six times, putting in words here, stops there; scratching through whole paragraphs; asking him to write whole new pages in particular places where I think the meaning is not clear; condensing, enlarging, polishing etc. In short I take very much greater liberties with his things than with any one else's, because there is no *amour propre* to be hurt in his case or mine, and I have complete confidence in him to reject my alterations if he does not really think them improvements....[36]

Since Mill submitted to Helen's criticism, how could Kate refuse? She took the article with her when she and Amberley went to stay with Mill and Helen in Avignon in the autumn of 1869. Helen, who presumably did a good deal of "condensing, enlarging, polishing etc.", persuaded her friend to work it up into a lecture, the "Claims of Women".

Kate spent the morning of 25 May 1870 reading the lecture aloud to her long-suffering husband: in the evening they drove from their Gloucestershire home to the Subscription Rooms in the market town of Stroud. The Amberleys and the chairman, the vice-president of the Mechanics Institute under whose auspices the meeting was being held, were alone on the platform. Now that the dreaded moment had arrived, Kate discovered, to her surprise, that she was not in the least nervous: she read her lecture with force and clarity. She compared the status of married women—even the happiest of them—with the lot of the domestic slave, "as she used to be in the southern States of America", sometimes treated by her owners with the greatest kindness, living a life of comfort and luxury while many of her fellow slaves starved. Women must be rescued from servitude, given absolute equality with men; if not, slaves they must remain: "That is your case, women of England, if you do not feel roused to help in this movement. It is not for you I urge any change, if you feel no need of it, though the fact of your indifference argues your need of enfranchisement. But though you and I may be happy it is no reason not to urge it on behalf of the millions of women in England and America who are not living in this blissful state of comfort and content."[37]

Despite her charm and sincerity, the audience remained apathetic. The lecture, she wrote to Helen, "seemed to fall very flat". Members of the audience,

were all so quiet, in fact much too quiet & respectable.... I had no sympathy at all with me—a Tory squire in the Chair who went I am told because he thought it w^d be good fun. Amberley made a little speech but he was the only sympathizer I really had. There were several county people lots of women & I think the whole thing was new to them all so in that way I may have done some good. Propaganda is always good & people expressed surprise to *me* afterwards to see that a woman c^d lecture & still look like a lady....[38]

Kate had intended that, after the lecture, signatures should be collected for a petition; but, owing to a misunderstanding, very few people realized what was expected of them. She had stipulated that the press should not be represented; nevertheless several reporters managed to worm their way into the hall. *The Times* report, though patronizing and critical, was not damning; but the local newspaper carried an abusive letter from "A He-Critter":

I read somewhere the other day that there are now three sexes—masculine, feminine, and Miss Becker. The latter model seems to be popular, and as the latest fashion is the breath of life to a large section of the female world, it is being followed . . . with a devotion second only to the worship of the last new thing in bonnets. When a peeress takes to the stump . . . and when the claims of the third sex are championed by public men like John Stuart Mill, Jacob Bright and Professor Fawcett, a factitious importance is given to the so-called "claims of women" . . . .

The "He-Critter" also noted in passing that "her ladyship was chaperoned by her liege lord", who listened patiently while she "denounced the marriage laws as barbarous, and protested against the idea of any 'subordination' on the part of the wife; and one of the funniest effects I ever heard was when his lordship gravely assured the audience that he had great pleasure in 'permitting' his wife to deliver her lecture".[39]

In the prevailing climate of opinion Mill's argument that the suffrage issue could be separated from the claim for complete equality was a wise one. There were innumerable opponents of complete equality of the sexes; and those people who were beginning to think that women really ought to have the vote might well look askance at the larger claim.

Mill and Helen understood the drawing-power of Kate Amberley's name and social position; they also knew that this made her a certain target for public abuse. "It is noble of you to be so brave and resolute", wrote Helen. "You have made a raid into the enemies [*sic*] country; got the ideas introduced among just the sort of people most difficult to get at...."[40]

Kate was behaving with nobility and increasing confidence. Not only was she made fun of at the Carlton Club but, at a party at Gladstone's, she was told that she was making her husband a laughing-stock. Husband and wife both received abusive letters. Neither gave way, Amberley encouraging Kate and continuing to play his own part in the movement.

From Helen came further strengthening letters. "It is so kind of you to speak to us poor young struggling workers as you do",[41] replied Kate gratefully. In March 1872 she took the chair at a public meeting in Bristol and made a speech. "I quite expected you to write & tell me I was very good to do such a public thing", she wrote afterwards to Helen. "I did not feel out of place nor did it ever occur to me that it was anything unusual , , , ,"[42] At the end of the meeting a woman came up and introduced herself as Mill's sister Mary Colman. She told Kate she would send her brother a full report of the proceedings.

The Queen, who was well known to disapprove of the women's rights movement, was disgusted by Kate Amberley's behaviour and sent a ferocious letter to Theodore Martin, the Prince Consort's biographer. It was written immediately after Kate's lecture at Stroud, but, when Martin's book was published nearly forty years later, and Kate, Mill and Helen were all in their graves, it was judged prudent for her to remain anonymous:

> The Queen is most anxious to enlist every one who can speak or write to join in checking this mad, wicked folly of "Women's Rights," with all its attendant horrors, on which her poor feeble sex is bent, forgetting every sense of womanly feeling and propriety. Lady —— ought to get a *good whipping*.
>
> It is a subject which makes the Queen so furious that she cannot contain herself. God created men & women different—then let them remain each in their own position . . . .[43]

CHAPTER 21

Intrigue and Dissension

The first rumblings of an impending storm in the suffrage movement were heard in 1869 when Josephine Butler experienced a call, which she believed came directly from God, to do battle against the Contagious Diseases Acts. Under a system of State regulation of prostitution, which had been initiated by Napoleon and adopted throughout Europe, women who lived in garrison towns could be dubbed "common prostitutes", whether they were prostitutes or not, and obliged, on pain of repeated terms of imprisonment, to submit to periodical medical examination. The authorities maintained that the examination, which was applied only to women, checked the spread of venereal disease and so guarded the health of members of the armed forces, who could not be expected to remain continent when separated from their wives.

The first Contagious Diseases Act was passed in England in 1864; a second Act, extending the scope of the provisions to new districts, was passed in 1866 and re-enacted in 1869. Two organisations for the repeal of the Acts were formed that year: the National Association for the Abolition of State Regulation of Vice, and a Ladies' National Association, led by Josephine Butler.

The state of public opinion was largely unknown, for, by tacit consent, the subject of prostitution was considered too abhorrent for open discussion. Josephine Butler, well aware that she was courting obloquy, gave up, that she might concentrate on the campaign, the work in which she had been engaged for the higher education of women. She was naturally anxious to gain the approval of so respected a champion of individual liberty as John Stuart Mill. His initial response to her inquiry was cautious. He considered "that every kind of effort, whether social or political, in favour of women should be encouraged, so long as it is honest and genuine"; but appended a corollary to the effect that right-minded people would learn by experience that the enfranchisement of women would prove to be the basis "and the safeguard of human worth and happiness".[1]

Mill pondered the question during the next few months and came to the conclusion that it was his duty to support the repeal of the Acts. In January

1870 he replied to a correspondent that the outcome of his "consideration is that I greatly deprecate any extension of the Contagious Diseases Act, and should highly approve of its repeal".[2] To another correspondent, the French feminist Julie Victoire Daubié, he described the association of women which had been formed to "excite opinion" against the "deplorable system. They are heartily seconded by men, and there is reason to hope not only that the upholders of the system will not venture to go further, but that they will be obliged to undo what they have done...."[3]

John Chapman of the *Westminster Review* had published several articles expressly designed to reinforce the campaign for repeal. To him Mill wrote that he heartily approved of the suggestion that Josephine Butler's Ladies' National Association should be reinforced with men. "I should be happy to be a member of an Association so constituted." He could not, however, act as president, a post the supporters of repeal would have been delighted for him to fill. He had too much work on hand to be able to spare sufficient time, and did not think it right in the circumstances "to hold myself out to the public as the head of the organisation, and the apparent guide and director of its proceedings".[4]

Among Josephine Butler's male supporters were two suffragist members of Parliament, Jacob Bright and James Stansfeld; among the women Mrs McLaren of Edinburgh and other members of Bright's family, Lydia Becker and Mrs Peter Taylor. Helen Taylor also joined. "I rejoice that you have given your name to the Ladies C. D. A. Association", wrote Clementia Taylor. Suffrage supporters in London, Manchester and Edinburgh were working "splendidly" for repeal, and she had been informed by a member of the Manchester suffrage society that "the infamy of the Act is opening women's eyes to the benefit of the franchise. Mrs Grey and Miss Shirreff are opponents to us in this. I grieve as they are both intelligent thoughtful women—they adopt the views of the medical world believing physicians better able to judge what is right and expedient in such matters — *really ignoring the principle....*"[5]

The official medical line was that the Acts, even though harsh and unpleasant, were beneficial because they helped to check the spread of venereal disease. Some doctors took a different line. Elizabeth Blackwell, who explained their implications to Kate Amberley, came out strongly for repeal. The Acts, she said, when extended to the civilian population, applied only to women. If women were to be medically examined, then why not men?

No one expected Elizabeth Garrett, whose work for women and children was so well known, to take the official line, but she was convinced, from three years' experience of dispensary work, that it was justified. She wrote a letter of explanation to the *Pall Mall Gazette,* and this, published in the issue of 25 January 1870, was used as anti-repeal ammunition by a society which had been formed for the purpose of extending the Acts. In it she argued that compulsory powers of arrest and treatment were essential, since women who knew they were infected were reluctant to enter hospital voluntarily. She stressed the inhumanity of exposing innocent women and their unborn children to contagion, and noted the large number of her patients who had been infected "through no fault of their own. I believe that among the poor, the number of innocent people who suffer from the worst and most lasting forms is greater than the guilty.... Degradation cannot be taken by storm and the animal side of nature will outlive crusades."[6]

That Elizabeth Garrett should support a measure which forced an indignity on women but not on men shocked some of her friends immeasurably. In an emotional outburst to Helen, Clementia Taylor cried that she had been "pained and saddened" by the letter. It "sickens and disgusts me with humanity—with life. Can I have loved and honoured the woman who wrote it?"[7]

The letter had saddened Millicent Fawcett even more. Mrs Fawcett believed that Elizabeth, her deeply loved and admired elder sister, was utterly wrong. She herself was convinced that the Acts were iniquitous and should be repealed; but she also thought that identification with a crusade which many people found revolting would harm the suffrage cause and so she decided to take no part in it. Some of the suffragists—especially the educationists—adopted the same attitude; others supported both causes, believing that one would help the other. It was the beginning of a split which threatened the future of the suffrage movement.

Mill, meanwhile, came out openly in support of repeal, telling the women precisely where their duty lay. In his speech at the Hanover Square Rooms on 26 March 1870, he had this to say:

> If women had had votes, we should not have had the "C. D. Acts;" under which the wives and daughters of the poor are exposed to insufferable indignities on the suspicion of a police-officer; and it must be so if the Acts are to be so enforced as to have any chance of being effectual for their object. If these Acts are repealed—if they are not extended to the whole country—it will be owing to the public spirit and courage of those ladies, some of them of distinguished eminence, who have associated themselves to obtain the repeal of the Acts.[8]

Agitation for repeal was increasing so rapidly that a Royal Commission to inquire into the operation of the Acts was set up the same year. Mill was invited to give evidence and did so in May 1871. When the Chairman asked if he thought the legislation justifiable on principle his answer was unequivocal:

> I do not consider it justifiable on principle because it appears to me to be opposed to one of the greatest principles of legislation, the security of personal liberty. It appears to me that legislation of this sort takes away that security, almost entirely from a particular class of women intentionally, but incidentally and unintentionally ... from all women

whatever, in as much as it enables a woman to be apprehended by the police on suspicion and taken before a magistrate, and then by that magistrate she is liable to be confined for a term of imprisonment which may amount I believe to six months, for refusing to sign a declaration consenting to be examined.

What he also said—and this was hard for some of the commissioners to accept—was that the men and not the women were at fault:

The object of the Act is not to protect those who voluntarily seek indulgence, but to protect the innocent from having these diseases communicated to them; that I understand to be the object. Now a woman cannot communicate the disease but to a person who seeks it, and who knowingly places himself in the way of it. A woman can only communicate it through a man; it must be the man who communicates it to innocent women and children afterwards. It seems to me, therefore, if the object is to protect those who are not unchaste, the way to do this is to bring motives to bear on the man and not on the woman, who cannot have anything to do directly with the communication of it to persons entirely innocent, whereas the man can and does.

He saw no reason why, if the authorities insisted on the examination of women, they should not also insist on the examination of men; and he suggested that severe penalties should be imposed on any man proved to have infected an innocent woman with a venereal disease.

"If", he was asked, "the Legislature did enact with a view to preventing such cases as this, that the woman affected should have the remedy of divorce, would your knowledge of human nature lead you to the conclusion that that remedy would be resorted to in one case in a hundred, or one case in a thousand?"

"A good many more than that", answered Mill, "though probably not the majority."

"Are you aware", asked the Chairman, "that for a man to give his wife a disease of that description would be adjudged cruelty by the Court of Divorce, and would be a ground of divorce, at all events *a mensa?*"

"Yes, but not complete dissolution of the matrimonial tie."

"Would you make it so?"

"Yes."

"You would make it *a vinculo?*"

"Yes, *a vinculo,* accompanied with heavy pecuniary damages for the benefit of the sufferers, the wife and children."[9]

This was an uncompromising statement, unlike others Mill was to make on the subject of divorce (see below, chapter 22). For some months, however, he had been troubled, not so much by the possibility of dissolving the marriage tie, but by the feeling that he might, by his outright support of repeal, be damaging the suffrage cause. His first doubts may well have been aroused by Charles Kingsley, who, in May 1879, had written a cryptic letter to Clementia Taylor:

> If I, as one who has the movement at heart more intensely than I choose to tell any one ... might dare to give advice, it would be, not in the direction of increased activity, but in that of increased passivity. . . . I say that a great deal which has been said and done by women, and those who wish to support women's rights, during the last six months, has thrown back our cause—I will not say, nay I utterly decline to, enter into details. But what I say is true, I know, and know too well . . . .

Mill, who had learned from Mrs Taylor that Kingsley was no longer attending suffrage meetings, wrote to ask him the reason. To a man, Kingsley felt he could be more explicit, even though he was not prepared to mention the Contagious Diseases Acts by name.

"There exist, in all ranks of the English ... women brave, prudent, wise ... whose influence ... is always exercised for good. . . . And unless we can get these ... to be 'the leaders of fashion,' ... we shall not succeed. . . . I know that what our new idea has to beware of ... is hysteria, male and female", wrote Kingsley, whose conjugal life was highly erotic (see Susan Chitty, *The Beast and the Monk: A Life of Charles Kingsley,* Hodder and Stoughton, 1975), defining hysteria in this context "as the fancy and emotions unduly excited by suppressed sexual excitement. It is all the more necessary to do this, if we intend to attack 'social evils', i.e., sexual questions, by the help of woman raised to her proper place. That you mean to do so I take for granted. That I do, I hope you take for granted . . . ." The women's suffrage movement should be conducted quietly and unobtrusively, without the interference of the press and, preferably, without the assistance of unmarried women. He strongly objected to the movement's "being mixed up with social, i.e., sexual questions" and deprecated, "most earnestly, all the meddling, however pure-minded, humane, etc., which women have brought to bear on certain questions during the last six months. I do not say that they are wrong. Heaven forbid! But I do say, that by so doing they are retarding, it may be for generations, the cause which they are trying to serve. And I do say ... that they are thereby mixing themselves up with the fanatical of both sexes; with the vain and ambitious, and, worst of all, with the prurient . . . ."[10]

Mill was in entire agreement with Kingsley that it was important as far as possible to confine the movement to well-bred, well-educated women whose morals were above reproach, although he did not wish to see it entirely in the hands of the upper classes. But how, if there was to be no publicity, could there be any progress? And how, if there were public meetings, could notoriety hunters be excluded? With regard to "the other movement", he continued delicately, "I believe that there has seldom been a movement of purer chivalry than this among respectable women who are exposing themselves to almost intolerable insult, wholly from the goadings of their conscience, and their belief that they are responsible if they do nothing for the horrible degradation of fellow-women".[11] Quite apart from its most laudable aims, "the other movement" had convinced many people, among them Mary Carpenter and Kingsley's friend Frederick Denison Maurice, a fellow Christian Socialist, that women should have the vote.

Kingsley's letter had made Mill uncertain of the course he should take. Helen, too, was doubtful. She had recently signed a repeal circular, "grateful for the opportunity of being able to join in a public demonstration of abhorrence both of the C. D. Acts and of the iniquitous system they are intended to prop up";[12] but to her, as to Mill, the suffrage issue must take precedence, and, if the two movements could not be worked in harmony, repeal must be sacrificed. It was noticeable that, when Mill spoke in Edinburgh in January 1871, to the waving of hats and handkerchiefs, he made no reference to the gallant women of the repeal crusade: his mind was made up; he could no longer lend his name and influence to repeal.

His decision was made at a moment of strife within the suffrage movement. In 1870 delegates from the provincial centres had attended a conference in London. At Mill's suggestion the centres had been linked in a union of sorts, each retaining independence of action, but the London National Society at the hub had been generally considered the most important, if not by the Manchester committee. The London centre was divided on the repeal issue, a majority taking the view adopted first by Millicent Fawcett and now by Mill and Helen, who were not of course on the executive, that their personal views, whatever they were, must not be expressed in public. Clementia Taylor, who had a fatal propensity for looking at both sides of a question, was sadly torn: her principles, her instincts, were all for Mrs Butler's crusade; her loyalty to the suffrage cause was indisputable. Caroline Biggs, at her right hand, had no such doubts: she was for repeal and for the suffrage and saw no reason why the twin issues should be divided. Jacob Bright and Lydia Becker, the Manchester delegates to the London conference, were pronounced repealers. Their object was to form a strong central suffrage committee with headquarters in London. It would supersede the existing London committee and represent the various branches.

Nothing was settled at the London conference, and so Bright summoned delegates from all the centres, London included, to reassemble. There had been internal disputes on the repeal issue, and both he and Miss Becker had noticed Mrs Taylor's agonizing uncertainty. They asked her to sign the circular letter of invitation to the second conference but had no intention of allowing her to take a prominent part. Before she had even heard that the conference was to take place she wailed to Helen, "Mrs Fawcett had agreed to take part in it—strongly advocated it". Millicent Fawcett's views were well known and respected. She was in favour of the conference in order to prevent the outside world from guessing that discord existed between the leaders of the movement; and neither Jacob Bright nor Lydia Becker expected her to modify her stand. Clementia Taylor, however, having signed the invitation, refused to attend the conference, because she had not been asked to speak. Her position in the society, she told Helen, "demanded that if present I should say a few words". Mr Bright had insulted her and the committee of which she was the acknowledged head. She "knew that all possibility of harmony existing between Manchester and London was over", and that nothing but her retirement from office would satisfy the Manchester delegates. They were, she averred, jealous of her position, their animosity increased "by the opinions expressed by almost every committee in England Scotland & Ireland that I was the leader—that I had founded their Societies". She had therefore made up her mind to resign from her executive committee. Her friend Caroline Biggs and a newly appointed joint secretary, Miss Eliza Orme, were more than capable of carrying on the work of the London centre. "Though no longer a member of the Executive, I shall still work for the cause I have so deeply at heart . . . ."[13] Her mood continued sombre and pessimistic: "I begin to despair of our gaining the suffrage for women till Mr Mill returns to Parliament and again becomes our Leader—*then* immediate victory would not surprise me".[14]

Mill, who had no intention of returning to Parliament, dismissed Mrs Taylor as a waverer of little or no use to the cause; but he was alarmed and agitated by the news that Jacob Bright was forging ahead with his plans for a central association, an association in which the issues of repeal and women's suffrage would be combined. As he wrote to his friend Professor Croom Robertson of the London executive committee, "The agitation for . . . repeal . . . should be in nowise mixed up with that for the Suffrage. To confound the two together, is to break faith with the members of the Suffrage Society, many of whom totally disapprove of the other agitation . . . . To make use of the one organisation as a tool to bring in money and influence for the other, is a breach of faith which I have the less hesitation in stigmatizing as it deserves, because I am myself in favour of both . . . ." Croom Robertson had asked for his advice on the action his committee should take when, as now seemed certain, the central association came into being. It was that London should refuse to join but retain its position as an independent and equal member of the original union of suffrage societies. This portion of his letter he was willing for Croom Robertson to read aloud at the next executive committee meeting; the rest was for his eyes alone. Any member of the committee, he added, the officers included, who had signified approval of Jacob Bright's intentions and a willingness for London to join a central association, "should at once be requested to resign, and, if necessary, removed".[15] Croom Robertson had written to him of a possible recruit to the executive. "I do not know which part [he] has taken in the CDA", Mill replied. "Henceforward I would admit no members of the Committee who are for their repeal, unless well known personally, and I hardly know [him] enough to answer for him . . . ."[16]

Jacob Bright, of course, knew nothing of this. At the annual general meeting of the Manchester Suffrage Society he announced with pride, "We are met today I believe with one single object, and that is to arrange for a central committee in London . . ., a committee that should represent all the committees throughout the kingdom that choose to be represented . . ., for the purpose of concentrating the movement, instead of having it scattered . . ." Its sole aim would be "to remove the political disabilities of women", an aim which could best be pursued by bringing concerted pressure to bear in Parliament. To this end, the new central organization would be responsible for forming provincial branches and would act as a centre for the collection and dissemination of information. "The purpose . . . is to aid and not to supplant"[17] the existing suffrage societies.

Twenty-four local societies pledged their support at this meeting for Bright's Central Committee for Women's Suffrage. The London National Society was not among them: Mill had made sure of that. He had by now embarked on a devious course of strategy, unworthy of a man who had always been rightly renowned for his integrity and honesty, his advocacy of individual freedom. He remained in the background, acting entirely through Croom Robertson, who sometimes showed faint signs of rebellion but always in the end capitulated to the demands of the apostle of liberty. Within the sepulchre at Avignon Harriet's dry bones must have rattled in protest!

The first to be purged from the London committee must be the honorary secretary, Caroline Biggs, "I know that Miss Biggs has been very far from judicious', wrote Mill to Croom Robertson, "and has either lent herself to, or has herself been the cause of, most unwise mingling . . . of the franchise with the C. D. A. agitation . . . ." She was, as he knew, wholehearted in her support of repeal and, as such, a menace. "It is not true that the Society owes her any obligation. She was thrust in by Mrs Taylor . . . who . . . made it a personal matter to herself. Civility and thanks are therefore all to which Miss Biggs has any just claim in return for her services . . . ."[18] Miss Biggs must be asked to resign; if she refused she must be dismissed.

The vacillating Mrs Taylor, whose threat of resignation had not yet been implemented, was shocked to receive from Helen a letter casting aspersions on Caroline Biggs, whose devotion to the suffrage cause had never been in doubt. Miss Biggs, Clementia assured Helen, "has intellect, energy, enthusiasm for our cause—and yet prudence that will ever prevent her from saying or doing a foolish thing. She is free from vulgarity—from any self-seekingness and an indefatigable worker. I feel very strongly that the Society would lose much by her retirement and to me the loss would be so great that I really do not know how I should manage to do without her— no *paid* Secretary could take her place . . . ."[19] Mrs Taylor was not alone in her estimate of Miss Biggs. Another suffrage leader, Miss Helen Blackburn, historian of the movement, described her "ready pen, methodical work and untiring industry [which] soon proved her an invaluable ally"; and wrote of "this serene and gentle nature who was the friend of all the workers at home and abroad; and of whom one may truly say she had 'the charity that suffereth long and is kind'."[20]

Miss Biggs needed all her charity. Neither Mill nor Helen had taken the slightest notice of Clementia Taylor's plea, nor of Croom Robertson, who appears to have been prevaricating. "I certainly feel as much astonishment as regret that a vote of censure, and of request to Miss Biggs to resign, was not passed at the last Committee meeting", wrote Mill to his accomplice. Although he advocated the use of polite language, using the word " 'change' etc in speaking of dismissal", if Miss Biggs refused to take the hint the word "dismissal" must be employed. It happened on occasion, especially with the Manchester people, "that blunt language is necessary for they can understand no other.... Moreover... if you have scruples in carrying your measures either in the absence of the others, or by simply overpowering them with votes by a majority, *however small,* you may as well give up the struggle ...."

Croom Robertson recanted, though not with any enthusiasm. "We can most heartily sympathise with your weariness and disgust at the contest which has been forced on you... I can only advise continuing to use your utmost efforts to weed the Committee of the obnoxious set",[21] wrote his master.

Within a week, justice, as Mill would undoubtedly have called it, had been done: a vote of censure was passed on Caroline Biggs, though not by a unanimous decision, and she resigned. On hearing the news, Mill wrote to Croom Robertson congratulating him on his success. At the same time he promised, in the event of an open breach between the London National Society and Jacob Bright's central association, to serve as president of a reformed London committee; and this he subsequently did.

Miss Biggs, who naturally transferred her allegiance to the new central association, continued, until her death in 1888, to work for the extension of the suffrage to women.

In the meantime, having successfully disposed of Miss Biggs, Mill turned his attention to the reform of the executive of the London National Society, continuing to work through Croom Robertson, who was forbiden to divulge any of his orders. He had no respect for Mrs Peter Taylor, whom he considered weak to the point of imbecility; but he did not wish to see her go. Owing to dissension in the ranks of the committee and to the callous treatment of Miss Biggs, she had stopped attending meetings. Mill was anxious for her to return. Her name, he said, was associated in the public mind with the original London society; if she departed she would be replaced by others, who would be looked on as usurpers. Released as she now was from the influence of Miss Biggs, Croom Robertson would find her malleable: if not, he could always defeat her by making sure that she was outvoted in committee. In other words, she was needed as a figure-head: "her age, her appearance, that very feminine weakness which is so evident about her, is invaluable for the purpose. Her bitterest enemy cannot accuse her of being a strong-minded woman ...."[22] She had another advantage, Mill reminded his friend: her home, Aubrey House, had always been used for meetings; if she departed for good he would have to find somewhere else.

Clementia Taylor was anything but strong-minded: she hesitated, changed her mind and worried over unimportant details; but she was liked and respected and she had served the cause faithfully to the best of her capacities. To her credit, when pressed to return, she resolutely refused. Nor, despite her sympathy with Josephine Butler's crusade, did she join Jacob Bright's association, many of whose members supported both causes. "Has Mr Mill received a letter from Mrs Butler . . . relative to a most terrible and painful subject—the C. D. Act?" she asked Helen. She herself had been on the point of offering to form a committee in London for the repeal of the Acts, but, on reflection, felt "I might injure our franchise cause by connecting myself with a Society which will be opposed by *very* many of our supporters *not* from any cowardice on my part—a woman has no right to shrink from a duty because painful", but because her first duty, whether in or out of office, was to the franchise, "which really goes to the root of all evils connected with women. . . . I have promised Mrs Butler all the help I can give silently", she added, hoping, no doubt, to placate her crusading friend; and she asked Helen, in the event of a repeal branch being formed, if she would be prepared to join: "Your name will have such weight and influence . . . ."[23] Helen had no intention of lending her name to any new committee advocating repeal. On this issue, where her stepfather had led she was prepared to follow.

Mill, meanwhile, was instructing Croom Robertson on the reform of the executive committee of the London National Society. He drew up a list of members on whose absolute loyalty he could rely: among them were Thomas Hare, who, however, was seldom available for meetings, and his daughter Katharine; W.T. Thornton; the secretary, Eliza Orme; and Croom Robertson himself. Three he marked as "doubtful". Among them was Mrs Charlotte Burbury, who corresponded extensively with Helen on suffrage affairs and was appointed honorary secretary when Miss Orme resigned in 1872 to study law. Many years later—in 1893—Mrs Burbury saw Mill's letter and slipped into it a note of her own: "The three marked *uncertain* were among the most certain. I was only reluctant to support the vote of censure on Miss Biggs." Of the two members marked by Mill "Perhaps hostile", one was Mrs Fawcett, who was, he understood, "a recent convert to the C. D. A. movement". It seems strange that he did not realize that, whatever her private opinions, she was not prepared to support Josephine Butler in public. He considered her "quite public spirited" but somewhat prosaic and, like her husband, "a little doctrinaire . . . . Hence she may at any time fancy that consistency demands what I might think foolish conduct . . . ."[24] Mill had, in fact, misjudged Millicent Fawcett: prosaic and a little doctrinaire she might be, but she was more consistent than he was himself.

The Central Committee of the National Society for Women's Suffrage met for the first time as an organization at the Langham Hotel, London, in January 1872. Mill's strategy had driven to follow Caroline Biggs's example several prominent members of the London National Society who were known to be in favour of repeal. Among them were Sheldon Amos, Professor of Jurisprudence at University College, a supporter of the higher education of women and a leader of Mrs Butler's crusade; Mrs James Stansfeld, whose husband risked his Parliamentary career by his outspoken advocacy of repeal; and Mrs Frederick Pennington, the wife of a member of Parliament. Frances Power Cobbe, who had earlier left the London committee, now joined Jacob Bright's organization; and there was a further division of the Garrett family when two enterprising young women, Agnes and Rhoda, sister and cousin respectively of Elizabeth and Millicent, also joined.

Mill had been relieved to see the departure of the dissident members. His faithful friends on the London committee had disapproved of the appointment of Mrs Pennington and Professor Amos; and Katharine Hare had gone as far as asking Helen if she should resign, "as their names are identified with the C. D. A. agitation, from which I am most anxious that ours should be perfectly distinct".[25] She had been told she would do more good by remaining; but she was now to be married and would be living out of London and suggested once again that she should resign. Mill instructed Croom Robertson to ask her to stay on: it would be difficult to find a suitable replacement. Emily Shirreff's sister Maria Grey might provide additional ballast. She had recently published a useful pamphlet, *Is the Exercise of the Suffrage Unfeminine?*, and had, of course, concluded that it was not. She was also, as Mill knew, opposed to repeal. "She is a lady, and her age gives weight, but we do not know much of her." Mrs Grey, who was fifty-five, was too busy with her educational project to take up suffrage work, however sympathetic she might feel. The problem, as Mill complained to Croom Robertson, was that "the ladies we could most rely on are unhappily more or less invalids". However, "now that you are freed from associates against whose faults we thought ourselves qualified to warn you . . . , I have no doubt you will find much fewer difficulties and much less need of advice".[26]

The Suffrage Bill which Jacob Bright introduced on 1 May 1872 was defeated by a larger majority than its predecessor had been. Professor Cairnes told Mill that only one vote had been lost by the association of women's suffrage with the agitation for the repeal of the Contagious Diseases Acts; but Mill was convinced that the defeat was due entirely to the identification of the suffrage movement "with the Bright and Becker set". This juxtaposition, as he told Cairnes, which Jacob Bright, "instead of disclaiming . . . did his utmost to confirm, is but one example of the total want equally of good taste and good sense with which they conduct the proceedings". It is true that, in his speech in the House, Bright had claimed that support for repeal would also give an impetus to the campaign for the vote. By this time Mill must have completely forgotten his own assertion that the enfranchisement of women would act as a spur to the agitation against the Acts as well as to the elimination of many other evils. In a passage in the manuscript draft of his letter to Cairnes he claimed that, during the four years in which the movement "was mainly under my daughter's guidance", it had been kept free from doubtful associations. But "my daughter's ill health leaving the way open to Mrs Taylor's visible weakness, the Jacob Brights and their set have become prominent in London & have already thrown back the question into that refrain of feminine contempt & ridicule out of which it was raised".[27]

Victorian women were, of course, prone to fall back on ill health as an excuse for inaction. Helen, though never robust, was equal to any amount of work; and Mill, in suppressing this passage, must have realized that it was a distortion of the truth.

It had been suggested by the remaining members of the executive of the London National Society that a public meeting should be held to reassure rank-and-file members that it was still in being, despite the existence of Jacob Bright's Central Committee. Mill was opposed to any such publicity. The London National Society must be prepared to bide its time, he told Croom Robertson. When the leaders of the Central Committee "let the reins drop, disgusted with the failure they have caused, or when they have fallen into such discredit with their followers that they can make no serious resistance to being superseded, then the time of the London Committee will have come".[28]

Once again Croom Robertson bowed to his master's commands. In July 1872 he reported that there was "no question of holding any such public meeting as you deprecated". Some fifty subscribers had attended the annual general meeting under the chairmanship of Thomas Hare. "The report of our year's action—containing no allusion to the dissensions—was unanimously approved of." Requests for information about the origins of the Central Committee were made and answered "more freely because only one reporter was present employed by ourselves". As a result, "a motion recommending or requiring us to come to terms with the Central Committee was withdrawn.... The meeting had the effect of removing from the minds of different members of our Comm. all scruples as to our position; & we shall now go on upon the old line with perfect confidence—working in our own fashion, and not regarding the action, whatever it be, of the other body ...."[29]

When Jacob Bright announced his intention of introducing his suffrage bill in Parliament for the third time, Croom Robertson invited members of his executive to register a protest against his repeal sympathies by dissassociating themselves from his efforts on behalf of the suffrage. Some members agreed to this divisive suggestion; others, so he told Mill, were "rather shocked at the notion of Jacob Bright not having the joy of leading the cause to triumph".[30]

Not that triumph was remotely in sight! Mill, who was relieved that a rumour which had reached him in Avignon of a union between the London National Society and the Central Committee was false, was strongly in favour of a protest. Croom Robertson had suggested submitting to Bright an address praying him to refrain from reintroducing his bill. In a letter, partly composed by Helen and reflecting their joint views, Mill replied, "We think that the great motive, and it is a powerful one, for making some sort of an address ..., is in order that we may influence members who are favourable to the suffrage, openly to stay away in considerable numbers if Mr Jacob Bright insists on a division. That is the only way we can see of breaking the fall which is sure to come: and if Mr Jacob Bright knows that your Committee recommends this policy, it will be more likely than anything else to check his folly, if anything would...."[31]

Mrs Burbury and Mrs Fawcett would have nothing to do with the protest; Mill advised Croom Robertson to ignore their objections. He had, he said, a poor opinion of Mrs Burbury's powers of judgement. As for Mrs Fawcett, she was "so far from being indispensable, that she is quite as detrimental as useful". If her views were to take precedence in committee he himself would resign from the London National Society. He conceded that she was a sensible, energetic young women, with plenty of self-confidence; but she lacked experience and was, "therefore, admirably calculated to fall headlong into mistakes. She never originated this movement, and is not likely to originate any." She was no organizer and, even if she were "twice her present age, she is quite unfit to be a leader".[32]

Mill had drawn a convenient veil over his original estimate of Mrs Fawcett, his praise of her speaking and writing abilities, of the value of a young, intelligent woman to the movement. If his present harsh judgement was based on the assumption that she was in collusion with "the Bright and Becker set", he was entirely wrong: whatever her sympathies, she had continued to remain aloof from the repeal agitation.

It is impossible to deny that Mill's actions during the past few years had fermented discord and dissension within the movement he had helped to create and lead, had sown confusion where they might have promoted unity and strength. The strife persisted after his death in 1873. The following year Jacob Bright and his Parliamentary colleague on the Central Committee, Edward Eastwick, lost their seats, and it was necessary to look elsewhere for a leader of the suffrage cause in Parliament. The London National Society wanted an uncontroversial figure to introduce the next suffrage bill. As Mrs Burbury wrote to her former colleague Miss Biggs, "Should the Bill be entrusted to any one whose name is well known in connection with the agitation against the C. D. Acts, our Com[tee] ... would publish in the newspapers an emphatic protest, to which many very influential signatures would be attached...."

Caroline Biggs, as secretary, replied that the Central Committee would welcome "any opportunity of cordial co-operation among all the Com[tees] "; but she was "sure that we could not accept any proposal which even *appeared* to convey a slight on the Members of Parliament to whom we have had so much cause for gratitude for their devoted conduct of the Bill, or attempted to impose conditions upon those who shall in future undertake it. You know that any other subject except Women's Suffrage is entirely and at all times ignored in our office; no work would otherwise be carried on, as we have members of Com[tee] of all shades of opinion upon those other matters."[33]

Charlotte Burbury sent her own letter and Caroline Bigg's reply to Helen and asked her where she stood on the leadership issue. Helen replied loftily, "I am quite prepared to sign a public protest, should you judge it necessary to make one. . . . I do not wish to be in any way a party to any combined action with the other committees; I might even prefer to retire if any combined action is decided upon. . . . I am sure I should approve any action you might take tending to separate our Committee more widely from the others, because I have not thought you sufficiently on your guard against them . . . ."[34]

This was too much for Millicent Fawcett, who had been disgusted by Charlotte Burbury's letter to Caroline Biggs. The prospect of the London National Society airing its grievance in public and attempting to force conditions on the movement's new Parliamentary leader led her to resign and to do what Mill had always suspected she might—join the Central Committee. Helen was invited to fill her place on the London executive and agreed: "I shall be glad to do anything in my power to replace Mrs Fawcett's aid . . . in any way."[35] Her advice as a committee member was precisely the same as the advice Mill had given Croom Robertson when the prospect of a public meeting was mooted: "I think our Committee can scarcely keep too quiet; it is not a time for action but for quiet waiting until others are tired of injudicious action, when . . . it will be for us to resume the lead".[36]

The new Parliamentary leader, Mr Forsyth, Conservative member for Marylebone, confounded everybody by inserting into his suffrage bill a clause expressly excluding married women from any voting rights which might be obtained. Under protest and, after a year spent in argument and discussion, the words "no woman under coverture" were substituted for "no married women" in the text of the bill. When the bill was finally introduced, however, it got no further than a second reading.

In 1877 Jacob Bright returned to the House of Commons. By that time the rabid opposition to Josephine Butler's crusade had been greatly diminished (the Contagious Diseases Acts were suspended in 1883 and repealed in 1886), and the London National Society was, in consequence, becoming less exclusive. Bright retired through illness in 1878, and his place as leader fell to a young Liberal member, Leonard Courtney (later Lord Courtney of Penwith). Courtney's immediate reaction was to invite the suffragists who had split on the issue of repeal to come together, and he more or less forced the warring factions to make peace.

When, some twenty years later, Mrs Fawcett was made president of the National Union of Women's Suffrage Societies, which consolidated the disparate committees in a single organization, she confounded Mill's final judgement by making an admirable leader. Though she lacked the dynamism of the suffragette idol, Emmeline Pankhurst, she did much to raise the prestige of the movement and guide it towards its ultimate success. For Mill she always had the greatest admiration and respect, looking on her invitations to Blackheath as a signal honour. It was fortunate that she never learned of his duplicity or—if she did—decided to keep very quiet about it. In 1927, nine years after English women over thirty had been given the vote, one year before they gained it on equal terms with men, the eighty-year-old Dame Millicent Fawcett paid Mill a final tribute. She walked, hand-in-hand with her sister Agnes, to place a sheaf of flowers at the foot of the bronze statue which had been erected to his memory on the Thames embankment.

CHAPTER 22

The Subjection of Women

Harriet's influence over the *Principles of Political Economy* and *On Liberty* was dominant; over his most controversial book, *The Subjection of Women*, it was crucial, although she did not live to see a word of it put on paper. It reflected her thoughts; it was rooted in her article "The Enfranchisement of Women". Written in 1861, Mill put it aside, revised it from time to time, and published it in 1869. As completed, it "was enriched with some important ideas of my daughter's, and passages of her writing. But in what was of my own composition, all that is most striking and profound belongs to my wife; coming from the fund of thought which had been made common to us both, by our innumerable conversations and discussions on a topic which filled so large a place in our minds."[1] Had Harriet lived, he maintained, eager as always to depreciate himself, *The Subjection* would have been a far better book. His object—and hers—was to set out as clearly as possible his preoccupation with sex inequality: "That the principle which regulates the existing social relations between the two sexes—the legal subordination of one sex to another—is wrong in itself, and now one of the chief hindrances to human improvement; and that it ought to be replaced by a principle of perfect equality, admitting no power or privilege on the one side, nor disability on the other."[2]

The Subjection contains echoes of Mary Wollstonecraft's *Vindication,* of William Thompson's and Mrs Wheeler's *Appeal of Women;* it is in the force of the argument, in the clarity and strength of the writing that it differs most from its predecessors. Some amelioration in the lot of women had since been achieved, but they were still subordinate to men. Mill dealt with this subordination under three heads—education, domestic life, and occupation. While many women accepted their disabilities uncomplainingly, some were beginning to rebel, even to the extent of petitioning Parliament for their admission to the franchise. Their claim to be educated as solidly, and in the same branches of knowledge, as men, is urged with growing intensity, and with a great prospect of success; while the demand for their admission into professions and occupations hitherto closed against them becomes every year more urgent. Though there are not in this Country, as there are in the United

States, periodical Conventions and an organized party to agitate for the Rights of Women, there is a numerous and active Society organized and managed by women, for the more limited object of obtaining the political franchise. Nor is it only in our own country and in America that women are beginning to protest . . . France, and Italy, and Switzerland, and Russia now afford examples of the same thing . . . .[3]

In the modern world human beings are—or should be—free to use their faculties and abilities to the best advantage. It should not be ordained that "to be born a girl instead of a boy, any more than to be born black instead of white, or a commoner instead of a nobleman, shall decide the person's position through all life—shall interdict people from all the more elevated social positions, and from all, except a few, respectable occupations".[4]

The subordination of women was an unjustifiable relic of a bygone age; yet every step made in the improvement of mankind had "been . . . invariably accompanied by a step made in raising the social position of women". The differences in the physical constitution of men and women had been "ascertained, to some extent", by doctors and physiologists; but woman's mental characteristics must remain largely unknown "so long as those who alone can really know it, women themselves, have given but little testimony, and that little, mostly suborned. It is easy to know stupid women." The stupidity of a man or woman can be gauged from the opinions of his or her intimate circle.

> Not so with those whose opinions and feelings are an emanation from their own nature and faculties. It is only a man here and there who has any tolerable knowledge of the character even of the women of his own family. . . . Many a man thinks he perfectly understands women, because he has had amatory relations with several, perhaps with many of them. If he is a good observer . . . he may have learnt something of one narrow department of their nature. . . . But for all the rest of it, few persons are generally more ignorant. . . . The most favourable case which a man can generally have . . . is that of his own wife: for the opportunities are greater, and the case of complete sympathy not so unspeakably rare. . . . But most men have not had the opportunity of studying . . . more than a single case: accordingly one can . . . infer what a man's wife is like, from his opinions about women in general. To make even this one case yield any result, the woman must be worth knowing, and the man not only a competent judge, but of a character so sympathetic in itself, and so well adapted to hers, that he can either read her mind by sympathetic intuition, or has nothing in himself which makes her shy of disclosing it. Hardly anything, I believe, can be more rare than this conjunction . . . .

In the vast majority of cases, however, "the knowledge which men can acquire of women . . . is wretchedly imperfect and superficial, and always will be so, until women themselves have told all that they have to tell".[5]

If women were permitted to compete on equal terms with men for entry to the professions and other occupations, said Mill, as he had said before, there need be no unfair competition between the sexes, for women would not seek to do any work for which they were not equipped. Nor would they shun the idea of marriage if the vocation of wife and motherhood seemed natural to them. Men were afraid, "not lest women should be unwilling to marry ...: but lest they should insist that marriage should be on equal conditions; lest women of spirit and capacity should prefer doing almost anything else, not in their own eyes degrading, rather than marry, when marrying is giving themselves a master, and a master too of all their earthly possessions".[6] Whether or not a woman chose to marry, her property and inheritance should be her own; but, in the case of a married woman, this need not interfere with the joint right of husband and wife to tie up their property by settlement for the benefit of their children.

To refuse women the vote, to exclude them from almost every form of lucrative occupation merely served to ensure their permanent subjection to men. "Under whatever conditions ... men are admitted to the Suffrage, there is not a shadow of justification for not admitting women to the same ...." There was no doubt, either, of women's ability

> not only to participate in elections, but themselves to hold offices, or practice professions involving important public responsibilities ... since any woman who succeeds in an open profession proves by that very fact that she is qualified for it. And in the case of public offices, if the political system ... is such as to exclude unfit men, it will equally exclude unfit women.... As long therefore as it is acknowledged that even a few women may be fit for these duties, the laws, which shut the door on these exceptions cannot be justified by any opinion ... respecting the capacities of women in general.[7]

The crux of the whole situation was, of course, the undeniable need to educate and train women for the responsibilities they were by nature perfectly capable of assuming. In marriage, as in professional life, an educated woman was an asset, as her husband's partner, her children's guide. Meanwhile, women "are declared to be better than men; an empty compliment, which must provoke a bitter smile from every woman of spirit, since there is no other situation in life in which it is the established order, and considered quite natural and suitable, that the better should obey the worse".[8]

One of the most significant and controversial problems raised, but not resolved, in *The Subjection of Women* was the possibility of divorce. In the past Mill and Harriet had inveighed against the injustice of an unhappy marriage in which the wife was victimized and all the rights and privileges held by the husband. In 1832, less than two years after they met, each wrote an essay on the subject, though not for publication;[9] and their arguments

were repeated in *The Subjection*. In his original essay Mill followed William
Thompson's plea for equal rights in marriage. He did not deny that for
centuries the indissolubility of the marriage tie had helped to protect the
wife; that, when the first transports of passion were ended, a woman could at
least keep her home and children and, generally, her husband's affection,
even if he went elsewhere for love. Most women accepted the existing state of
marriage and were averse to the idea of divorce. They enjoyed one advantage
over single women: as wives and mothers they were looked on as useful
members of society; their single sisters had to establish—if they could—a
claim to recognition on their merits alone. Yet, to Mill, it was utterly wrong
that marriage should be based on anything but mutual happiness of man and
wife; it must be a marriage of equals, not of a superior and an inferior being.

There were, as he knew, cases in which the dissolution of a marriage
would benefit both husband and wife, always provided the wife was given
equality of rights with her former husband. Early marriage led all too often to
disillusionment, but, while the resultant misery was a powerful argument in
favour of divorce, this remedy must never be lightly invoked, especially
where there were children of the marriage. Mill therefore believed that a
sensible married couple would not start a family until they were as certain as
they could be that their marriage was stable. (Since birth control was virtually
impossible, such a statement lends credence to the argument that Mill was
under-sexed or even impotent.)

Although he believed in the sanctity of marriage, especially where
children were concerned, he thought a marriage might be ended when
incompatibility of temperament made it impossible for husband and wife to
continue to live together, or if one or other of them had fallen irretrievably in
love with some one else. In these circumstances he maintained (and he could
only have been thinking of his own) he could advance no argument which
would convince him that the marriage tie should be forcibly adhered to.
Women were ready for equality, but talk of equality would remain farcical so
long as the marriage tie remained virtually indissoluble.

Harriet Taylor's thoughts, expressed in a more fragmentary and random
form than Mill's, were in some ways more realistic. So long as women lacked
the necessary education to give them self-confidence they would be inclined
to timidity and dependence. It would therefore be unwise to invoke divorce,
since a woman left to fend for herself might well seek another protector.
Harriet was in no doubt that the vast majority of men were sensualists, while
women, on the whole, were not. The miseries endured by so many women
would be greatly reduced, their happiness heightened, by equality in
marriage; but equality was impossible so long as girls were trained only *for*
marriage and given no clear idea of its obligations and limitations. Education
in its true sense was the key to equality; but, under existing conditions, to
offer women equality, which would be equality only in name, and to relax the
laws which protected them, might well act not to their advantage but to their
detriment. It was for John Stuart Mill, she said, as the most worthy exponent

of the highest virtues, to teach the true values of equality to the world.

If Mill had his own predicament in mind in 1832, it was not long before his views began to fluctuate. In 1842, so he reminded Auguste Comte, "Je vous ai déjà dit que la question du divorce est pour moi indécise ...."[10] By 1855, however, he had become more positive. As he wrote to another correspondent, "My opinion on Divorce is that though any relaxation of the irrevocability of marriage would be an improvement, nothing ought to be ultimately rested in, short of entire freedom on both sides to dissolve this like any other partnership. The only thing requiring legal regulation would be the maintenance of the children when the parent could not arrange it amicably—& in that I do not see any considerable difficulty."[11]

In *The Subjection of Women* he inveighed against the institution of marriage, in which husband and wife "are called 'one person in law', for the purpose of inferring that whatever is hers is his, but the parallel inference is never drawn that whatever is his is hers". Since 1858 the Court for Divorce and Matrimonial Causes had been empowered to dissolve a marriage by divorce; but divorce was still an extreme measure. As Mill pointed out, if a wife was driven by cruelty to leave her husband, she could "take nothing with her, neither her children nor anything which is rightfully her own". If he chose he could force her to return:

> It is only legal separation by a decree of a court of justice, which entitles her to live apart. ... This legal separation, until lately, the courts of justice would only give at an expense which made it inaccessible to anyone out of the higher ranks. Even now it is only given in cases of desertion, or of the extreme of cruelty; and yet complaints are made every day that it is granted too easily. Surely, if a woman is denied any lot in life but that of being the personal body-servant of a despot, and is dependent for everything upon the chance of finding one who may be disposed to make a favourite of her instead of merely a drudge, it is a very cruel aggravation of her fate that she should be allowed to try this chance only once. The natural sequel and corollary from this state of things would be, that since her all in life depends upon obtaining a good master, she should be allowed to change again and again until she finds one.

At this point Mill began to hedge, to burke the issue: "I am not saying that she ought to be allowed this privilege. That is a totally different consideration. The question of divorce, in the sense of involving liberty of remarriage, is one into which it is foreign to my purpose to enter."[12]

Such ambiguity could not pass unnoticed. "Even his friends thought [the] argument overstrained", wrote W. L. Courtney; "for it has a depth and intensity of passion in the language which could only be understood if the author were advocating divorce, pure and simple, in the case of ill-assorted unions. But this is exactly what Mill does not do."[13]

Leslie Stephen's brother, James Fitzjames Stephen, who described the book as "a work from which I dissent from the first sentence to the last", found something positively unpleasant, if not indecent, "in prolonged and minute discussions about the relations between men and women". As to separation or divorce, "it is impossible to avoid the inference that marriage, like other partnerships, may be dissolved at pleasure. The advocates of women's rights are exceedingly shy of stating this plainly. Mr Mill says nothing about it . . . ."[14]

The anonymous editor of *The Grosvenor Papers,* who invited communications "in confidence from ladies", was equally vehement. Mill's thesis led inescapably to divorce as a means of relief for a wronged wife, "and it will not do for him to avoid the contingency. . . . We insist on almost indefinite power of divorce being the logical corollary of equality in the marriage relations as sketched out by the author. If he is dissatisfied by this let him complete his plan and argue the question . . . ."[15]

Mill continued to sit on the fence. The object of the book, he explained to an Australian correspondent, Henry Keylock Rusden, was to uphold women's claim to equality with men both in and out of marriage. He had "carefully avoided giving any opinion as to the conditions under which marriage should be dissoluble, for the very good reason that I have not formed . . . a well-grounded opinion on the subject".[16]

It is not difficult to find an excuse for Mill's caution. Helen would have reminded him—if he was in any danger of forgetting—of the furore aroused by his championship of Bradlaugh the previous year and warned him of the perils involved in another controversial subject. He was, of course, aware that few people approved of the idea of divorce or easier separation; but he might well have been less open to censure if had allowed himself to be more explicit.

Over all, the reaction to *The Subjection of Women* was mixed. Leslie Stephen, more balanced in his judgement than his brother, considered that none of Mill's previous books had been "more emphatically marked by generosity and love of justice". He noted, however, "a certain shrillness of tone [which] marks the recluse too little able to appreciate the animal nature of mankind. Yet in any case he made a most effective protest against the prejudices which stunted the development and limited the careers of women."[17]

The editor of *The Grosvenor Papers* was violently antagonistic. Since the beginning of the world, "or at least since 'The Fall', it has been understood to be the intention of the Creator that women should be in subjection to man". The world had acted "with diminishing strictness" towards women: all that was now required was a law, or laws, to curb man's abuse of his powers; the powers themselves should not be disturbed. The demand for equal opportunities in education sounded highly suspicious. The editor magnanimously conceded that he had no quarrel with education as such; most men found the companionship of an educated wife congenial. But many people were opposed to higher education for women on the grounds that "the advanced educational party are known to have ulterior objects in view".

The nature of these "objects" was not stated, but the editor was presumably referring to the demand for the vote and the advance towards complete equality. His conclusion was that Mill's entire argument was "the crudest and most illogical that even the present age, so prolific in such, has produced".[18]

One of Mill's warmest admirers, Alexander Bain, gave, in his biography, a critical reception to *The Subjection*. Mill "leads us to suppose that the relations of men and women between themselves may work on a purely voluntary principle", he commented suspiciously. His "handling of the mental equality of the sexes is...open to exception.... He grants that women are physically inferior, but seems to think that this does not affect their mental powers"; and he found the terms on which Mill advocated equality of the sexes stronger "than people generally would be willing to accept".[19]

On publication of *The Subjection,* Bain had written Mill a letter of cautious appreciation. "I am very glad you are so well pleased with the new book", Mill replied. If his friend thought he had been a little too positive in his central theme, Mill maintained that it was necessary not merely to convert the general public, but "to stir up the zeal of women themselves" on their own behalf. The infant suffrage movement had already converted many people to the cause of women's education. "That point is conceded by almost everybody & we shall find the education movement for women favoured & promoted by many who have no wish at all that things sh^d go any further....'[20]

Mill was naturally interested in the comments of his personal friends. To Charles Eliot Norton he wrote that it was "a great satisfaction that you not only agree so completely with the little book, but think so highly as you do of its probable influence".[21] Once again he was surprised and pleased by the reaction of Charles Kingsley, who found his argument "unanswerable, and certain, from its moderation as well as from its boldness.... I shall continue to labour ... in the direction which you point out; and all the more hopefully because your book has cleared and arranged much in my mind which was confused and doubtful."[22]

Mill's worshippers in the women's movement were suitably reverential, although Kate Amberley wished that the necessary reforms could be made without too much talk. She realized that this was impossible, "and so I suppose that we must be discussed and turned inside out for the next 20 years & then lawmakers will begin to see that they had better give in & let us manage our own affairs & keep our own property and be guardian to our own children".[23] She and her husband were "so enchanted with seeing such a high ideal of marriage ... put before people. It seems to me to be a view of it quite overlooked & a blessing so wonderfully rare. I wonder if more education in the women will help to bring it about." She promised to study the book well, "that I may get all the arguments into my head & have them ready for any scoffers".[24]

Some of Mill's friends were worried in case the book went unnoticed.

Jessie Boucherett, so concerned for the employment prospects for women, hoped, so she told Helen nervously, that the book "will be reviewed in many periodicals, but I am afraid our enemies will think it the best policy to pass it over in silence".[25] She need not have been worried on that particular score: the book was not ignored, even if it received some savage reviews. *Blackwood's Magazine* in September 1869, for example, thundered at Mill for "his intense arrogance, his incapacity to do justice to the feelings or motives of all from whom he differs, his intolerance of all but his own disciples".

Elizabeth Garrett, in the process of taking her medical degree at the University of Paris, wrote to Helen of her pleasure that the tone of the book "is aggressive against slavery rather than apologetic for freedom: it will excite far more discussion & do far more good than any more cautious statement of the case on the side of women would have done".[26]

"I have never thanked Mr Mill for that book because I have felt and feel so strongly about it that I cannot express myself", confessed Barbara Bodichon. 'It is almost painful to be so dumb! & to feel not ever in any way [able] to repay what even to me personally Mr Mill has done of good. Then it is a great subject of rejoicing to feel the book is written & Mr Mill is on our side for ever & ever . . . ."[27]

The strangest, and certainly the most touching, of all the tributes from Mill's female admirers came from Russia. In the summer of 1869 Moncure Conway spent a holiday with his friend Eugene Schuyler, the American chargé d'affaires in Moscow, and Schuyler took him to call on a wealthy baron and his family who lived some twenty miles from the city. They arrived to find the baroness and her four daughters, who ranged in age from twenty-three to seventeen, "enjoying sherbet and cigarettes". Cigars, vodka and caviare were provided for the guests; and, after an interval for refreshment and polite conversation, Schyler informed the girls that Conway was a personal friend of John Stuart Mill. At that, Conway recorded, the girls "all came and bowed low to me, declaring (in perfect English) that Mill's book demanding freedom for women was their Bible. 'Yes', said the eldest, 'I sleep with that book under my pillow."[28]

The Subjection of Women seems to have had a more direct influence on the women's rights movement overseas than it did, initially at any rate, in Britain. In Denmark, for instance, it was translated by the well-known critic Georg Brandes and widely read. Indeed, said one of the leaders of the movement, its progress "was probably due in no small measure to Mill's famous book".[29]

"You have perceived that . . . whatever there is in it which shews any unusual insight into nature or life was learnt . . . from my wife, and subsequently also from her daughter",[30] wrote Mill to the American women's rights leader Isabella Beecher Hooker, who had sent him an appreciative letter. How much of the book was in fact Helen's work we do not know; but she had unquestioningly given him the same kind of advice and help as her mother had done.

By the end of the century *The Subjection* was suffering an eclipse in England. Elizabeth Blackwell wrote to Helen asking if she could not arrange for the publication of a new edition "of our venerated champion's work. . . . It would surely . . . be most valuable, that the noble words of one who has left us, should be used to instruct a new generation. [It] would be like fresh air let into a close hospital ward."[31]

The eclipse was only temporary: the book has been reprinted many times and is still in print today. The specific rights for which Mill, together with Harriet and Helen, campaigned have long since been taken for granted; but he would have given a wry and bitter smile had he known that, more than a hundred years after his death, it would be necessary to introduce a Sex Discrimination Bill in Parliament and to hold an International Women's Year in 1975. To the Women's Liberation Movement it is almost as much of a bible as it was to the young Russian noblewomen of 1869. It continues, writes the American sociologist and feminist, Alice S. Rossi, "to be a powerfully effective essay, which people in the 1970s can find as stimulating as those who read it for the first time in the 1870s. It is grounded in basic libertarian values that ring as true today as then. . . ."[32]

CHAPTER 23

Last Works

On Saturday 3 May 1873, Mill took the train from Avignon to Orange to spend an energetic and satisfying day walking and botanizing. He returned home in the cool of the evening, looking and feeling exceptionally well for a man of sixty-seven who had been suffering for years from tuberculosis. By the Monday he was feverish and Helen sent for Monsieur Chauffard, the local doctor. Chauffard was puzzled and so Dr Gurney was summoned by telegram from Nice. Mill's face and neck were swollen and Gurney diagnosed erysipelas, a disease endemic in the district. In Mill's case it was fatal, and on Wednesday 7 May the great man died.

Two trusted friends, the young Protestant pastor Louis Rey and his wife, came at once to see Helen, who, though naturally distressed, was perfectly calm and self-controlled. When Rey asked her if her stepfather, who had been delirious and rambling towards the end, had left any clear testimony, she replied that he had: " 'You know that I have done my work.' Vous savez que j'ai achevé mon oeuvre—ou mon ouvrage."[1]

Pastor Rey had not expected any words of religious significance. Dr Gurney, on the other hand, is reported to have said later that Mill died "a believer". Algernon Taylor's daughter Mary, who had grown up to be more like her aunt Helen than anybody else, took violent exception to this pronouncement. Dr Gurney, she said, "would, of course, have wished to believe in his illustrious patient's conversion", despite the fact that she was convinced that he did not know the first thing about Mill's religious convictions. "I never asked my aunt Helen . . . because I never thought such a question worth asking. She often alluded to her own *hope* in another life as something to which she clung, in spite of the beliefs of those she had lived with for so long. . . ." Louis Rey, who felt it his duty to take part in the altercation, declared that, in his honest opinion, Mill had lived and died an agnostic. "I would not for anything in the world tamper with the truth in regard to the last moments of his life. . . ." Although a respectful crowd of people had gathered at the cemetery gates, only five were present to see Mill's body interred in Harriet's tomb: they were Helen, the pastor and his wife, and the two doctors, Gurney and Chauffard. The simple service, conducted by

Rey, was, he said, "of a religious character … though I should certainly not have celebrated this, and Miss Taylor would not have authorised me to do so, if we had thought it in the least degree in contradiction with his thoughts or offensive to his memory".[2]

In 1871 Mill had reluctantly consented to act as a pall-bearer at the funeral of George Grote in Westminster Abbey. Afterwards he told Alexander Bain that his own funeral would be very different. It will be remembered that he had always refused to answer questions on his attitude towards religion; but Bain and other friends assumed, like Rey, that he was an agnostic if not an atheist. Helen Taylor, who knew him better than any one, was indignant when she learned that a memorial committee had been formed and that an effort was to be made to bring his remains to London for burial in the Abbey. As she wrote to Croom Robertson, "It seems to me that the idea of the Memorial Committee is utterly foolish and unsuitable for one who so disliked and scorned such things and who certainly does not need them to perpetuate his name." Nor, she added, disregarding the fact that three of his sisters were still living, "is there any one surviving to be soothed and comforted by such evidences".[3]

An analytical writer has questioned the precise meaning of Mill's famous last words. She translates them as "You know that I have done my duty", not, as Louis Rey remembered from what Helen told him, "You know that I have done my work." She asks if they were the valediction "of the wise old man of mature intellect who left his legacy complete … or the anxious, fearful, defensive words of the little boy who never grew up, seeking approval—his father's, Harriet's, Helen's?", and rightly concludes that "there is no way of knowing".[4] Mill had always been subservient; he had needed a mother-substitute, and had found her first in Sarah Austin; then, to perfection, in Harriet, who was both mother and wife; and finally in Helen, his mother and daughter. But his last words, especially if we accept Louis Rey's interpretation, require no psychological interpretation: he had, indeed, completed his work; there was nothing more he wished to say.

In some ways he owed even more to Helen than he had to Harriet. She had kept house for him for fourteen years, organized his private life, listened to tales of his cough and expectoration, his diarrhoea, and the swallowing of the pills his doctors had ordered. She had accompanied him on his travels and exhausted herself scrambling up hills. She had been his secretary and assistant, his editor and critic; she had taken on work for which he had no time, the burden of Buckle's literary remains. He had loved his "dearest Lily"; he had respected her competence almost as much as her intellect and drive. In practical matters he remained a child to the end of his life. Harriet had once sighed that he could not even be relied on to secure seats on a train. Once, on a journey with Helen through France and Switzerland, *he* complained that the sight of his name on the luggage labels invariably aroused curious, appraising stares. "Why not put Taylor?" asked Helen, "no one will take any notice of that." "Dear me, what a good idea. I should never have thought of that."[5] He had consulted her at every turn, asked her advice as he had once asked Harriet's. When, for instance, repairs were needed at Blackheath in the brickwork above "the darling's" window, he had postponed the decision between one builder and another until her return from Avignon. Haji was with him at the time but his advice was as nothing compared with Helen's.

The close relationship and community of interests between Mill and his Lily is illustrated in the most interesting and revealing manner in a letter from his sister Jane Ferraboschi. Helen had written to advise her of his death, and she replied, "your handwriting is so like my brother's that I thought it was a letter from him".[6]

Mill was mourned as one of the great men of his time; but reaction to his campaign for the equality of the sexes was mixed. *The Times,* for example, commented sourly that "of late years Mill has not come before the world with advantage. When he appeared in public it was to advocate the fanciful rights of women . . . or something equally impracticable. . . ."

Members of the women's suffrage movement were desolated by the loss of a man who had been a friend as well as a leader. Charlotte Burbury of the London National Society, of which Mill had been president after his purge of the "undesirable" element, wrote to Helen of the calamity which had befallen all those who were "earnestly striving" to follow his "counsels of wisdom and justice". The society regarded him "as the originator and founder of their association, — and his name as President constituting in a great measure their claim to public appreciation. In their future work . . . it will be their great encouragement to look back to the time when he was their leader and their endeavour to pursue that moderate and judicious course of action which has the sanction of his arguments and precepts . . . ."[7]

Lydia Becker, blissfully unaware of the harsh things he had written of the "Bright and Becker set", called on the women of England to follow where their hero had led. "His was the hand which dealt the first effectual blow at the political slavery of women. . . . Let them . . . honour Mill by the one tribute and the one duty which women alone can give. Men can raise memorials to his memory; men can labour . . . for the removal of electoral disabilities; but Mill could not give—and men cannot give—political freedom to women, unless they themselves come forward to claim and exercise it . . . ."[8]

Mrs Peter Taylor, also ignorant of Mill's opinion, sent Helen a conventional note of sympathy on a loss "great to all who knew him personally, a loss to the world who knew him through his writings—his deeds".[9]

The aged Harriet Grote, with whom Mill had quarrelled and been reconciled, was "deeply affected". For a day or two after she received the news, "I was", she told her friend Dean Stanley, "incapable of busying myself with anything, and lay fallow, as it were, hoping the pain would grow bearable after a space, which of course it has done, though I still mourn my old friend deeply."[10]

Mrs Grote, forceful and outspoken to the end, was becoming a trial to her friends. As Helen told Kate Amberley a few months later, there were moments "when I feel so cross with her that I feel inclined never to see her again; and then others when she seems so kind . . . that I am angry with myself for feeling so".[11] One of her grievances was that the old lady insisted on saying grace after dinner!

Many of the letters which flooded in on Helen might equally well have been written to a sorrowing widow. "All England, all Europe will mourn the death of a great man", wrote Emily Shirreff, one of the less emotional of her correspondents, "but *I* think of *you* . . . & truly I grieve for you more than I could easily express. After the privilege of such companionship you must pay the penalty of a painful isolation . . . ."[12]

"Oh! my Helen! *What* can I do!" cried faithful, loving Fanny Stirling. Not so long before, on a visit to the south of France, she had called unexpectedly at St Véran and had been told by the servant that Helen was not at home. Mill was in the garden and she "couldn't resist speaking to him, tho' I saw he didn't know me from Adam". And now he was dead. "*What* is to be done? I cannot get thro' my work for thinking of you. . . . *What* would life have been to such a nature as his without you . . . ."[13]

One of the most deeply affected of Mill's women admirers was Kate Amberley. She had read in the newspapers that Mill was critically ill and wrote at once to Helen, although her letter, like many others, did not arrive until after his death. "I am thinking of you & feeling with you at your watch by that bed . . . ."[14] When all was over she wrote again: "I cannot bear to think of you in your grief & desolation, for what must be the loss to you when it is so great to those who knew him only as a friend. It is quite irreparable to us both. One so kind, so true, so sympathizing, so encouraging, so tender, so lenient, I never shall know again . . . ."[15]

Kate longed to comfort Helen; and Helen longed to see Kate—far more than she wished to see her own brothers or Mill's bustling sister Mary Colman, who came out to Avignon for a few days. It was only when Mary had gone "and I am alone again", she wrote to Kate, "that I am beginning to realize what it is that I have undergone and that I have to take up the burden of life again as best I can".[16] She had been a prey to fearful guilt when her mother died: now, once again, she was filled with quite unnecessary remorse. "It is bitter to think he might have been with us yet but for a hot day's walk and a cold evening drive", she wrote on black-edged paper to Professor Croom Robertson. "I was not well enough to go with him. Perhaps had I been with him . . . I might have been able to avoid the chill, and he might be with us still . . . ."[17] To her uncle Arthur Hardy she wrote, without a trace of cynicism, comparing John Stuart Mill with the long-dead and half-forgotten John Taylor. She had lost one who had done all that he could "to replace to me my own dear father by his unfailing & never varying kindness & with whom fourteen years of the closest intellectual and home companionship have only served to increase my respect for a most rare integrity & purity of purpose".[18]

Helen's brother Haji sent with his sympathy a suggestion that she should take up Greek as an antidote for grief. She did not respond. Haji, who had relinquished any idea of becoming a monk, had consulted Dr Gurney about his numerous ailments and, in 1860, had married Gurney's sister Ellen. After the birth of a son and two daughters Ellen Taylor was desperately ill. ". . . the hand of death is upon her", Haji had written to his sister. "Yesterday the sweet creature said 'Is Lily coming to see me?' I answered that you were at Avignon."[19] Helen had not been prepared to leave Mr Mill and, even if she had undertaken the journey to England, she would have been too late. She besought her brother to think of his children, all under four: Cyprian, who had almost died in infancy, Elizabeth Mary (known as Nelly), and Mary. "Let them give you strength to bear your loss, although I know how vain it would be to talk of their consoling you . . . ."[20] Helen had no children to consider and so Haji had thought of Greek as an opiate. Now he invited his sister to stay for "as long as you can make yourself comfortable".[21]

Helen came to England but could not make herself comfortable, as she explained to Kate Amberley. "If you c^d have a change from y^r brother & come to us", wrote Kate, "we are always alone & quiet & I sh^d so like to help to soothe you . . . ."[22] She would come as soon as she decently could, replied Helen. In the meantime, since Kate was planning a visit to London, she offered her the use of the flat (10, Albert Mansions, Victoria Street) which she and Mill had shared since 1871, when they gave up the large, dilapidated house at Blackheath. She would join Kate in London or visit her later in the country, just as Kate wished. Her immediate sense of loss and desolation was so acute that, spurning Greek, she now sought an entirely unrealistic outlet. "I should be so glad if I could be of any use with the children, could I? Could I hear them their lessons while the Governess is away? You know I always said I should like to be a governess."

Once, in the course of a quarrel with Harriet over money, she had said that, had it been necessary, she would have earned money as a governess in order to realize her ambition to go on the stage; but never, in her strangest dreams, had she looked on teaching as a career. She was over forty now and her beauty had hardened into severity. She might look the part of a conventional governess; she had no desire to become one. What she yearned for was the balm and comfort of Kate's gentle affection to help bridge the agonizing gap between the present and the uncertain future. "I should like to see you, to be with you, or near you", she wrote. "I *do* feel solitary—not in mind or even in spirits, but in heart, and my heart turns to you; I wish to live for I feel as though I could do some work, but I do not think I can endure life if I cannot love somebody." She dared not allow herself to become too fond of her brother's children, appealing as she found them, "for there is a great deal in his way of managing them which is very painful to me and yet it would be worse than useless for me to interfere".[23]

In September 1873 Helen went to stay with the Amberleys in the country and saw her year-old godson, Bertrand, his brother and sisters. "Your visit was such a pleasure to us all",[24] wrote Kate when she had gone, and urged her to come and see them all again soon.

Helen had told Kate that she must live to see Mill's posthumous papers published. She also assured her uncle Arthur that "whatever time & health may remain to me for the future, I shall apply to furthering by every means that may lie in my power the same political and philosophical opinions".[25]

It came as no surprise to her friends that she should postpone any decision on her own future until she had put Mill's work in order. "Think dear, dear one", wrote Caroline Lindley in one of her most splendid effusions, "how many look to you as Mr Mill's representative and *for him* you live as you have done, ready to answer those quite ignorant of the high and pure motives by which our honoured and much lamented Friend was ever actuated...."[26]

Helen had been appointed Mill's executor and, in addition to editorial work and arrangements for publication, there were various legacies to be considered. She was, of course, pleased to know of his generosity to the cause of women's education. Although in the past he had given a fillip to Girton by setting an examination paper for the students in political economy, he had made no special provision for the college, as a protest against its sectarian religious services. Instead, he left instructions for £3,000 to be set aside for the "first University in England to open its degrees to women", and a further £3,000 to endow scholarships "exclusively for females". The remainder of the money from his estate (total, about £14,000) went to members of his own family and Harriet's.

Helen, who had inherited money from both her parents, was now affluent enough to live as she pleased. Her first task was to edit the *Autobiography,* begun so many years before and written with Harriet's guidance and approval. There was editorial work to do also on Mill's *Three Essays on Religion,* on a fourth volume of *Dissertations and Discussions,* and on his *Chapters on Socialism.* By 1879 all had been published.

The *Autobiography* came first, and over this Helen had a head-on clash with Mill's friend and future biographer Alexander Bain. Bain had been holidaying in Italy with his wife when he learned of Mill's fatal illness and death. "The heart for touring died away in me", he wrote to Helen, after which he set out for Avignon, stopping for a night at Nice to discuss details with Dr Gurney. At Avignon he had long talks with Helen and also interviewed Dr Chauffard and Pastor Rey; then he went to Paris to see Jane Ferraboshci and her sister Clara Digweed, who was with her.

Bain was, of course, amassing material for his biography, and for this the *Autobiography* was all-important. "A herculean labour will be thrown upon you", he assured Helen solemnly. "I shall be anxious to hear what instructions and intentions you have respecting his memory. This will be useful for my own guidance."[27]

Mill had left it entirely to Helen's discretion whether the *Autobiography* should be published or not. This put her in a quandary, for the manuscript contained the most flattering references to herself, as well as the adulatory descriptions of her mother. Should she delete the references to herself or, as Mill had intended, leave them in? She consulted several friends. One was Mill's disciple John Elliot Cairnes, by that time retired from his post as Professor of Political Economy at University College, London. Mrs Cairnes replied for her husband and herself. Helen "should publish the book without modification", she wrote. It was her duty as editor "to retrench nothing which could in any way impair the correctness of the picture". Mill's respect for her "intellect and character" was absolutely genuine. "His devotion to you has long appeared to us as one of the most beautiful and touching of his noble nature. . . . The general impression . . . does not go a jot beyond what both Mr Cairnes and myself have heard him express while he was still among us . . . ."[28]

Kate Amberley, on the other hand, was dubious. Helen had shown her the manuscript during her visit. Now, with some hesitation, she suggested the omission of a passage which named Helen as his "instructor" and one or two other "laudatory remarks".[29] She was anxious, she added, to learn the outcome of an interview her friend was to have with Alexander Bain, who had read the manuscript section by section as it was submitted to him.

Bain was extremely forthright: he objected not only to the passages about Helen but also to some of those about Harriet. "Of course I know well the strength of his admiration for her great and various gifts, and I counted on him expressing himself very strongly. But I greatly doubt the propriety of your printing those sentences where he declares her to be a greater poet than Carlyle, and a greater thinker than himself—and again, a greater thinker than his father (or at all events an equal)." Since Bain did not quarrel with Mill's remark that Shelley was but a child to Harriet as she became, he evidently had no great appreciation of the poet. He felt, however, as readers through the years have felt, that the paragon of Mill's heart had never existed—and could never exist. "I think that your mother, yourself and Mr Mill, will all be placed in a false position before the world by such extreme statements." He did not ask Helen to remove the entire eulogy of her mother, merely to omit "those three phrases of comparison. The incredulous world will be sufficiently startled by what still remains, although for all that we are prepared." To warn her of what had already been said by those who had seen the dedications to the *Liberty* and *Dissertations and Discussions*, he quoted the remark of George Grote, "the gentlest of human kind, and Mr Mill's tenderest friend . . . that 'only John Mill's reputation could have survived such an exhibition' ". If the general public were to gain the impression that he "was liable to exaggerated judgments when his feelings were concerned they will be apt to set aside his authority on questions generally".[30] Surely Helen could see that to publish the offending phrases would be to desecrate a great man's memory? He had no quarrel with Mill's praise of Harriet's influence on his work. This, he said, was "most striking, and satisfies our reason while wakening up our sympathetic interest. It is exactly the vein that suits the occasion."[31]

While Helen was cogitating over this letter Bain wrote again: this time his task was even more delicate. The *Autobiography* was "truly a noble monument, and will last for many ages"; but, as Helen was aware, she as well as her mother had been "commemorated" in "lofty terms". It would therefore be unwise for this commemoration to be published during her lifetime. One passage in particular seemed to him inadmissible: "Whoever, either now or hereafter, may think of me and the work I have done, must never forget that it is the product not of one intellect and conscience, but of three, the least considerable of whom, and above all the least original, is the one whose name is attached to it."[32] "I would suggest", said Bain, "...the danger of too pointed comparisons. I would recommend to you...to decline the compliment, for yourself, of being more original than Mr Mill...."[33]

Helen's riposte was a lengthy letter of justification. The earlier parts of the book had been revised at least twice during Mill's lifetime; and she must have known, although she did not mention it, that her mother had seen and approved all but the final passages about herself and those concerning her daughter. Helen refused to admit that it could be right "to tone down the deliberate, and reiterated statements of the impressions of a remarkable man.... The idea that what Mr Mill has written is the fairest indication of his character, has induced me to leave a great part of what he has written about myself.... I never saw these passages until it was too late to ask him to erase them, but I know he agreed in the rule that nothing known from private intercourse ought to be published if it gives pain to living persons." No one would be hurt if these passages were included; the expression of his feelings "must be gratifying in its own nature even if he only thought so from affectionate prejudice; but as published by myself they may be supposed to indicate a ridiculous vanity in me". What, then, should she do? She had not the slightest intention of removing a single sentence or phrase about her mother; but with herself it was different. She did not agree with Mill's expressions of praise "& would rather not publish them, but I am so hardened to what I dislike that I would publish them or not with equal indifference, & should be glad of your advice to help me to form a judgment as to the least of three evils—to suppress the particular passages—to publish them—or to keep the book back altogether".[34]

Bain refused to be drawn. Naturally the book must be published, and she had a perfect right to include in it everything she wished. "I will not take the responsibility of pressing upon you any slight mutilations, which after all would not materially affect the general result. Nor would I advise the total omission of the passages relating to yourself...."[35]

Helen, normally so incisive, could not make up her mind, and he wrote once again, "If you are still hesitating I would say, omit the whole, and reserve it for a future day. The difference between the living and the dead is vital in such a question...."[36]

She took the hint, and the *Autobiography* appeared in 1873 without

Mill's loving tribute to his stepdaughter. Kate Amberley, who had seen it in manuscript and tactfully suggested some curtailment but not the total omission, was disappointed. "I am very sorry you decided as you did, but you thought it well over so I like to say no more, but some day it must be repaired." She would preserve the *Autobiography* "among my sacred books, & a very sacred one it is. I wish there were more of you in it, but indirectly you are there . . . ."[37]

Mrs Grote found the book intensely moving—or so she told Helen. "The *power* of the mind which planned this frank narrative stands out in full light. . . J. Mill's name will always be held in reverence by his countrymen; & above all by his Countrywomen."[38] To Alexander Bain she was more frank, more like her old self: "If anything could make intellectual culture odious and terrible, it is the ensample of that overstrained infant", she commented on Mill's upbringing and education. She had, of course, turned eagerly to the passages about Harriet: "The revelations which we had been led to expect as to the relations between himself and Mrs Taylor come to nothing at all. He says: 'We liked each other; we lived much together; we travelled together; and when the good man departed, we got married and "lived happy ever after", till her death; but since we did not overstep the limits of propriety, no one has a right to find fault with her or with me' . . . ."[39]

Mill's sister Harriet Isabella told Helen that she had "read the book with much painful interest".[40] To the Rev. J. Crompton she was a good deal more explicit:

> I fear my brother will make but a queer impression on the public by his exaltation of his wife. The best I can say is this: it shews *what* his ideal of excellence was, and that it was not until he had clothed this woman in those attributes that he could bow down and worship. No doubt she must have had "cleverness" to begin with; then by constant intercourse with him she educated herself, caught his ideas, and I have no doubt that he, in his perfect, childlike simplicty, was struck by the wonderful similarity of *her* views to his! He was always the most unsuspicious of mortals and knew less of the "world" and its ways than any one I ever met with. The step-daughter has had good enough taste to erase the eulogies upon herself.[41]

Mill's sister could not have known the truth about Harriet's intellectual domination: had she been told it—and she was not—she would probably still have rejected the notion as nonsense. She must have learned from Alexander Bain of his correspondence with Helen about the disputed eulogies.

Bain was also in difficulties with Helen over Mill's *Three Essays on Religion: Nature, the Utility of Religion and Theism*. As early as 1854 Harriet had suggested in sincere but confusing words that he should write something on the utility of religion, as "one of the subjects you would have most to say on—there is to account for the existence nearly universal of some religion (superstition) by the instincts of fear, hope and mystery etc., and throwing over all doctrines and theories, called religion, and devices for power, to show how religion and poetry fill the same want . . . —how all this must be superseded by morality deriving its power from sympathies and benevolence and its reward from the approbation of those we respect".[42]

Mill naturally found her idea beautiful and asked her to enlarge it—as well he might—on the grounds that "a few paragraphs will bring me to the end of all I have got to say on the subject. What would be the use of my outliving you! I could write nothing worth keeping alive except with your prompting . . . ."[43]

Harriet could prompt, she could inspire, but she could not write the essay. Under her direction her loving husband set to work. Religion, he wrote, could not be defended on the base of truth and utility:

> If religious belief be indeed so necessary to mankind, as we are continually assured that it is, there is great reason to lament, that the intellectual grounds of it should require to be backed by moral bribery and subordination of the understanding. Such a state of things is most uncomfortable even for those who may, without actual insincerity, describe themselves as believers; and still worse as regards those, who, having consciously ceased to find the evidences of religion convincing, are withheld from saying so lest they should aid in doing an irreparable injury to mankind.

He did not seek to deny that religion might "be morally useful without being intellectually sustainable"; nor that there "are states of mind in which the idea of religious punishment acts with the most overwhelming force". The prospect of hell fire was "the vulgarest part" of religion. Its value "as a supplement to human laws . . . is not that part of its claims which the more highminded of its votaries are fondest of insisting on". Nevertheless, "belief . . . in the supernatural . . . cannot be considered to be any longer required, either for enabling us to know what is right and wrong in social morality, or for supplying us with motives to do right and abstain from wrong". Religion and poetry, he said, supplied the same want, but—and here he veered away from Harriet's interpretation—religion, "as distinguished from poetry, is the product of the craving to know whether these imaginative conceptions [common to both] have realities answering to them in some other world than ours". This seemed to him unlikely in the extreme. "History, so far as we know it, bears out the opinion, that mankind can perfectly well do without belief in a heaven."[44]

"Theism", which dates from 1869, was written much later than the other two *Essays on Religion,* and by the time that Mill came to write it his attitude towards religion, especially Christianity, had undergone a change. He now claimed, so he told a correspondent in 1861, that in none of his works had he had any intention "of undermining Theism". "I am far from thinking that it would be a benefit for mankind in general, if . . . they could be made disbelievers in all religion; nor would I willingly weaken in any person the reverence for Christ, in which I myself very strongly participate. I am an enemy to no religions but those which appear to me to be injurious either to the reasoning powers or the moral sentiments . . . ."[45]

In "Theism" Mill conceded that, while no proof existed for belief in an all-powerful God, "I think it must be allowed that . . . the adaptations of Nature afford a large balance of probability in favour of creation by intelligence". Available evidence "points to the creation, not indeed of the universe, but of the present order of it by an intelligent Mind, whose power over the materials was not absolute, whose love for his creatures was not his sole actuating inducement, but who nevertheless desired their good". Although there was no assurance of immortality, "the possibility of life after death rests on the same footing—of a boon from this powerful Being who wishes well to man, may have the power to grant, and which if the message alleged to have been sent by him was really sent, he has actually promised. The whole domain of the supernatural is thus removed from the region of Belief into that of simple Hope." The essential part of Christianity, the "holding up in a Divine Person a standard of excellence" was "available even to the absolute unbeliever and can never more be lost to humanity". It remained "a possibility that Christ actually was what he supposed himself to be—not God, for he never made the smallest pretension to that character, and would probably have thought such a pretension as blasphemous as it seemd to the men who condemned him—but a man charged with a special, express and unique commission from God to lead mankind to truth and virtue".[46]

Mill's own disciples, who had approved of his earlier stand, now accused him of deserting the true faith of an agnostic. Alexander Bain, who was convinced that his change of heart rested on a longing for a spiritual reunion with Harriet, admired his honesty but rightly feared its effect. Helen, suspicious by nature, was convinced, quite wrongly, that, with the connivance of the publishers, Bain would emasculate Mill's thesis immediately the book was out of her hands. She herself, it will be remembered, had spoken to her niece Mary of her hope in a future existence. To Mill, Helen was a being second in excellence only to her mother; her influence over him was immense. It is not unreasonable, therefore, to suppose that she had communicated to him her own hope in another life, a life in which some communion with Harriet would be possible.

Helen had with reluctance erased from the *Autobiography* the eulogy with which Mill had discharged his debt to her, but she left instructions that an unabridged version should be published within a year of her death. These instructions were ignored, and an incredulous world had to wait until 1924 to read Mill's tribute. Throughout the months of misery and desolation which followed Harriet's death, he wrote,

I was not alone: she had left a daughter, my step-daughter, Miss Helen

Taylor, the inheritor of much of her wisdom, and of all her nobleness of character, whose ever growing and ripening talents from that day to this have been devoted to the same great purposes, and have already made her name better and more widely known that was that of her mother, though far less so than I predict, than if she lives it is destined to become Of ... what I owe in the way of instruction to her great powers of original thought and soundness of practical judgment, it would be a vain attempt to give an adequate idea. Surely no one ever before was so fortunate, as, after such a loss as mine, to draw another prize in the lottery of life—another companion, stimulator, adviser, and instructor of the rarest quality. Whoever, either now or hereafter, may think of me and of the work I have done, must never forget that it is the product not of one intellect and conscience, but of three, the least considerable of whom, and above all the least original, is the one whose name is attached to it.[47]

Mill was as correct in his assessment of Helen's intellectual domination as he had been in his assessment of Harriet's. Mother and daughter were intellectually advanced in their own day and would have been advanced had they been alive today. In his submission and respect Mill may have overvalued their brilliance and potential, but his chief error was to overestimate their characters. Their letters speak for themselves: they reveal two highly intelligent women, with strong, sometimes undisciplined, affections, domineering, dogmatic and ruthless. In other words, they possessed the very combination of qualities which Mill lacked. Is it so surprising, then, that he needed these very qualities to complete himself?

CHAPTER 24

Helen Alone

Helen had been hoping to visit Kate Amberley again. If she did so it must have been within a year of Mill's death. In 1874 Kate, who was nursing her six-year-old daughter, caught diptheria from the child and both died from the disease. It speaks well for Lord Amberley that, in the midst of his own unbearable grief, he found a moment to write to Helen: "Infinitely as I have suffered myself, I have not forgotten to feel for you in the loss of a friend who was so truly anxious to do all in her power to make your life a little less unhappy."[1] Without his beloved Kate, the young man, it seems, lost the will to live, and in less than two years he, too, was dead.

As Amberley had realized, Helen felt this second blow intensely. "It has changed the aspect of life", she wrote to Mrs Cairnes; "taken out of it what cheerfulness was left to me personally, independent of myself."[2] Yet now, as before, she found solace in work. The *Autobiography* had been published; she had not yet completed her editorial work on the remainder of Mill's papers, and, when this was done, she planned to publish a selection of his letters. She lived on for more than thirty years; and, since her life—bizarre as it sometimes became—was firmly rooted in her long association with him, it seems relevant to give it a place here; relevant also to say something of Harriet Taylor's sons and of Algernon Taylor's children, of whom one—Mary—also had a part to play.

Helen was still working on Mill's *Chapters on Socialism* when she received an invitation which she would have been too busy to accept during his lifetime. When the school boards were first thrown open to election in 1870 Mill had been invited to stand as radical candidate for the Southwark district of London. He refused, with "regret that the pressure of other occupations puts it out of my power to perform the duties of that most important trust".[3] In 1876 Southwark invited Helen to stand: she accepted, much to the approval of her friends in the women's suffrage movement. Millicent Fawcett wrote at once with an offer to speak at one of her meetings. "You are the first radical woman, I think, who has stood . . . and your success would be a great service both to radicalism and to the women's cause . . ."[4] She pointed out, however, in case Helen disagreed, that, while she and her husband favoured the widest spread of education, they thought—as Mill had thought—that wherever possible parents should be expected to pay.

Mrs Fawcett spoke once and, as always, well. Helen then asked Professor Fawcett to address two meetings of working men to be held in different parts of the district on one evening. This he politely declined to do. He had, he said, already had to turn down invitations to speak for school-board candidates in his own consituency and it would be unfair on his constituents if he agreed to speak for her. Helen was incensed, so angry that she sat down and wrote him the kind of letter she had written to her stepfather when he championed Bradlaugh, although, as she did not know the professor so well, it was couched in less violent terms:

> I hope you will not think me egotistic if I venture to say that I do not think there is any one who would be surprised or hurt to find you doing what might appear somewhat marked in honour of Mr Mill. For my own part though I have spent thirty years of my life in working for the radical cause I do not presume to have any claim to help on this first occasion in my life that I have ever asked anything of any one, and although there are large numbers of working men who think me more qualified than any other candidates [to] work for them on the School board it is not on this ground that I ventured to suppose you might be willing to do more for me than the other applicants for your assistance. I am quite sure that if you do consent to speak twice in aid of my candidature and not at all for any other candidate, the reason will be universally supposed to be your respect for Mr Mill, and this is a supposition from which I should have supposed you would not shrink.

If Professor Fawcett would not undertake to address the two meetings—"and all whom I have seen are of opinion that you would be doing a great service to my candidature"[5]—would he at least condescend to speak at one?

Tact, as Helen herself was ready enough to admit, was not her strong point, and she never took the trouble to try to acquire it. Henry Fawcett, irritated as he must have been to be reminded of his duty in such a way, gave in meekly but promised to address only one of the meetings. "I am sure you know my reverence for Mr Mill is so great that I should be the last to show any disinclination to avail myself of any opportunity of doing honour to his memory . . . ."[6] Had he agreed to speak at both meetings, he added, the candidates in his constituency would justifiably argue that the second meeting should have been for them.

The election was fiercely fought, for Helen, an extreme radical, was opposed by a section of liberals who found her views too far to the left. But, with the help of Miss Trevor and the force of her own personality, she was elected at the head of the poll by the largest majority yet gained by any member of the London School Board. She was to repeat this success in 1879 and again in 1882.

Helen's health and strength were stimulated by excitement and controversy. Released from her duties to Mill, however congenial she had found them, her vitality seemed boundless. Until 1884, when she pleaded ill health as an excuse for standing down, she scarcely missed a school-board meeting. She campaigned energetically for universal free education, for smaller classes and the abolition of corporal punishment. She pressed for higher spending, more especially on the provision of free food, shoes and stockings for necessitous children. When this was not forthcoming she provided from her own pocket a midday meal and a pair of boots for the children most in need. As a member of the endowment committee of the school board, she was instrumental in persuading the charity commissioners to restore some of the educational endowments which had been alienated from their original purpose.

Although her motives were strictly humanitarian she could never resist a fight, and on one occasion her pugnacity and reforming zeal brought her into the law courts. In 1873 a hundred boys had been admitted to the newly opened St Paul's Industrial School in Southwark. At the request of the London School Board, Helen, accompanied by a Mrs Surr, made routine inspections of the school in 1879 and 1881, but it appears that they noticed nothing untoward. In September 1881, however, eight boys were caught ineffectually trying to set fire to the school building, as a protest, it was said, against the miserable conditions in which they were kept, and six of them were brought before a magistrate. Helen was not present at the hearing, but Mrs Surr, who had been conducting investigations on her own, assured her that, if any of the boys were brought to trial, it was most unlikely that a jury would convict. She only wished that Helen had been in court to hear the "prevarications & contradictions" of the warden, Mr Hinchcliffe. "His own side were quite ashamed of him & he was most severely reprimanded by the Magistrate for birching the boys before they came into court". Mr Fitch, "our" lawyer, "made him admit that he did not enter putting on handcuffs in the Punishment bk. He would not own to foot-manacles.... I had heaps of witnesses there to cruelty & neglect whom I could not bring up. One boy had been kept for 9 days on bread & water with hands & feet manacled ...." A Home Office representative informed Mrs Surr that he would produce a witness who would report favourably of the school. "I said, if you do so, I shall speak *ill* of it. . . ."[7]

Presumably Mr Hinchcliffe, advised in advance that the school was to be inspected, had managed to conceal all evidence of cruelty and had threatened the pupils that, if questioned by Miss Taylor or Mrs Surr, they were to say nothing. The case of the young arsonists, according to *The Times,* "touched the heart of many.... The Home Secretary was touched and ... rushed into print with a letter which certainly did ample justice to his head".[8] although, as it was pointed out, he was really precluded by the nature of his office from an intervention of this kind. More practically, he set up a committee of inquiry into conditions in the school, from which the eight boys had wisely been removed.

The committee of inquiry, like so many others, seemed to be taking its time and achieving nothing. Helen, lacking the restraining hand of her mother or Mill, took the law into her own hands. "The C^{ttee} is a whitewashing C^{ttee} ", she told Mrs Surr; "and if you can lay the facts before the public in any less laborious and equally effectual way, you may bring pressure to bear on the B^{d}better than through such a sham C ^{ttee}". What she proposed to do was to put a motion to the school board that Thomas Scrutton, chairman of the industrial schools sub-committee and manager of St Paul's School, be prosecuted for taking money on false pretences. If this was rejected—and it was obvious that it would be—a second motion could be introduced accusing Scrutton of having accepted certain sums of money from the board for the upkeep of boys not in the school on the dates for which the accounts had been presented. "Such a motion would very possibly be carried, after the revelations we could make",[9] she added darkly.

For some reason Helen was absent from the meeting at which the motions were put. She was given an opportunity to withdraw them but refused. Instead, she wrote a letter to a member of the board, a Mr Upton, accusing Thomas Scrutton not only of accepting money on false pretences but also of culpability in the deaths of thirteen boys who had died since the school was opened:

> Mr Scrutton has been sole acting manager ... for at least five years. . . . In my opinion there is little doubt that there is moral guilt of manslaughter for the death of many of the boys, although I do not think it may be easy to bring it home to Mr Scrutton. I do not think he ought to escape by throwing some of the blame on his subordinate Mr Hinchcliffe. I believe, but do not know, that Mr Scrutton supplied some of the miserable adulterated food himself to the school and there can be little doubt that the children were kept there only to make money by their work . . . .[10]

In the circumstances it is scarcely surprising to learn that Mr Scrutton decided to bring an action for libel against Helen Taylor. The judge at the hearing, which lasted four days, was Sir Henry Hawkins; Scrutton was represented by Mr Charles Russell (later Lord Russell of Killowen), Helen by Mr (later Sir) Edward Clarke. Miss Taylor, Mr Russell conceded, was "a woman of great benevolence who held strong views on many subjects [such] as the rights of women and the amelioration of her sex". Mr Scrutton had started the school "in order to meet a serious want which had previously been felt . . . in relation to industrial apprentices", and had contributed to the venture money of his own to supplement a grant from the London School Board.

Clarke's submission that the plaintiff had no case to go to the jury was overruled. He then proceeded to extol Helen's many and varied charitable activities and went on to describe how Mrs Surr, at the instigation of the board, had investigated conditions in the school and become aware of "systematic neglect of all precautions to guard the health and welfare of the children". Mr Scrutton, who, Clarke claimed, had indeed accepted money on false pretences over a period of five years during which he had been solely responsible for the school, was "morally guilty . . . and morally responsible for the conduct" of his subordinate. Miss Taylor had herself paid for the defence of the two boys who had actually been put on trial for arson; and, as a direct result of that trial, the Home Secretary had ordered Hinchcliffe to be dismissed. Since his departure conditions in the school had noticeably improved.

Helen must have guessed that she had lost her case when the judge pointed out that to complain of bad conditions in the school was one thing, to accuse Scrutton of fraud was another; and it was on the latter issue he had brought his action. "Mismanagement of the school", he remarked, "is a different thing from the plaintiff's dishonesty."[11] Even Scrutton's counsel agreed that Helen had not acted from malice but from a genuine, though mistaken, belief that the charges of dishonesty could be substantiated. Her case broke down on the plea of justification and, by consent, she paid into court the large sum of £1,000 to cover the plaintiff's costs and damages; but the action, which had drawn public attention to the deficiencies of one of London's industrial schools, led to much-needed reforms in others.

It is unlikely that Mill would have approved of so rash an act: had he been alive he would probably have cautioned Helen to proceed with restraint. But Helen, like her mother, went to extremes, as she did in the case of Ireland. Both Mill and Harriet had been keenly interested in Ireland's future. In her zeal for the revolution in France of 1848, Harriet had written to Mill of her hopes for an Irish revolution: "The Irish w^d I sh^d hope not be frightened but urged on by some loss of life."[12] Mill had been much occupied with the question of land reform while in Parliament; and Helen now adopted his ideas with tremendous zest. If "Mr Mill were alive", she declared, "he would have been heart & soul with the Irish in their struggle."[13] So, too, would Harriet, had she had the opportunity, although in public she would have been less vociferous than her daughter.

Helen despised Gladstone's government for its policy of coercion. She made no secret of her contempt, but showed it, according to a press report, by publicly calling the Prime Minister "a dastardly recreant, who had forsaken the true policy and pathway of Liberalism". She was, of course, a practised speaker and was much in demand by the various causes she had adopted. But a woman

who can speak to a Society of Quakeresses and other religious women on the imperishable virtues of Christianity; a woman who can hold an aristocratic audience spell-bound in a Duke's drawing-room, when speaking on the dignity of labour; a woman who can command the breathless attention of three or four thousand working men . . . , such a woman is no unworthy relative, disciple, and expounder of John Stuart

Mill, and should not waste time in flinging abusive epithets at Mr Gladstone or anyone else . . . .[14]

As part of her anti-government protest Helen became the life and soul of the English branch of the Irish Ladies' Land League. Hearing a rumour that the League might be proscribed, she rushed off to Dublin and offered to take charge of the movement, on the grounds that it would embarrass the government far more to have to arrest an English, rather than an Irish, woman. Her offer was made in good faith but it was not accepted.

Her zeal for the nationalization of land and the taxation of land values brought her to prominence in the Land Reform Union and the League for Taxing Land Values. It also earned her the friendship of one of Mill's disciples, the American exponent of land reform and the single tax, Henry George, who lectured in England during 1881 and 1882, and called Helen "one of the most intelligent women I have ever met, if not the most intelligent".[15] George and his wife stayed with Helen in her London home, at that time 13 Harrington Gardens, South Kensington; and his lecture tour gave a fresh impetus to the socialist ideals expressed in Mill's *Principles of Political Economy*. It will be remembered that, at Harriet's dictation, Mill had deleted the strictures on socialism and communism that he had made in the first edition and reversed the whole of his argument. During this period of "my mental progress", he wrote, "which now went hand in hand with hers, my opinions gained equally in breadth and depth, I understood more things, and those which I had understood before, I now understood more thoroughly". He had turned his back on his former opinions. In the old days,

I had seen little further than the old school of political economists into the possibilities of fundamental improvement in social arrangements. Private property, as now understood, and inheritance, appeared to me, as to them, the *dernier mot* of legislation: and I looked no further than to mitigating the inequalities consequent on these institutions, by getting rid of primogeniture and entails. The notion that it was possible to go further than this in removing the injustice—for injustice it is, whether admitting of a complete remedy or not—involved in the fact that some are born to riches and the vast majority to poverty, I then reckoned chimerical, and only hoped that by universal education, leading to voluntary restraint on population, the portion of the poor might be made more tolerable. In short, I was a democrat, but not the least of a Socialist. We were now much less democrats than I had been, because so long as education continues to be so wretchedly imperfect, we dreaded the ignorance and especially the selfishness and brutality of the mass: but our ideal of ultimate improvement went far beyond Democracy, and would class us decidedly under the general designation of Socialists. . . . The social problem of the future we considered to be, how to unite the greatest individual liberty of action, with a common ownership in the raw material of the globe, and an equal participation of all in the benefits of combined labour . . . .[16]

Harriet had carried him with her as far to the left as it was possible to go. Yet, despite his assertions to the contrary, he remained at heart more of a democrat than a socialist, even though, in his *Chapters on Socialism*, he prophesied the rise of socialism as an outcome of universal suffrage. Helen, his editor, followed her mother's left-wing views. In 1881 she took part in meetings organized by the advocates of a truly socialistic programme which led to the formation of the Democratic Federation (it was renamed the Social Democratic Federation in 1883) and was a member of its first executive committee.

Prior to the establishment of the Federation she had given practical help and encouragement to the first Labour candidates for Parliament. The original contender was the trade union leader George Odger, the man who had roused his fellow working men to enthusiasm at Mill's election meeting in 1865. Odger, who died in 1877, made no fewer than five attempts to enter Parliament; and Helen was with him during his final illness.

In 1884 she retired from her school-board activities on the plea of ill health. The following year she took the most histrionic step in an extraordinary career: she decided, as a gesture, to stand for Parliament. Her decision arose from the action of the Liberals of the London constituency of North Camberwell to set aside the nomination of the secretary of one of her pet organisations, the Vigilance Association. In protest against this high-handed action she offered herself as radical candidate, as which she was duly accepted.

Henry George wrote from New York in a spirit of unrealistic optimism:

Your election, and I trust there is no doubt of that, will seem to me a greater triumph, and more potent for good than that of any other single individual could be. It will mean not merely a vote but a voice. . . . It is only of late years, and largely since I first met you that I have come to realize the importance of women taking their part in politics. . . . It makes me almost wish I were an Englishman that I might have the privilege of voting and working for you. . . . I hope by the bye that one of your first motions will be for the removal of that grating on the woman's gallery that seems to me such a suggestive eye sore.[17]

Helen, one may be sure, would have been glad to lead an army of women to tear down the grating with their own hands. She had received a number of contributions towards her election expenses and offers of help, notably one from George Jacob Holyoake; and it says much for the radicals of North Camberwell that they were willing to take her campaign seriously. She herself argued that, despite the fact that women had no vote, there was nothing in the existing state of the law to debar a woman from sitting in the

House of Commons. She reminded members of the North Camberwell Radical Club that it was precisely twenty years since John Stuart Mill had been invited to stand for Westminster. "It was with great reluctance that he consented, but he felt there were questions which he alone was prepared" to advocate in Parliament. "Among them especially was the question of equal rights of men and women"[18] Outlining her own programme—and, like all candidates with no prospect of success, she could afford to be over-ambitious—she said that the first was universal suffrage, which she defined as the right to vote of every man and woman who had not been convicted of any crime. She would also campaign for the restoration of the land to the people; a fair day's wage for a fair day's work; the reorganization of labour on a co-operative basis, the workers being empowered to elect their own managers; direct taxation, with a graduated system of income tax for all incomes above £300 a year, rising by degrees to 19 shillings in the pound for incomes of £100,000. Justice and education should be free for all; and alienated charitable endowments should be restored; members of Parliament should be allowed to claim their election expenses; wars should be outlawed unless waged with the consent of the people. Last, but by no means least, she would campaign for home rule and legislative independence in Ireland.

In October 1885 she held her one and only public meeting: it was a sensational affair. The only man among a bevy of women on the platform was Holyoake. In the chair was Mrs Ethel Leach of the Great Yarmouth School Board, who "described with taste and spirit some incidents in Miss Taylor's career of public service".[19] Helen herself "spoke with eloquence and behaved with courage".[20] It seems doubtful that she managed to make herself heard, for the local Liberals, incensed by the effrontery of the radical left in putting up a candidate against them, had packed the hall with hooligans, who "made all the ruffianly noises they knew, and their proficiency . . . was considerable". At length, tiring of ruffianly noises, they rushed the platform and pushed the women roughly to the floor, injuring some of them in the process. What part, if any, Holyoake played we do not know; but several working men in the audience closed the doors and began to help the women to climb through the windows. When Helen eventually left the hall she was mobbed in the street, but some obliging workmen stopped a cab "in which she was able to drive away until her own brougham was conveniently at command". Throughout the ordeal she had contrived to appear "quite unperturbed".[21] "I am for fair play", declared a male spectator. "Women . . . are not yet admitted to civil or political equality and ought not to be fought like men . . . ."[22]

The meeting, and the behaviour of the women, was a foretaste of the suffragette meetings to come. Had Helen been younger and willing to come forward, she would have proved a formidable rival to Emmeline Pankhurst for the leadership of the militant wing of the suffrage movement.

The day after the meeting she received an unexpected offer of help. George Odger was dead, but another Odger, John, came forward to offer her protection:

> I read with much indignation about the ruffianism displayed at your meeting & was glad to see your determination to fight them. It is a great battle to fight, & . . . they must be stopped from breaking up your Public Meetings. I have some experience in organising parties to stop disturbances of that kind. . . . At these sort of meetings you must have a proper bodyguard, who are not afraid of anybody. . . . I can get about 20 respectable men to come with me, who will act under my instructions so that all the speakers will have a proper hearing and nothing to fear . . . .[23]

Helen did not call on Odger for protection, and her campaign ended with the proverbial whimper. On nomination day she duly presented herself before the returning officer. He refused the proffered papers, so she explained to a well-wisher, on the grounds that "he could not accept the name of a woman as Candidate for the House of Commons".[24] In offering herself for election, however, she had done what no other woman would attempt for years to come. What more could Mill or Harriet have asked of her?

CHAPTER 25

The Younger Taylors

Of John and Harriet Taylor's three children only Helen, the youngest, made any mark in the world. She had grown up under the tutelage of the mother she both loved and resented and of John Stuart Mill whom she admired above all men. It was only natural that a girl of intellect and drive should have striven to surpass her mother and win the respect and affection of the man who became her stepfather.

The inadequacy of the boys, Herbert and Algernon, must, at any rate in part, be attributed to their mother's neglect. It is true that she came to London in their school holidays and that they sometimes travelled abroad with her or stayed in her country house. What they thought of Mill's friendship with their mother we do not know; but they were aware that their parents were estranged and that Helen, never separated from Harriet, was her favourite child.

From the age of seventeen Herbert made business trips to America. Over the complicated issue of Harriet's marriage settlement, Mill had accused him of being contradictory, Harriet of siding with the enemy, and so she saw far less of him than of Haji. Herbert never shared the Blackheath house: he married young and had children, but the marriage was unhappy and he separated from his wife. Unlike his father, Herbert was a poor business man: he went bankrupt and, according to Helen, played ducks and drakes with money held in trust for his Taylor relations. In 1888 Helen told Haji that she had heard rumours that he was about to be sued by his wife for an income of £1,500 a year which he had undertaken to pay her. He "is living in Piccadilly, keeps up membership of his club and has gone into business again. . . . A man who makes such an agreement, leaving his children to his wife, and himself leads a bachelor life . . . while bankrupt does not inspire me with confidence." She had no wish to see her elder brother again. His "very name brings to my memory with an undying pang all that he inflicted upon my beloved mother, and the shadow that his heartlessness cast on my youth. . . . Bad son, bad brother, and now it would seem bad husband and bad father. Ought you and I . . . to sit still with our hands folded . . . ?"[1]

Sitting still with folded hands was second nature to Haji. Years

225

before—in 1860—Mill, returning to Blackheath leaving Helen in Avignon, had been pleasantly surprised to find him "looking pale but . . . with a more animated (or rather less dead) expression of countenance than usual".[2]

Haji had not changed: he was content to lean on his daughters. His son, Cyprian, had gone into the Navy and was a midshipman at the age of fifteen; but a promising career was curtailed by ill health and a series of mental breakdowns. Cyprian lived to be nearly eighty, but at thirty-eight he was judged to be hopelessly insane and was confined in a mental home. Of late, Haji informed Helen in 1900, "he has shown a disposition for breaking glass and tearing up postal orders sent him. . . . The Doctor seems to think badly of the case . . . ."[3]

Elizabeth Mary (Nelly) was eccentric, though not to the point of destroying postal orders. Helen, who would herself have profited greatly from a university education, offered to pay for Nelly to go to Newnham in 1878. "I am much indebted to you for your kind and liberal offer", replied Haji. "As the matter may require a little consideration, I am not able to reply today, but will take an early opportunity of doing so . . . ."[4] After due thought Haji rejected the well-intentioned offer on his daughter's behalf. Nelly had already undergone a "long and systematic study embracing the ancient and modern languages and several branches of mathematics, besides subsidiary subjects";[5] additional study would be too arduous, he feared.

Whether or not the school provided Nelly with such a comprehensive course of study, it is clear that Haji was concerned to keep her at home. She may, of course, have been consulted and decided to reject the offer, but, had she gone to Cambridge, the course of her life might well have been different. In the event she adopted religion with even more fervour than her father; and, far from remaining at home, disappeared from his life into a community of religious friends who lived in Canada.

Baulked in her hopes for Nelly, Helen transferred the offer to Haji's younger daughter, Mary. It would be most advantageous for the girl to attend one of the women's colleges, she told her brother. Owing to the pioneer work of Emily Shirreff, Maria Grey and their colleagues, there were now in existence "a large and increasing number of High Schools for Girls of which the post of Head Teacher is very highly considered. . . . To take these it will be almost essential in the future to have passed the Examinations. Other openings are also being made for educated women, for which the *imprimatur* of the degree is of great value . . . ."[6]

If Haji's daughters were as well grounded as he claimed, there was no reason why Mary should not succeed, but he would have none of it. In the circumstances, it was unjust of him to grumble later on that she had developed a "hysterical tendency. . . . She needs work. . . ."[7] Despite the lack of qualifications, Mary did teach for a time, and, according to her father, she was "rewarded by a fair measure of success."[8]

Whether teaching or not, Mary was obliged to devote most of her time to an increasingly demanding father. Haji, though still a churchgoer, had found a new religion—vegetarianism. He had, he said, been converted by "the force of good example of the village Schoolmaster where I lived and his wife";[9] and when he moved to Devon and gave up a house of his own he refused to stay anywhere unless he could have his special diet. "I care about Vegetarianism more than any other subject or cause",[10] he told Helen. He had extracted a promise from a reluctant Mary "that she would not without my consent join the ranks of the flesh-eaters"; but, after a subversive holiday at a Young Women's Christian Association hostel, she rebelled. Returning to their temporary home, Chudleigh Vicarage, she asked his permission to eat the same food as the vicar and his family, who did not stint themselves. "I replied that she must please herself", sighed Haji, "but in that case the cup of heaviness which to me it was to sit daily at meals with those partaking of stews, roasts, bacon, fish and other highly seasoned dishes, together with sherry and claret...that this cup of repulsion, full already, would overflow...."[11] It is not to be wondered at that his younger daughter had an hysterical tendency or, as Helen was told by a cousin, Mrs Lord (née Ley), with whom they also stayed in Devon, "a terrible temper".[12]

Mary found comfort in close friendships with other women. The most permanent,"my other half", as Mary fondly called her, was Mary Ann (Molly) Trimble. The two of them went to Avignon to stay with Helen, whom Mary hardly knew. Helen, who was spending more and more time alone at St Véran, was fast becoming a recluse; letters remained unanswered; invitations were either ignored or curtly refused. In 1888 Mrs McLaren of Edinburgh wrote to express disappointment on behalf of the women's suffrage movement that Helen had not seen her way to cross the Atlantic to attend a great Women's Rights Convention in Washington, where she would have been suitably honoured. "Seeing that such honours would have been reflected upon the women of your country itself—and seeing that such honours were intended as a mark of reverence for and grateful remembrance of your great Father in Law [i.e. stepfather] I cannot help asking are you right to...deprive us of this?"[14]

Helen, though still under sixty, could not contemplate the journey. Nor did she respond two years later when Dr Elizabeth Blackwell advised her that an invitation was on its way from Worcester, Massachusetts, and gave her the text of the letter:

It will be forty years in October since the first National Woman's Rights Convention was held in Worcester. We intend to celebrate it.

That Convention grew out from Mr John Stewart [sic] Mill, a remarkable article in the *Westminster Review*, siding with the movement and stating its grounds. Now we think it would be the best and most desirable thing to have Miss Helen Taylor attend this Anniversary. She is one of the best known and most highly esteemed English women, on this side—she would command respect for the cause....[15]

In 1893 Helen received a third invitation from the United States, this time to visit Philadelphia as the guest of the National Council of Women: this, too, was ignored or refused. If she was still a personality in the States, in her own country, if she was remembered at all, it was only as a passionate eccentric.

In 1902 she made the effort to go to England to see Haji, who was not at all well. He wrote to her afterwards that he would always look back on the visit "as among the most agreeable episodes of my life . . . , recalling so many past incidents of which you enumerated not a few in detail".[16] He wrote again to remind her of the Roman Catholic services they had once attended together. Nowadays, when he had the strength to travel to the nearest Catholic church, the service was heard "without a sympathetic and appreciative listener, or, indeed, any better company than my own!"[17]

It was the last time brother and sister met, for Haji died the following year, after an operation. His daughter Mary and the devoted Milly Trimble, who had escorted Helen back to France, now took up their abode with her. They found that her most faithful servant had left to get married and the house and garden were in an appalling state of neglect and confusion. In the diary which she kept from 20 February 1904 to 4 July 1906, Mary described her sense of helplessness and shock and noted, among other horrors, that the remaining two servants were exploiting her unsuspecting aunt and extorting money from her: "The house is in a forlorn state, most of the rooms, except the servants' bedrooms, are kept under lock and key, in a filthy condition. The garden is a perfect scene of desolation." Helen was not only eccentric but growing senile. Her sole occupation now "consisted of picking up leaves and twigs".[18] She was no longer capable of keeping herself clean and tidy, and had grown gaunt from a diet consisting chiefly of hot chocolate and soup.

Mary, doing her best to tidy the house or, perhaps, merely inquisitive, discovered a will—luckily still unsigned—in which her aunt left the ungrateful servants two years' wages and all her property in France. When taxed with injustice towards her own family, Helen assured her that she knew nothing about the will, "but I cannot believe this".[19] Helen told Mary that she would not be forgotten, but that Nelly in Canada and Herbert, still presumably living a bachelor existence in Piccadilly, would receive nothing.

Mary and her "other half" were longing to get back to England and their home in Torquay, but they could not leave Helen, who clung to the house in which she had once been so happy and important. Day by day she grew more querulous, and suspicious to the point of paranoia. Knowing her love of animals, Mary bought her a dog. This was a disastrous move, for the little creature elected to sleep with Mary and Molly, and Helen came bursting into their bedroom at all hours of the night to make jealous scenes and address Molly Trimble "as though she were of inferior breeding". After a particularly noisy scene, the two younger women, "now thoroughly wound up . . . breathed out nearly all that was in our minds". Mary informed her aunt that "living with her was enough to drive anybody mad"; while Molly, normally more compliant, "said that our life with her was dreadful",[20] and ordered her out of the room.

Eventually they wore down Helen's resistance. She gave her niece power to deal with her business affairs, though she "hated doing what reminded her of death", yet "her existence at Avignon was almost death in life, a living death".[21] Aware, in her confused and muddled mind, that she could no longer live alone, she accepted the inevitable and accompanied the two friends to England at the end of 1904.

Helen, who had spent so many winters in the south of France, felt perished with the cold of an English winter. "She made a resolution yesterday to stay indoors always, as an old woman should, or might fairly be supposed to do", noted Mary grimly. "This because she felt cold under her skirts. Have bought a 6/11d. flannel petticoat and tacked it inside the other one. Also knickers, which I am trying to get her into."[22]

While Helen, docile in the face of Mary's resolution, was endeavouring to acclimatize herself to this strange new life, Molly Trimble and some local friends, "dear Mr and Mrs Joll", went to Avignon to clear and close the house. They "have done the work of three months in three weeks", wrote Mary. "Half a ton of letters to be sorted, all manner of rubbish to be separated from useful things, books to be dusted and selected from, arrangements to be made for sale, and 18 boxes to be packed."[23]

In this way a great deal of valuable material was casually dispersed, for Helen had never begun her self-imposed task of editing a selection of Mill's correspondence for publication. Part of their library was still in London and, when she had chosen a few books for herself, she willingly presented 1,500 to Somerville, one of the first two women's colleges in Oxford.

Molly Trimble and the Jolls had arranged some sort of payment for the unsatisfactory servants. Pastor Louis Rey was given power of attorney to sign for the sale of the house and property; and the sum of 3,000 francs was donated to the town of Avignon for the upkeep in perpetuity of the marble tomb. Their work completed, Molly and Jolls returned to Torquay; and, cried Mary, "how glad I was when I got my darling back again".[24]

Mary was as authoritative as Helen had been in her prime, but, under her sway, the old woman settled down surprisingly well. "No twig ever suggests itself now as needing to be picked up", her niece recorded. "But she finds plenty of more exhilarating occupations.... We are very busy making petticoats for the wives and children of the unemployed at West Ham."[25] There were short walks in the spring sunshine, afternoon visits to the Jolls and other friends and occasional shopping expeditions. Aunt "is quite changed in many ways. We have no difficulty in getting her to change her underlinen, and she is quite pleased to wear the nice things I get her." Sometimes they went out in a pony carriage; sometimes, greatly daring, "we get into the motor omnibus ... and go for a drive in the evening through the gaily lighted streets of Torquay".[26] During the summer months, even more daring, "Aunt ... goes out in a trailer behind a tricycle.... She is fond of the trailer."[27] Occasionally they attended a concert; and there was a memorable visit to the popular illusionist display of Maskelyne and Devant. Aunt "said it was all so harmless, and yet so entertaining that one could not help laughing. She has grown very plump and rather rosy, and so fond of us both and full of trust in us, that life has become very pleasant."[28]

During these sunset days Helen, in some confused way, was fond of recalling the past. By 1906 she was spending most of the day in bed, but "she still takes a great interest in all questions of reform", Mary wrote to a friend, "though it is now a passive rather than an active interest".[29] Mary and Milly had both become confirmed socialists. "As for Aunt, she has long been deeply tinctured with socialist sentiments, though I had not quite understood her hints in that direction."[30]

One incident above all reminded Helen of the past. A man called at the front door carrying a magnificent bouquet of roses. He would not give his name but wrote on a card that he was a great admirer of Mill's books and hoped that she would accept a few flowers from his garden. "Aunt", wrote Mary, "was much gratified."[31]

Helen died in Torquay on 29 January 1907. Mary died eleven years later. Like her brother Cyprian she had become mentally disturbed, and she spent the last months of her life in an institution.

After Harriet's death Mill had told her brother Arthur that he and Helen would spend much of their time in the cemetery at Avignon "until our turn comes for being buried along with her".[32] Evidently Mary did not know of this intention or, if she did, considered it unnecessary, for Helen was buried in the cemetery at Torquay. The simple inscription on her tombstone reads, tersely, "She fought for the people." It is an inscription which sums up most aptly the life of Harriet Taylor's daughter, John Stuart Mill's spiritual child.

References

The manuscript collections to which reference is made are as follows:

The Mill-Taylor Collection(MTColl.) in the British Library of Political and Economic Science. (References by volume and item number.)
The Keynes Library at King's College, Cambridge.
The Library of University College, London.

Authors are identified by surname only, except where this might cause confusion.
Publication details of works cited are given in the Bibliography.

CHAPTER 1

1. Bain, *James Mill: A Biography*, p. 59.
2. Ibid.
3. Conway, *Autobiography*, p. 14, note.
4. Bain, *James Mill*, p. 59.
5. *The Amberley Papers*, ed. B. and P. Russell, vol. I, p. 421.
6. Bain, *James Mill*, p. 334.
7. J. S. Mill, *Autobiography*, definitive edition, p. 22.
8. Ibid., p. 7.
9. To the Rev. J. Crompton, 26 October 1873 (Library of King's College, Cambridge).
10. Bain, *John Stuart Mill: A Criticism*, p. 28.
11. *The Early Draft of John Stuart Mill's Autobiography*, ed. Stillinger, p. 181.
12. Ibid., pp. 184-5.
13. J. S. Mill, *Collected Works*, vol. XII (first vol. of *The Earlier Letters, 1812-1848*, ed. Mineka), p. 6.
14. Wallas, *The Life of Francis Place, 1771-1854*, second edition pp. 73-4.
15. Library of King's College, Cambridge.
16. Wallas, *Life of Francis Place*, pp. 72, 73, 75.
17. *Early Draft*, pp. 183, 56, note 184.
18. Library of King's College, Cambridge.
19. Solly, *These Eighty Years*, vol. I, p. 147.
20. Bain, *James Mill*, p. 334.
21. Froude, *Thomas Carlyle: A History of his Life in London, 1834-1881*, vol. I, p. 79.
22. Solly, *These Eighty Years*, vol. I, p. 147; vol. II, p. 404.
23. Bain, *James Mill*, p. 355.
24. Notes of a conversation between the Rev. J. Crompton and A. S. West at Norwich in April 1875 (Library of King's College, Cambridge).

CHAPTER 2

1. Waterfield, *Lucie Duff Gordon*, p. 32.
2. Ross, *Three Generations of English-women*, vol. I, p. 37.
3. Ibid., vol. I, p. 65.
4. J. S. Mill, *Collected Works*, vol. XII, p. 11.
5. Ibid., p. 116.
6. MTColl. II, 280.
7. Thompson, *The Appeal of Women*, pp. vii-viii, 16, 17, 210-12.
8. J. S. Mill, *Autobiography*, p. 73.
9. *The Woman Question in Europe*, ed. Stanton, p. 4.
10. Stephen, *The English Utilitarians*, vol. III, p. 18, note.
11. *The Amberley Papers*, vol. II, p. 248.
12. Bain, *John Stuart Mill*, p. 39.

CHAPTER 3

1. Bain, *John Stuart Mill*, p. 38.

2. Stephen, *The English Utilitarians*, vol. III, p. 22.
3. J.S. Mill, *Autobiography*, p. 95.
4. J. S. Mill, *Collected Works*, vol. XII (first vol. of *The Earlier Letters, 1812-1848*, ed. Mineka), p. 30.
5. J. S. Mill, *Autobiography*, pp. 104, 99.
6. A. W. Levi, *The Mental Crisis of John Stuart Mill;* quoted in Mazlish, *James and John Stuart Mill: Father and Son in the Nineteenth Century*, p. 210.
7. *Early Draft*, p. 183.
8. J. S. Mill, *Collected Works*, vol. XII, p. 149.
9. Ibid., 210.
10. Froude, *Thomas Carlyle: A History of the First Forty Years, 1795-1835*, vol., II, p. 465.
11. Mineka, *The Dissidence of Dissent: The Monthly Repository, 1806-1838*, p. 191.
12. Garnett, *The Life of W. J. Fox*, p. 66.
13. Mineka, *The Dissidence of Dissent*, pp. 192-3.
14. Conway, *Centenary History of the South Place Society*, p. 89.
15. J. S. Mill, *Collected Works*, vol. XVII (fourth vol. of *The Later Letters 1849-1873*, ed. Mineka and Lindley), p. 1960.
16. Taylor, *Memories of a Student*, p. 11.
17. *Early Draft*, p. 193.
18. Mazlish, pp. 284, 196.
19. T. Carlyle, *Reminiscences*, ed. Froude, p. 182.
20. Packe, *The Life of John Stuart Mill*, p. 116.
21. MTColl, XXVIII, 143.
22. MTColl. XXIX, 260.
23. Duffy, *Reminiscences and Conversations with Carlyle*, p. 168.
24. Roebuck, *Life and Letters*, ed. Leader, pp. 38, 28.
25. Norton, *Letters*, p. 497.
26. Duffy, *Reminiscences and Conversations with Carlyle*, p. 168.

CHAPTER 4

1. Martineau, *Autobiography, with Memorials by Maria Chapman*, vol. II, p. 299.
2. J. S. Mill, *Autobiography*, pp. 130-2.
3. Ibid., p. 173, note.
4. Ibid., p. 124.
5. Wilson, *The Life of Carlyle*, vol. II, p. 400.
6. Bain, *John Stuart Mill*, p. 43.
7. J. S. Mill, *Collected Works*, vol. XII, p. 114.
8. J. S. Mill, *Autobiography*, p. 131.

9. Garnett, *The Life of W. J. Fox*, p. 98.
10. J. S. Mill, *Collected Works*, vol. XII, p. 178.
11. Ibid., pp. 186-7.
12. Hayek, p. 54.
13. MTColl, XXVIII, 147.
14. J.S. Mill, *Autobiography*, p. 131.
15. Tomalin, *The Life and Death of Mary Wollstonecraft*, p. 235.
16. J. S. Mill, *Collected Works*, vol. XIV (first vol. of *The Later Letters*), pp. 137-8, 154, 159.
17. Hayek, *Mill and Harriet Taylor*, p. 196.
18. J. S. Mill, *Collected Works*, vol. XIV, p. 166.
19. J.S. Mill, *Autobiography*, pp. 160-1, 168.
20. J. S. Mill, *Collected Works*, vol. XV (second vol. of *The Later Letters*), pp. 523-4.
21. J. S. Mill, *Collected Works*, vol. XIV, p. 476.
22. Borchard, *John Stuart Mill the Man*, p. 66.
23. John Stuart Mill, *Bibliography of the Published Writings of*, ed. MacMinn et al., pp. 60, 62, 71.
24. J. S. Mill, *Collected Works*, vol. XIV, pp. 42-3.
25. Hayek, *Mill and Harriet Taylor*, pp. 99-100.
26. Ibid., pp. 45, 105.
27. J.S. Mill, *Collected Works*, vol. XII, p. 227.
28. Hayek, *Mill and Harriet Taylor*, p. 95.

CHAPTER 5

1. J. S. Mill, *Collected Works*, vol. XII, pp. 213-14, 215, 227.
2. MTColl, XXVII, 33.
3. MTColl. XXVII, 37.
4. MTColl. XXVII, 23.
5. MTColl. XXVII, 39.
6. MTColl. XXVII, 28.
7. MTColl. XXVII, 30.
8. MTColl. XXVII, 27.
9. J.S. Mill, *Collected Works*, vol. XII, p. 229.
10. Garnett, *The Life of W. J. Fox*, pp. 166-7.
11. Ibid., p. 186.
12. Conway, *Centenary History*, pp. 86, 93.

CHAPTER 6

1. P. W. Wilson (ed.), *The Greville Diaries*, vol. II, p. 3.
2. Froude, *Carlyle: The First Forty Years*, vol. II, pp. 194-5, 205.

3. J. S. Mill, *Collected Works*, vol. XII, p. 85.
4. Froude, *Carlyle: The First Forty Years*, vol. II, p. 243.
5. L. and E. Hanson, *Necessary Evil: The Life of Jane Welsh Carlyle*, p. 160.
6. D. A. Wilson, *The Life of Carlyle*, vol. II, p. 359.
7. Froude, *Carlyle: The First Forty Years*, vol. II, p. 445.
8. Froude, *Thomas Carlyle: A History of his Life in London, 1834-1881*, vol. I, p. 26.
9. Froude, *Carlyle: The First Forty Years*, vol. II, pp. 230, 458.
10. Carlyle, *Letters*, ed. Norton, vol. II, p. 200.
11. Froude, *Carlyle: The First Forty Years*, vol. II, pp. 465, 484.
12. Carlyle, *Reminiscences*, p. 177.
13. Roebuck, *Life and Letters*, p. 38.
14. H. Grote, *The Philosophical Radicals of 1832*, p. 45.
15. Roebuck, *Life and Letters*, pp. 38, 40.
16. MTColl. VIII, 29.
17. Bain, *John Stuart Mill*, p. 164.
18. J. S. Mill, *Collected Works*, vol. XIII, p. 572.
19. Ibid., vol. XIV, p. 123.
20. J. S. Mill, *Collected Works*, vol. XIV, p. 133.
21. Ibid., vol. XII, pp. 140-1.
22. Haight, *George Eliot and John Chapman*, p. 213.
23. Bain, *John Stuart Mill*, p. 164.
24. J. S. Mill, *Collected Works*, vol. XII, p. 152.
25. Ibid., pp. 352-3.
26. Ibid., p. 342.
27. Ibid., pp. 349-50.
28. Hayek, *Mill and Harriet Taylor*, pp. 103-4.
29. *Jane Welsh Carlyle, Letters and Memorials of*, vol. I, p. 138.
30. D. A. Wilson, *The Life of Carlyle*, vol. II, p. 310.
31. Bain, *John Stuart Mill*, p. 42.
32. Froude, *Carlyle: A History of his Life in London*, vol. I, pp. 79-80.
33. J. S. Mill, *Collected Works*, vol. XII, p. 321.
34. MTColl. II, 295.
35. J. S. Mill, *Collected Works*, vol. XIII, pp. 486-7.
36. Mazlish, *James and John Stuart Mill*, p. 318.
37. J. S. Mill, *Collected Works*, vol. XIII, pp. 620-1.
38. Ross, *Three Generations of Englishwomen*, vol. I, p. 195.
39. J. S. Mill, *Collected Works*, vol. XIII, p. 622.
40. Ross, *The Fourth Generation*, pp. 74-5.
41. J. S. Mill, *Collected Works*, vol. XV, p. 671.
42. Ibid., p. 675.
43. *Early Draft*, p. 148.

CHAPTER 7

1. D. A. Wilson, *Life of Carlyle*, vol. II, p. 321.
2. J. S. Mill, *Collected Works*, vol. XII, p. 184.
3. Ibid., pp. 181-2.
4. Froude, *Carlyle: The First Forty Years*, vol. II, p. 463.
5. T. Carlyle, *Letters to John Stuart Mill, John Sterling and Robert Browning*, ed. A. Carlyle, p. 104.
6. Norton, *Letters*, vol. I., p. 496.
7. Froude, *Carlyle: A History of his Life in London*, vol. I, p. 27.
8. Garnett, *Life of Thomas Carlyle*, p. 76.
9. Froude, *Carlyle: A History of his Life in London*, vol. I, p. 27.
10. Duffy, *Conversations with Carlyle*, p. 169.
11. Garnett, *Life of Thomas Carlyle*, p. 76.
12. Froude, *Carlyle: A History of his Life in London*, vol. I, pp. 28-9.
13. T. Carlyle, *Reminiscences*, vol. II, p. 178.
14. J. S. Mill, *Collected Works*, vol. XII, p. 252.
15. T. Carlyle, *Letters to John Stuart Mill . . .*, p. 107.
16. Ibid., p. 110.
17. J. S. Mill, *Collected Works*, vol. XII, p. 253.
18. Marston, *The Life of John Stuart Mill*, p. 9.
19. Quoted in J. S. Mill, *Collected Works*, vol. XII, p. 252, note.
20. Guernsey, *Thomas Carlyle, His Life—His Books—His Theories*, p. 87.
21. Norton, *Letters*, ed. Norton and Howe, vol. I, p. 496.
22. Quoted in J. S. Mill, *Collected Works*, vol. XII, p. 252, note.
23. T. Carlyle, *Letters to John Stuart Mill . . .*, p. 108.
24. Norton, *Letters*, vol. I, p. 496.
25. Collis, *The Carlyles: A Biography of Thomas and Jane Carlyle*, p. 73.
26. Campbell, *Thomas Carlyle*, pp. 102-4.

CHAPTER 8

1. T. Carlyle, *Letters to John Stuart Mill...*, pp. 125, 196-7.
2. Duffy, *Reminiscences and Conversations with Carlyle*, p. 168.
3. *Jane Welsh Carlyle: A Selection of her Letters*, ed. Bliss, p. 60.
4. Duffy, *Reminiscences and Conversations*, p. 169.
5. Diana Trilling, in *Partisan Review*, vol. XIX; quoted in *Early Draft*, ed. Stillinger, p. 25.
6. T. Carlyle, *Letters to John Stuart Mill...*, p. 225.
7. MTColl. XXVII, 2.
8. T. Carlyle, *Letters to John Stuart Mill...*, pp. 179-80.
9. Norton, *Letters*, vol. I, p. 499.
10. Duffy, *Reminiscences and Conversations*, p. 166.
11. Norton, *Letters*, vol. I, pp. 499-500.
12. Ibid., p. 496.
13. Duffy, *Reminiscences and Conversations*, p. 170.
14. Ibid., p. 169.
15. J. S. Mill, *Collected Works*, vol XIV, p. 180.
16. Ibid., pp. 180, 188.
17. T. Carlyle, *Letters to John Stuart Mill...*, p. 183.
18. D.A. Wilson, *Life of Carlyle*, vol. V, p. 21.
19. J. S. Mill, *Collected Works*, vol. XV (second vol. of *The Later Letters*), p. 557.
20. Ibid., vol. XVII, p. 1590.
21. Norton, *Letters*, vol. I, pp. 495-6.
22. J. S. Mill, *Autobiography*, pp. 123-4.
23. Froude, *Carlyle: A History of his Life in London*, vol. II, p. 449.

CHAPTER 9

1. Roebuck, *Life and Letters*, p. 39.
2. Bain, *John Stuart Mill*, p. 173.
3. Ibid., p. 172.
4. Cranston, *John Stuart Mill*, p. 16.
5. J. S. Mill, *Autobiography*, p. 174.
6. Neff, *Carlyle and Mill: An Introduction to Victorian Thought*, p. 328.
7. J. S. Mill, *Collected Works*, vol. III (second vol. of *Principles of Political Economy*), p. 763.
8. J. S. Mill, *Autobiography*, p. 174.

9. J. S. Mill, *Collected Works*, vol. XIV, p. 17.
10. Hayek, *Mill and Harriet Taylor*, pp. 119-22.
11. J. S. Mill, *Collected Works*, vol. III, p. 978, note.
12. Ibid, vol. XIV, p. 8.
13. J. S. Mill, *Collected Works*, vol. III, p. 978, note.
14. Ibid., vol. XIV, pp. 8-9.
15. J. S. Mill, *Collected Works*, vol. III, p. 978, note.
16. Ibid., vol. II.
17. Ibid. vol. XIV, p. 9.
18. J. S. Mill, *Collected Works*, vol. II, p. 208.
19. Ibid., vol. II, p. 980, note.
20. Ibid., vol. XIV, p. 9.
21. J. S. Mill, *Collected Works*, vol. XIV, p. 11.
22. Ibid., pp. 18, 21.
23. J. S. Mill, *Collected Works*, vol. II, p. 207.
24. Ibid, vol XIV, pp. 149-50.
25. J. S. Mill, *Collected Works*, vol. XIV, p. 185.
26. Howe (ed.) *Holmes-Laski Letters, the Correspondence of Mr Justice Holmes and Harold Laski, 1916-1935*, pp. 571, 676.
27. J. S. Mill, *Autobiography*, p. 176.

CHAPTER 10

1. Bain, *John Stuart Mill*, p. 90.
2. MTColl. XXVIII, 177.
3. MTColl. XXVIII, 179.
4. MTColl. XXVIII, 186.
5. Hayek, *Mill and Harriet Taylor*, p. 130.
6. MTColl. XXVIII, 200.
7. Hayek, *Mill and Harriet Taylor*, pp. 150-1.
8. Ibid., pp. 153.
9. Ibid., p. 153-4.
10. Ibid., p. 155.
11. Ibid., p. 158.
12. Ibid., p. 156.
13. Ibid., p. 162.
14. Ibid., p. 163.
15. MTColl. XXVII, 57.
16. J. S. Mill, *Autobiography*, p. 168.
17. J. S. Mill, *Collected Works*, vol. XIV, p. 43.

CHAPTER 11

1. Hayek, *Mill and Harriet Taylor*, p. 114.

2. J. S. Mill, *Collected Works*, vol. XIII, p. 615.
3. Bain, *John Stuart Mill*, p. 74.
4. J. S. Mill, *Collected Works*, vol. XIII, p. 739.
5. Ibid., vol. XIV, p. 144.
6. J. S. Mill, *Collected Works*, vol. XIV, p. 175, 183-4.
7. J. S. Mill, *Collected Works*, vol. XIV, p. 13.
8. J. S. Mill, *Collected Works*, vol. XIV, p. 49.
9. Mrs Stuart (*sic*) Mill, *Enfranchisement of Women* reprinted from the *Westminster Review* for July 1851, Trübner, London, 1868), pp. 3-22.
10. J. S. Mill, *Collected Works*, vol. XIV, pp. 47-8, 55-6, 66, 69.
11. J. S. Mill, *Collected Works*, vol. XIV, pp. 189-90.
12. Ibid., p. 148.
13. J. S. Mill, *Dissertations and Discussions*, vol. II, p. 411.
14. Gaskell, *The Life of Charlotte Brontë*, p. 344.
15. Quoted in Haldane, *Mrs Gaskell and Her Friends*, pp. 267-8.
16. J. S. Mill, *Collected Works*, vol. XV, pp. 628-9.
17. Quoted in Haldane, pp. 269-71.
18. J. S. Mill, *Collected Works*, vol. XV, pp. 629-30.
19. Ibid., vol. XV, pp. 509-10.
20. Ibid., vol. XVI (third vol. of *The Later Letters*), p. 1059.
21. Ibid., vol. XVI, pp. 1106-7.
22. Ibid., vol. XVII, pp. 1670-1.
23. Ibid., vol. XVII, p. 1748.

CHAPTER 12

1. Bain, *Autobiography*, p. 222.
2. J. S. Mill, *Collected Works*, vol. XII, p. 308.
3. C. Fox, *Memories of Old Friends*, ed. Pym, second edition, vol. I, pp. 132-3, 146.
4. Ibid., pp. 188-9, 300, 316.
5. J. S. Mill, *Collected Works*, vol. XIII, p. 603.
6. To the Rev. J. Crompton, 26 October 1873 (Library of King's College, Cambridge).
7. J. S. Mill, *Collected Works*, vol. XIV, p. 61.

8. Quoted in J. S. Mill, *Letters*, ed. Elliot, vol. I, pp. 158-9.
9. Hayek, *Mill and Harriet Taylor*, pp. 171-5.
10. Bain, *John Stuart Mill*, p. 166.
11. MTColl. XLVII, 13.
12. MTColl. XLVII, 14.
13. Hayek, *Mill and Harriet Taylor*, pp. 175-6.
14. J. S. Mill, *Collected Works*, vol. XIV, pp. 73-4.
15. Hayek, *Mill and Harriet Taylor*, p. 177.
16. A. S. West. Notes of a Conversation with the Rev. J. Crompton. (Library of King's College, Cambridge.).
17. Hayek, *Mill and Harriet Taylor*, pp. 180-1.
18. J. S. Mill, *Collected Works*, vol. XIV, p. 82.
19. Ibid., p. 83.
20. Ibid., p. 195.
21. MTColl. XLVII, 26.
22. J. S. Mill, *Collected Works*, vol. XIV, p. 197.
23. MTColl. XLVII, 29.
24. MTColl. XLVII, 30.
25. J. S. Mill, *Collected Works*, vol. XIV, p. 196.
26. Ibid., p. 135.
27. Ibid., pp. 207-8.
28. MTColl. XLVII, 32.
29. MTColl. XLVII, 33.
30. MTColl. XLVII, 34.
31. J. S. Mill, *Collected Works*, vol. XIV, p. 209.
32. Ibid., p. 220.
33. Ibid., p. 223.
34. MTColl. XLVII, 37.
35. J. S. Mill, *Collected Works*, vol. XIV, pp. 231, 234.
36. MTColl. XLVII, 39.
37. MTColl. XLVII, 40.
38. J. S. Mill, *Collected Works*, vol. XV, p. 547.
39. To the Rev. J. Crompton (Library of King's College, Cambridge).
40. J. S. Mill, *Collected Works*, vol. XV, p. 583.
41. MTColl. XLVII, 43.
42. J. S. Mill, *Collected Works*, vol. XV, pp. 584-5.
43. MTColl. XLVII, 45.
44. J. S. Mill, *Collected Works*, vol. XV, p. 589.
45. MTColl. XLVII, 47.
46. A. S. West (Library of King's College, Cambridge).

47. J. S. Mill, *Collected Works*, vol. XV, pp. 785-6.
48. Ibid., vol. XVI, p. 1079.
49. MTColl. II, 283.
50. J. S. Mill, *Collected Works*, vol. XVII, p. 1946.
51. MTColl. VIII, 92.
52. Quoted in J. S. Mill, *Letters*, ed. Elliot, p. xlvi.
53. MTColl. VIII, 73.
54. MTColl. VIII, 67.

CHAPTER 13

1. Norton, *Letters*, vol. I, p. 329.
2. Taylor, *Memories of a Student*, p. 144.
3. Taylor, *Memories of a Student*, pp. 10-11.
4. J. S. Mill, *Collected Works*, vol. XIV, pp. 96-7.
5. Ibid., pp. 108, 111.
6. J. S. Mill, *Letters*, ed. Elliot, vol. II, pp. 357-8.
7. J. S. Mill, *Collected Works*, vol. XIV, p. 168.
8. Ibid., pp. 153-4.
9. Hayek, *Mill and Harriet Taylor*, p. 195.
10. J. S. Mill, *Autobiography*, pp. 176-7.
11. Courtney, *The Life of John Stuart Mill*, p. 121.
12. Bain, *John Stuart Mill*, p. 171.
13. Himmelfarb, *On Liberty and Liberalism: The Case of John Stuart Mill*, p. 260.
14. J. S. Mill, *Collected Works*, vol. XIV, pp. 294, 300, 320, 332.
15. J. S. Mill, *Autobiography*, p. 170.
16. J. S. Mill, *Collected Works*, vol. XV, p. 581.
17. J. S. Mill, *On Liberty*, fourth edition, pp. 21-2, 27, 188, 190-3.
18. J. S. Mill, *Collected Works*, vol. XV, pp. 597, 598.
19. Conway, *Autobiography*, vol. I, p. 346.
20. J. S. Mill, *Collected Works*, vol. XV, p. 632.
21. Fox, *Memories of Old Friends*, vol. II, pp. 267-70.
22. Himmelfarb, *Victorian Minds*, p. 141.
23. Himmelfarb, *On Liberty and Liberalism*, p. 338.
24. J. S. Mill, *Utilitarianism, On Liberty, Essay on Bentham*, ed. Warnock, p. 19.

CHAPTER 14

1. MTColl. XIII, 221.
2. J. S. Mill, *Autobiography*, p. 130 and note.
3. *The Amberley Papers*, vol. I, p. 372.
4. MTColl. XLIV.
5. MTColl. XXVII, 70.
6. MTColl. XXVII, 48.
7. MTColl. LIV, 1.
8. MTColl. XXIV, 705.
9. MTColl. LI, 3.
10. MTColl. LI, 6.
11. MTColl. LI, 7.
12. MTColl. LI, 8.
13. MTColl. LI, 9.
14. MTColl. LI, 10.
15. MTColl. LI, 11.
16. MTColl. LI, 14.
17. MTColl. LI, 12.
18. MTColl. LI, 14.
19. MTColl. LI, 17.
20. MTColl. LI, 13.
21. MTColl. LIV, 5.
22. MTColl. LI, 24.
23. MTColl. LI, 30.
24. MTColl. LI, 34.
25. MTColl. LI, 37.
26. MTColl. LI, 34.
27. *Bell's British Theatre*, vol. I.
28. MTColl. LI, 35.
29. MTColl. LIV, 7 and 8.
30. MTColl. LI, 36.
31. MTColl. LI, 50.
32. MTColl. LI, 56.
33. MTColl. LI, 60.
34. Ibid.
35. MTColl. LI, 67.
36. MTColl. LI, 69.
37. MTColl. LI, 70.
38. MTColl. LII, 76.
39. MTColl. LIV, 12.
40. MTColl. LII, 104.
41. MTColl. LII, 122.
42. MTColl. LII, 109.
43. MTColl. LII, 118.
44. MTColl. LII, 124.
45. MTColl. LIV, 19.
46. J. S. Mill, *Collected Works*, vol. XV, pp. 521-2.

CHAPTER 15

1. MTColl. LIV, 23.
2. MTColl. LIV, 25.

3. MTColl. LIV, 27.
4. MTColl. XXVII, 87.
5. MTColl. XXIV, 706.
6. MTColl. LIV, 28.
7. MTColl. LIV, 29 and 30.
8. MTColl. LIV, 30.
9. MTColl. LIII, 1.
10. MTColl. LIII, 3.
11. MTColl. LIII, 12.
12. MTColl. LIII, 20.
13. MTColl. LIII, 24.
14. MTColl. LIII, 26.
15. MTColl, XXIV, 708.
16. *Later Letters*, vol. XV, p. 574.
17. Ibid., p. 582.
18. MTColl. XXIII, 632 and 633.
19. MTColl. XXIX, 298.
20. MTColl. XXIX, 713.
21. Hayek, *Mill and Harriet Taylor*, p. 267.
22. MTColl. XLV, 38.
23. Garnett, *The Life of W. J. Fox*, p. 99.
24. Solly, *These Eighty Years*, vol. II, p. 404.

CHAPTER 16

1. MTColl. XXIII, 651.
2. J. S. Mill, *Collected Works*, vol. XV, p. 677.
3. Ibid., pp. 854-5.
4. Ibid., pp. 862-3.
5. J. S. Mill, *Collected Works*, vol. XVII, p. 1655.
6. Lewin (ed.), *The Lewin Letters: A Selection from the Correspondence and Diaries of an English Family*, vol. II, p. 242.
7. MTColl. XXI, 294.
8. *The Amberley Papers*, vol. I, pp. 297, 304-5.
9. MTColl. XIX, 11.
10. *The Amberley Papers*, vol. I, p. 374.
11. MTColl. XXI, 291.
12. *The Amberley Papers*, vol. I, p. 372.
13. MTColl. XIX, 9.
14. The Fawcett Library.
15. *The Amberley Papers*, vol. I, pp. 479, 513, 475.
16. MTColl. XIX, 45.
17. Quoted in *The Amberley Papers*, vol. II, p. 495.
18. MTColl. XIX, 46.
19. *Frances Power Cobbe, Life of, as Told by Herself*, pp. 458, 456, 400.
20. Norton, *Letters*, vol. I, p. 330.

21. *Chicago Tribune*, 15 March 1868.
22. J. S. Mill, *Collected Works*, vol. XIV, pp. 139-40.
23. Ibid., vol. XV, p. 958.
24. Ibid., vol. XVII, p. 1549.

CHAPTER 17

1. J. S. Mill, *Considerations on Representative Government*, pp. 160-2.
2. MTColl. Additions Series, Letters I II, 2/1/4.
3. MTColl. Additions Series, Letters 1 II, 2/1/17.
4. MTColl. Additions Series, Letters 1 II, 2/1/19.
5. MTColl. XVII, 53.
6. MTColl. XVII, 55.
7. Ibid.
8. Quoted in St Aubyn, *A Victorian Eminence: The Life and Works of Henry Thomas Buckle*, p. 78.
9. MTColl. XVII, 56.
10. MTColl. XVII, 57.
11. MTColl. XVII, 63.
12. MTColl. XVII, 65.
13. St Aubyn, *A Victorian Eminence*, p. 24.
14. *The Amberley Papers*, vol. II, p. 375.

CHAPTER 18

1. J. S. Mill, *Collected Works*, vol. XVI, pp. 1005-6.
2. Ibid. p. 1050.
3. Ibid., vol. XV, p. 588.
4. Ibid., p. 787.
5. Ibid., pp. 864-5.
6. *The English Woman's Journal*, vol. VI, no. 31, 1 September 1860.
7. MTColl. XIV, 102.
8. J. S. Mill, *Collected Works*, vol. XV, p. 683.
9. Quoted in Strachey, *The Cause*, p. 103.
10. MTColl. XIX, 11.
11. Quoted in *The Amberley Papers*, vol. I, p. 434.
12. J. S. Mill, *Collected Works*, vol. XVI, p. 1060.
13. MTColl. Additions Series II Speeches 1 11, 1/12.
14. Quoted in *The Amberley Papers*, vol. I, p. 437.
15. J. S. Mill, *Autobiography*, p. 199.
16. MTColl. XIX, 12.

17. A Scrapbook containing cuttings on political subjects, chiefly by J. S. Mill (British Library, shelf-mark C. T. 4. 8d). 8d).
18. MTColl. XII, 40.
19. J. S. Mill, *Collected Works*, vol. XVI, pp. 1163-4.
20. MTColl. XII, 41 (draft).
21. MTColl. XIII, 190.
22. Blackburn, *Women's Suffrage*, p. 55.
23. Quoted in *Englishwoman's Review*, no. 1, October 1866.
24. MTColl. XIII, 181.
25. MTColl. XIII, 183.
26. Quoted in B. Stephen, *Emily Davies and Girton College*, pp. 113-14.
27. Norton, *Letters*, vol. I, p. 400.
28. MTColl. XII, 49.
29. MTColl. XIII, 262 (draft).
30. *Parliamentary Papers 1867-68, XXVIII, part 2, vol. II, pp. 62-5.*
31. J. S. Mill, *Collected Works*, vol. XVI, p. 1260.
32. Extract from Mill's speech "The Admission of Women to the Electoral Franchise", spoken in the House of Commons, 20 May 1867. (MTColl. XLV, 12.)
33. Nightingale, *Notes on Nursing*, p. 135.
34. J. S. Mill, *Collected Works*, vol. XV, p. 707.
35. Quoted in Woodham Smith, *Florence Nightingale*, p. 486.
36. J. S. Mill, *Collected Works*, vol. XV, p. 710.
37. MTColl. XIV, 10 (copy).
38. MTColl. XLV, 12.
39. MTColl. XIV, 11.

CHAPTER 19

1. J. S. Mill, *Autobiography*, p. 213.
2. MTColl. XLV, 12.
3. J. S. Mill, *Collected Works*, vol. XVI, p. 1272.
4. Quoted in *Englishwoman's Review*, no. 4, July 1867.
5. MTColl. XIV, 11.
6. MTColl. XIII, 62.
7. MTColl. XXI, 293.
8. MTColl. XXII, 434.
9. Quoted in B. Stephen, *Emily Davies and Girton College*, p. 118.
10. MTColl. XII, 54.

11. Quoted in B. Stephen, *Emily Davies and Girton College*, p. 118.
12. J. S. Mill, *Collected Works*, vol. XVI, p. 1299 ff.
13. Ibid., p. 1315.
14. MTColl. XIII, 302.
15. MTColl. XIII, 279.
16. MTColl. XIII, 280 (draft).
17. MTColl. XII, 74.
18. MTColl. XIII, 282.
19. MTColl. XIII, 284.
20. MTColl. XIII, 286.
21. J. S. Mill, *Autobiography*, p. 214.
22. MTColl. XII, 12.
23. MTColl. XII, 3.
24. MTColl. XII, 16.
25. MTColl. XII, 22 (draft).
26. MTColl. XII, 26.
27. MTColl. XII, 29.
28. MTColl. XII, 20.
29. MTColl. XII, 23.
30. MTColl. XIII, 295.
31. *Charles Kingsley: His Letters and Memories of his Life*, ed. Mrs F. Kingsley, vol. II, p. 295.
32. J. S. Mill, *Collected Works*, vol. XVI, p. 1352.
33. *Chicago Tribune*, 15 March 1868 (MTColl. Box V,4).

CHAPTER 20

1. J. S. Mill, "Thoughts on Parliamentary Reform" (February 1859), in *Dissertations and Discussions*, vol. III, pp. 37-8.
2. J. S. Mill, *Collected Works*, vol. XVI, pp. 1458-9.
3. Ibid., pp. 1483-4.
4. MTColl. LIII, 53.
5. MTColl. LIII, 55.
6. MTColl. XXIII, 652.
7. J. S. Mill, *Collected Works*, vol. XVI, pp. 1503-4.
8. Ibid., p. 1521.
9. MTColl. LIII, 56.
10. MTColl. LIII, 57.
11. MTColl. XIV, 12.
12. MTColl. XIII, 300.
13. MTColl. XXIII, 653.
14. MTColl. XXII, 438.
15. MTColl. XXII, 439.
16. MTColl. XII, 93.
17. J. S. Mill, *Collected Works*, vol. XVII, p. 1649.

Conway, Moncure Daniel, *Autobiography, Memories and Experiences* (Cassell, 1904).

    Centenary History of the South Place Society (Williams & Norgate, 1894).

    Thomas Carlyle (Harper, 1881).

Courtney, W. L. *The Life of John Stuart Mill* (Walter Scott, London; Thomas Whitaker, New York; W. J. Gage, Toronto: 1889).

Cranston, Maurice, *John Stuart Mill. Writers and their Work* series no. 99 published for the British Council and the National Book League, Longmans Green, 1958).

Duffy, Sir Charles Gavan, *Reminiscences and Conversations with Carlyle* (Sampson Low, 1892).

Early Draft of John Stuart Mill's Autobiography, ed. Jack Stillinger (University of Illinois Press, Urbana, Ill., 1961).

Eastlake, Lady, *Mrs Grote, a Sketch* (John Murray, 1880).

Findlater, Richard, *The Lady of the Old Vic* (Allen Lane, 1975).

Fox, Caroline, *Memories of Old Friends,* ed. Horace N. Pym, second edition, (Smith Elder, 1882).

Fox, Franklin (ed.), *Memoir of Mrs Eliza Fox* (Trübner, 1869).

Froude, J. A. *Thomas Carlyle, a History of the First Forty Years, 1795-1835* (1882; new impression, Longmans Green, 1901).

    Thomas Carlyle, a History of his Life in London, 1834-1881 (Longmans Green, 1891).

Fulford, Roger, *Votes for Women* (Faber and Faber, 1957).

Garnett, Richard, *Life of Thomas Carlyle* (Walter Scott, 1887).

    The Life of W. J. Fox (John Lane the Bodley Head, London; John Lane, New York: 1910).

Gaskell, Elizabeth Cleghorn, *The Life of Charlotte Bronte* (1857; Everyman Edition 1919).

George, Henry, Jr, *The Life of Henry George* (Heinemann, 1900).

Gérin, Winifred, *Elizabeth Gaskell, a Biography* (Clarendon Press, Oxford, 1976).

Grosvenor Papers, The: An Answer to Mr J. Stuart Mill's "Subjection of Women" (Darton and Co., 1869).

Grote, Harriet, *The Personal Life of George Grote* (John Murray, 1873).

    The Philosophical Radicals of 1832 (Savill and Edwards, 1866).

Guernsey, Alfred H., *Thomas Carlyle, His Life—His Books—His theories* (D. Appleton, New York, 1879).

Haight, Gordon S., *George Eliot and John Chapman* (Yale University Press, New Haven, Conn., Oxford University Press: 1940).

Haldane, Elizabeth, *Mrs Gaskell and Her Friends* (Hodder and Stoughton, 1931).

Hamilton, Mary Agnes, *John Stuart Mill* (Hamish Hamilton, 1953).

Hanson, Laurence and Elizabeth, *Necessary Evil, the Life of Jane Welsh Carlyle,* (Constable, 1952).

Hayek, F. A., *John Stuart Mill and Harriet Taylor, their Correspondence and*

Subsequent Marriage (Routledge & Kegan Paul, London; University of Chicago Press, Chicago, Ill.; British Book Service, Toronto: 1951).

Himmelfarb, Gertrude, *On Liberty and Liberalism, the Case of John Stuart Mill* (Alfred A. Knopf, New York, 1974; Secker and Warburg, London, 1975).

Himmelfarb, Gertrude, *Victorian Minds* (Weidenfeld and Nicolson, 1968).

Holme, Thea, *The Carlyles at Home* (Oxford University Press, 1965).

Howe, Mark DeWolfe (ed.), *Holmes-Laski Letters, the Correspondence of Mr Justice Holmes and Harold Laski, 1916-1935* (Oxford University Press, 1953).

Kamm, Josephine, *Hope Deferred, Girls' Education in English History* (Methuen, 1965).

Indicative Past, a Hundred Years of the Girls' Public Day School Trust (Allen and Unwin, 1971).

Rapiers and Battleaxes, the Women's Movement and its Aftermath (Allen and Unwin, 1966).

Kingsley, Charles, his Letters and Memories of his Life, ed. Mrs Fanny Kingsley (Henry S. King, 1877).

Lewin, Thomas Herbert (ed.), *The Lewin Diaries, a Selection from the Correspondence and Diaries of an English Family* (Archibald Constable, 1909).

Longford, Elizabeth, *Victoria RI* (Weidenfeld and Nicolson, 1964).

Manton, Jo, *Elizabeth Garrett Anderson* (Methuen, 1965).

Mary Carpenter and the Children of the Streets (Heinemann Educational, 1976).

Martin, Theodore, *Queen Victoria as I knew Her*, second impression (William Blackwood, 1908).

Marston, Mansfield, *The Life of John Stuart Mill* (F. Farrah, 1873).

Martineau, Harriet, *Autobiography, with Memorials by Maria Chapman* (Smith Elder, 1877).

Mazlish, Bruce, *James and John Stuart Mill, Father and Son in the Nineteenth Century*. (Basic Books, New York; Hutchinson, London: 1975).

Mill, Harriet and John, *Essays on Sex Equality*, ed. Alice S. Rossi (University of Chicago Press, Chicago, Ill., 1970).

Mill, John Stuart, *Autobiography*, ed. Helen Taylor (1873).

Autobiography, ed. with a Preface by Harold Laski (Oxford University Press, 1924).

Autobiography, definitive edition, with a Preface by John Jacob Cass (Columbia University Press, New York, 1924).

Autobiography, The Early Draft of John Stuart Mill's, ed. Jack Stillinger (University of Illinois Press, Urbana, Ill., 1961).

Bibliography of the Published Writings of John Stuart Mill, ed. Ney MacMinn, J. R. Hands, James McNab McCrimmon (North Western University, Evanston, Ill., 1945).

Collected Works, vols II-III (*Principles of Political Economy*), introduction by V. W. Bladen, textual editor J. M. Robson (1965); vols XII-XIII (*The*

Earlier Letters of John Stuart Mill, 1812-1848), ed. Francis E. Mineka (1963); vols XIV-XVII (*The Later Letters of John Stuart Mill, 1849-1873*), ed. Francis E. Mineka and Dwight N. Lindley (1972). Publishers (all vols): University of Toronto Press, Toronto, and Routledge and Kegan Paul, London.

   Considerations on Representative Government (Parker, Son and Brown, 1859).

   Dissertations and Discussions (John D. Parker, 1859).

   Essential Works of John Stuart Mill. ed. and introduced by Max Lerner (1961; Bantam Books, New York, 1971).

   The Letters of John Stuart Mill, ed. Hugh S. R. Elliot. (Longmans Green, 1910).

   Nature, the Utility of Religion and Theism (Reeder and Dyer, 1874).

   On Liberty (1859; fourth edition, Longmans Green, 1869).

   On Liberty, Representative Government; The Subjection of Women ed. and introduced by Millicent Garrett Fawcett (Oxford University Press, 1912).

   Principles of Political Economy, ed. and introduced by Sir W. J. Ashley, new impression (Longmans Green, 1921).

   The Subjection of Women, ed. with Introductory Analysis by Stanton Coit (Longmans Green, 1906).

   Utilitarianism, On Liberty, Essay on Bentham, ed. and introduced by Mary Warnock (Fontana Library of Philosophy, Collins, 1962).

Mineka, Francis E., *The Dissidence of Dissent, the Monthly Repository, 1806-1838*. (University of North Carolina Press, Chapel Hill, NC, 1944).

Neff, Emery, *Carlyle and Mill, an Introduction to Victorian Thought* (Columbia University Press, New York, 1926).

Nightingale, Florence, *Notes on Nursing* (Harrison, 1859).

Norton, Charles Eliot, *Letters of*, ed. Sarah Norton and DeWolfe Howe (Constable, 1913).

Packe, Michael St John. *The Life of John Stuart Mill* (Secker and Warburg, 1954).

Rey, Louis, *John Stuart Mill en Avignon*, an address given on 23 April 1921 (Macabet Freres, Vaison)

   Le Romain de John Stuart Mill (Monzein, Paris, 1913).

Roebuck, John Arthur, PC, QC, MP, *Life and Letters of*, ed. Robert Eadon Leader (Edward Arnold, 1897).

Ross, Janet, *Three Generations of Englishwomen* (John Murray, 1888).

   The Fourth Generation (Constable, 1912).

Rossi, Alice S., *The Feminist Papers* (1973; Bantam Books, New York, 1974).

Russell, Bertrand, *Autobiography*, vol. I (Allen and Unwin, 1967).

St Aubyn, Giles, *A Victorian Eminence, the Life and Works of Thomas Buckle* (Barrie, 1958).

Sinclair, Andrew, *The Better Half, the Emancipation of American Women* (Cape 1966).

Solly, Henry, *These Eighty Years* (Simpkin Marshall, 1893).

Stanton, Theodore (ed.), *The Woman Question in Europe* (Putnam, London and New York, 1884).

Stephen, Barbara, *Emily Davies and Girton College* (Constable, 1927).

Stephen, James Fitzjames, *Liberty, Equality, Fraternity* (Smith Elder, 1873).

Stephen, Leslie, *The English Utilitarians* (Duckworth, 1900).

Strachey, Ray, *The Cause* (G. Bell, 1928).

     Millicent Garrett Fawcett (John Murray, 1931).

Taylor, Algernon, *Memories of a Student* (Simpkin Marshall, 1895).

Thompson, William, *The Appeal of Women* (Longman, 1825),

Tomalin, Clare, *The Life and Death of Mary Wollstonecraft* (Weidenfeld and Nicolson, 1974).

Wallas, Graham, *The Life of Francis Place, 1771-1854* (1898; revised edition, Allen and Unwin, 1918).

Waterfield, Gordon, *Lucie Duff Gordon* (John Murray, 1937).

White, Carlos, *Ecce Femina, an Attempt to Solve the Woman Question* (Lee and Shepherd, Boston, Mass., 1870).

Wilson, David Alec, *The Life of Carlyle*, 6 vols (Kegan, Paul and Trench, 1923-1934). (Vol. 6 by D. W. MacArthur.)

Wilson, P. W. (ed.), *The Greville Diaries* (Heinemann, 1927).

Woodham Smith, Cecil, *Florence Nightingale* (Constable, 1950).

Wollstonecraft, Mary, and Mill, John Stuart, *Mary Wollstonecraft, The Rights of Women, and John Stuart Mill on the Subjection of Women,* introduction by Pamela Frankau (Dent's Everyman Library, 1954).

Index

property, 95; 97–8, 101, 107–9, 115, 117,
119–23, 127, 128; submits to her
domination, 26, 29, 34, 41–2, 51–3, 67–8,
71–5, 79–80, 83–4, 88, 102–2, 109–10, 129,
205, 221–2; helps with her pamphlet "The
Enfranchisement of Women", 83–91, 163,
167; his concern for her health, 55, 88,
108–9, 124–5; his enduring agony at her
death, 104, 110, 129–30, 132; spends part of
each year at Avignon in order to be near her
tomb, 131–2; and his friends and close
acquaintances: studies with John Austin,
19, 56; his affection for Sarah Austin,
18–19, 51, 54–6, 205; parts from and
criticizes, 54, 56–7; friendship with G.J.
Graham, 23–4; coldness towards, 51;
friendship with J. A. Roebuck, 23–4;
quarrels with him about Harriet, 50–1;
friendship with John Sterling, 26, 65, 80;
hint of a romance with Eliza Flower, 28–9;
47; his reputed love for Lady Harriet
Baring, 30, 48; friendship with W.J. Fox,
28–30, 34, 37–8, 44, 46–7; friendship with
Thomas Carlyle, 26–7, 62; with Thomas
and Jane, 48–9, 64; breach with Carlyle,
66–7, 69–71; and Carlyle's *The French
Revolution*, 58–64; friendship with Charles
Buller, 48; with Comte, 55–6; crosses
swords with him, 83–4; 199; dislikes
Harriet Martineau, 30, 52–3; friendship
with Edwin Chadwick, 90, 145, 169; with
Caroline Fox, 93–4; with George Grote, 13,
135–6; with Mrs Grote, 13; alienation from
her, 30, 51, 93; continued friendship, 69,
135, 129, 169; and Theodor Gompmerz, III,
134–5; friendship with W. T. Thornton,
129, 137–8; accepts Harriet's strictures on
him, 139; recruits him to women's suffrage
movement, 162; friendship with Thomas
Hare, 140, 147; consults him on girls'
education, 155–6, 173; and Charles
Kingsley: recruits him to women's suffrage
movement, 166; 184–5; and Alexander
Bain, 25, 51–2, 54, 71, 78, 83–4; and John
Eliot Cairnes, 161; recruits him to women's
suffrage movement, 162; 190; and Helen
Taylor: is influenced by her, 56, 133–4, 138,
140, 144, 170, 202, 205–6, 214–15;
influences her, 115, 142, 176–7, 225; values
her help and companionship, 130–1,
133–9, 172; friendship with the Amberleys,
135–6; is godfather to their son Bertrand
Russell, 137–8; 143–4, 148–9, 161, 169; and
Charles Eliot Norton, 138, 154; and
Parliament: election to, 47, 51, 105, 140,
145, 147–9, 223; presents petition to

enfranchise women, and introduces follow-
up motion, 151–2; prepares and introduces
amendment to Reform Bill to enfranchise
women property owners, 155–8, 159–61;
presents petition on married women's
property, 168; supports Bradlaugh, 168–9,
171; election defeat, 168, 171–2; and Irish
land reform, 137, 220–1; and the Jamaica
problem, 69, 137; and the representation of
minorities, 147–8; and birth control, 22–3,
72, 169, 198, 221; and divorce, 87, 183,
197–200; and Communism and Socialism,
72, 75–6, 85, 221; and the working classes,
72–3, 77, 148, 222; and religion, 58, 103,
138, 169, 204–5, 212–14; and the inferior
status of women, 21, 85–7, 111, 155–6,
159–60, 168, 195–7, 199; and the need for
the better education of girls and women,
111–13, 146, 155–6, 159, 195, 197, 221;
approves of election of women to school
boards, 173; campaigns for women's
medical training, 157–8; supports higher
education for, 146, 209; and women's
suffrage: 22, 35–6, 140, 145–67; recruits
influential supporters, 162; claims that
Helen Taylor initiated the movement, 164,
190–1; 168–9, 172–6, 178, 206; the adverse
effect on the movement of his ambiguous
attitude towards repeal of the Contagious
Diseases Acts, 180–93; and the London
National Society for Women's Suffrage,
161–4, 166, 184–92; and prominent
suffragists: Frances Power Cobbe, 138,
145–6, 163–4; Henry Fawcett, 146–7, 151,
174, 178; Barbara Bodichon, 146–7, 151,
162; Isa Craig, 147, 162; Emily Davies,
146–7, 151–4; Bessie Rayner Parkes,
146–7; Elizabeth Garrett, 157–8, 161, 172;
Millicent Fawcett, 174–5, 189, 192;
Clementia Taylor, 172, 173–5, 184, 188–9,
191; Lydia Becker, 164–5, 190–1; Croom
Robertson, 175, 186–92; Jacob Bright and
the Central Committee for Women's
Suffrage, 185–91; Caroline Biggs, 187–8;
and the Woman's Rights Movement in the
United States, 85, 87, 90–1, 163, 167, 195–6,
202, 227–8; Works: *Autobiography*, 12–13,
15, 25–7, 29, 34–7, 39–40, 56–7, 61, 69–70,
72–3, 81, 108, 110, 116, 140, 164, 195,
209–16, 221; *Considerations on
Representative Government*, 140;
Thoughts on Parliamentary Reform, 148;
On Liberty, 89, 109–14, 116, 129, 136, 195;
Principles of Political Economy, 72–7, 78,
85, 109, 114, 195, 221; *Dissertations and
Discussions*, 88, 140, 209; *Chapters on*